TAKING THE SOVIET UNION APART ROOM BY ROOM

A volume in the NIU Series in

Slavic, East European, and Eurasian Studies

Edited by Christine D. Worobec

For a list of books in the series, visit our website at cornellpress.cornell.edu.

TAKING THE SOVIET UNION APART ROOM BY ROOM

Domestic Architecture before
and after 1991

Kateryna Malaia

NORTHERN ILLINOIS UNIVERSITY PRESS

AN IMPRINT OF CORNELL UNIVERSITY PRESS   ITHACA AND LONDON

Publication of this book was made possible, in part, by a grant from the First Book Subvention Program of the Association for Slavic, East European, and Eurasian Studies.

First published 2023 by Cornell University Press

Librarians: A CIP catalog record for this book is available from the Library of Congress.

ISBN 9781501771200 (hardcover)
ISBN 9781501771217 (pdf)
ISBN 9781501771224 (epub)

To Ukraine

Contents

Figures

Acknowledgments

I am endlessly grateful to my parents, Liudmyla and Leonid. They have always been on my side and are behind everything I have ever accomplished. Furthermore, they are the primary reason this book exists. When I was a child in Kyiv in the 1990s and first years of the 2000s, they took on remodeling our apartment not once but twice. That meant going to hardware stores, endlessly picking tile, wallpaper, flooring, light fixtures, and kitchen cabinets. As a child, I hated the hardware stores more than the commotion of remodeling itself. In fact, remodeling was a bit of an adventure: all of our belongings had to be moved to one room, including the piano, blocked by dozens of boxes and bags that effectively put my much-hated music practice on hold. Sometimes we had no floors in the kitchen; once, for a couple of days, we had no windows. Another time we had no doors to the bathroom or toilet and hung blankets instead while waiting for new doors to be installed. For our first remodeling, our apartment gained a near-permanent presence: Petia, a handyman, who enthusiastically took over any kind of apartment construction, often to redo it later after the first attempt failed. Petia clearly spent more time at our home than he did at his own. At some point, our indoor cat Tikhon caught fleas from the sand and cement that inevitably accompanied our renovation project. Turns out these childhood adventures shaped my life for years to come.

The irony strikes me to this day: what I sincerely hated as a child became the subject of my research and an inspiration for me as an adult. This would have been impossible without my adviser at the University of Wisconsin–Milwaukee—Arijit Sen. It is Arijit's vision of the life of everyday spaces that I channel in everything I do. His continuous support through multiple disruptions, including one global pandemic, one partial and one full-scale invasion of my home country, several major life crises, a couple of cross-country moves, and multiple minor hurdles made this project possible to complete.

I also thank my mentors Christine Evans and Jennifer Jordan at the University of Wisconsin–Milwaukee for their support, their patience with my sometimes-chaotic writing, and their readiness to always offer encouragement on the way toward this project's completion. I thank the Center for Urban History of East Central Europe in Lviv for hosting me as a fellow and providing me with the opportunity to work in Lviv archives and share my work with peer researchers. I thank the Leibniz Centre for Contemporary History and the Legacies of

Communism Group at the University of Potsdam, Germany, for hosting me as a fellow and, thus, offering me time for uninterrupted writing. I also thank ZZF scholars—Juliane Fürst, Corinna Kuhr-Korolev, Jan Behrends, and many others—for discussing my work, for their encouragement, and for precious suggestions on emphasizing normalcy as an important quantifier in the post-socialist everyday life.

I thank my friend and colleague Chelsea Wait for offering the earliest idea for this project's structure when I was struggling with organizing chapters, each of which seemingly pertained to each room of any given apartment. I also thank Chelsea and Cindy Anderson for being a part of the extremely helpful reading group we have maintained throughout the years of me writing this work. And I thank my friend Joseph Witt for his readiness to edit my writing any time of day or night.

I am grateful to the University of Wisconsin–Milwaukee for the institutional support and dissertation fellowship resources it provided, and to Mississippi State University School of Architecture for the generous research support offered to junior faculty. I am also grateful to the Society of Architectural Historians and the Association for Slavic, East European, & Eurasian Studies for letting me present and receive feedback on this project from its earliest stages.

I am thankful to my interviewees: apartment residents who invited me to their homes and explained the history of their remodels, architects and engineers who practiced in residential construction and interior design, construction workers who made remodeling ideas come true, and many others.

Finally, I thank archives and archivists in Kyiv and Lviv, Ukraine, for their help with locating materials I used in my research. This includes Tsentral'nyi Derzhavnyi Kinofotofonoarkhiv Ukrainy, Tsentral'nyi derzhavnyiiy arkhiv vyshchykh organiv vlady ta upravlinnia Ukrainy, and Desrzhavnyi Oblastnyi arkhiv L'vivs'koi oblasti. It also includes specialists from Kyivproekt and librarians from Derzhavna naukovo arkhitekturno-budivel'na biblioteka imeni V. H. Zabolotnoho.

I am lucky to have been born and grown up in such a peculiar place—Kyiv—and during the time of change—the collapse of the USSR and the post-Soviet 1990s. I am even luckier that I was able to partially abstract from my personal experience and conduct broad research of the era that shaped my post-Soviet generation. I am lucky that I have not been killed in the war the Russian Federation started against Ukraine. And finally, to end this long list of acknowledgments, I am thankful for change, which may be scary but without which life would be stale.

Romanization

First names and place names are Romanized according to the original language of the country and commonly used international spellings. For example, Kyiv is Romanized according to the United States Board on Geographic Names. Lviv is Romanized without an apostrophe since it is a commonly used international spelling of this city's name. Due to the nature of the subject and geography—the post-Soviet world—most foreign words are Romanized from Russian, while some are Romanized from other post-Soviet languages. A note on the original language is provided for languages other than Russian. Some commonly used Russian words, such as perestroika and glasnost, are spelled in the way they are commonly spelled in the international media.

All interviewee names have been changed according to the requirements of human subject research. Therefore, there was no spelling preference for the interviewee pseudonyms. Instead, they were Romanized according to the Library of Congress Romanization Table for Ukrainian language, as these interviews were collected in Ukraine.

apartment building series—A package of architectural and engineering design documents, or the buildings constructed according to the package. These designs were meant for practically unlimited industrial reproduction. Attempts to create a universal housing unit were first undertaken in the early Soviet years, and many standardized residential buildings were built under Joseph Stalin. But the heyday of standardized mass housing in the USSR happened after the 1954 Central Committee and the Cabinet of Ministers of the USSR decree "On the development of prefabricated reinforced concrete structures and components production." Starting in 1954, the absolute majority of housing everywhere in the Soviet Union was built based on the centrally developed projects. Each project could be reproduced an unlimited number of times with only minimal adjustments or variations dependent on the place of construction. At the same time, every residential project with an individually designed plan, section, or façade had to be approved by the Gosgrazhdanstroi (State Committee on Civil Construction and Architecture of the USSR in Moscow).

apartment reconstruction—A type of single apartment remodeling that involves refitting slabs and load-bearing elements in old or worn-out buildings. This term is used by construction professionals.

babushatnik (from babushka, Russian for grandmother)—An apartment that has not been remodeled since the Soviet times. A *babushatnik* is likely to be populated with Soviet furniture and objects. It may be run down or well cared for yet outdated.

Biuro tekhnicheskoi inventarizatsii (BTI; Bureau of Technical Documentation)—State or municipal organizations responsible for real estate record and stocktaking, like the Recorder of Deeds in the United States.

compact housing (*malogabaritnoe zhil'e*)—Typically used to describe small Soviet apartments built in the Khrushchev and post-Khrushchev eras.

compaction (*uplotnenie*)—Confiscation of housing space above the established nine-square-meter norm from bourgeois homeowners in favor of the working class in the first years after the 1917 Bolshevik Revolution.

cosmetic remodeling (*kosmeticheskii remont*)—Remodeling that does not affect the apartment layout or structural elements. Typically, it involves changing wallpaper, painting windowsills, and other minor renovations.

evroremont—Remodeling done using imported materials or materials produced under foreign standards and according to Western quality standards, as imagined by the post-Soviet populations. Additionally, *evroremont* often meant a particular type of aesthetics and spatial organization, derived from the post-Soviet idea of how Western housing looked and functioned. A typical example of this spatial organization and aesthetics is the deconstruction of a partition wall separating the kitchen from the rest of the apartment spaces and a resulting transition to an open-/semi-open-plan apartment. The term *evroremont* emerged in the late 1980s and early 1990s.

improved plan apartments—Umbrella term used to describe apartment building series in which apartments had bigger floor areas, bigger kitchens, and more storage space than the early prefabricated series. In terms of architectural series, improved plan apartments typically refer to the second generation of prefabricated apartment building construction starting in 1963. Philipp Meuser and Dimitrij Zadorin, *Towards a Typology of Soviet Mass Housing: Prefabrication in the USSR 1955–1991* (Berlin: DOM publishers, 2015), 267.

khrushchevka—Early apartment building series built when Nikita Khrushchev was the general secretary of the Communist Party of the USSR and several years after. This term is typically used for five-story apartment buildings built between 1954 and 1968.

kommunalka—A communal apartment; typically, an apartment in a building built prior to the 1917 Bolshevik Revolution that has since been subdivided into parts and populated by unrelated families as the result of compaction. In most post-Soviet cities, the number of communal apartments has gradually decreased to near zero since the collapse of the USSR; the only exclusion is Saint Petersburg, where, due to the dominance of pre-1917 apartment housing, *kommunalkas* are still unexceptional.

lived and auxiliary spaces—Soviet bureaucracy divided domestic space into the so-called auxiliary spaces (kitchens, bathrooms, lavatories, hallways, and storage) and lived spaces (everything else).

mikroraion—A neighborhood built according to the Soviet method of urban planning that entailed calculating and building both housing and social infrastructure, such as schools, daycares, grocery stores, and clinics, all together.

pereplanirovka (replanning)—A remodeling where partitions and/or walls are demolished and/or new partitions are constructed. The term is typically used for private, rather than governmental, endeavors of changing an apartment plan. Replanning became popular in the 1990s.

perestroika—The course of economic and political reforms announced by Mikhail Gorbachev in 1985.

Plattenbau (German)—Prefabricated panel housing construction in the German Democratic Republic (GDR); similar prestressed concrete panel housing in Czech and Slovak languages is called *panelák*.

remont—Remodeling; in this work, particularly in relation to home improvement. In several post-Soviet languages, remont can stand for both the process of remodeling and the resulting interior design.

sanitary block (*sanitarnyi uzel*, or *sanuzel* for short)—In Soviet and post-Soviet terms, a space specialized for hygiene needs. In a Soviet apartment, a sanitary block was typically composed of a bathtub, a sink, and a toilet. These three fixtures could be placed in the same room (combined sanitary block) or separately (separate sanitary block, with the bathtub and the sink in one room and the toilet in another).

shabashniki—Construction laborers working short-term jobs. A detailed overview and the history of shabashniki can be found in *Broad Is My Native Land* by Siegelbaum and Moch. In this book shabashniki are defined as "temporary workers earning money 'off the books' in the late Soviet Period."

Sovok—A derogatory synonym for the Soviet Union, or a person who is nostalgic about the USSR or was never able to adjust to the post-Soviet times and lives in the past. See Alexander Genis, "Sovok" *in Russian Studies in Literature.*

stalinka—Apartments in individually designed or limited series buildings constructed during Stalin's rule (1922–1952).

Zhilishchno-ekspluatatsionnaia kontora (ZhEK)—Residential Maintenance Office; a communal organization responsible for maintenance of several apartment buildings and their shared infrastructure, such as heating and gas supply.

TAKING THE SOVIET UNION APART ROOM BY ROOM

INTRODUCTION

The social importance and acuteness of the housing problem have predetermined a serious attitude to it. To provide every family with a separate flat or house by the year 2000, is, in itself, a tremendous but feasible undertaking.

—Mikhail Gorbachev, *Political Report of the CPSU Central Committee to the 27th Party Congress*, 1986

The first post-Soviet decades were accompanied by a near-pathological desire for home improvement. Domestic upgrade advertisements were everywhere;[1] domestic gadgets were given to the winners of popular television shows;[2] and architecture and construction professionals shifted from large-scale state commissions provided through their institutions to small-scale private remodeling and construction services. It was as if the entire metropolitan population decided to fix up their apartments on a scale from modest, do-it-yourself renovations to the majestic gold- and marble-finished homes of the New Russians.[3] Building and finishing material stores, as well as fancy furniture salons, started popping up around urban centers to satisfy the needs of the remodeling clientele. Residential interior designers, a profession that had not existed in the Soviet Union, came to a quick fruition after the state fell apart.[4]

The 1990s, just like the decades after the 1917 Bolshevik Revolution, had its newspeak, such as *evroremont* (literally Euro-remodeling, or remodeling done according to European standards as envisioned by post-Soviet populations)[5] and *pereplanirovka* (replanning, or change of apartment layout). For a while, domestic remodeling seemed to be the new "blue jeans" of the post-Soviet world: the defining cultural trend of the era. Inevitably, homes went through substantial transformations, often invisible through the uniform facades of the urban apartment blocks. This book shows that such seemingly chaotic transformations followed clear spatial and cultural principles and were strictly characteristic of the post-Soviet condition: for apartment dwellers, domestic change was among the ways of gaining a new post-Soviet identity and the newly redefined social success.

1

This work about urban apartment homes during perestroika (1985–1991) and the first post-Soviet decades (1991 through the first decade of the 2000s) asks: how does a dwelling transform along with and under the pressure of historical upheaval? And how does a dwelling help in understanding large-scale changes that may be otherwise difficult to comprehend? Despite its interest in the dissolution of the USSR, this book does not focus on the dramatic events of 1990–1991, such as the secession of republics from the Soviet Union or the removal of the Communist Party from governance. Judy Attfield wrote: "authenticity and ephemerality can be said to materialise the relation between time and change in ordinary things like houses and garments."[6] This work is concerned with the lived experiences materialized through everyday space transformations and continuities that took place in the years leading to the collapse of the USSR and after.

My inquiry starts in the 1980s, because it is impossible to speak about the collapse of the Soviet Union without first speaking about perestroika (rus. rebuilding). The 1980s were a checkered decade in the history of the USSR: it started with Brezhnev's stagnation (*zastoi*), continued with the two fastest-dying general secretaries in Soviet history—Andropov and Chernenko—and ended with the energetic reformer Mikhail Gorbachev. Gorbachev defined his years in office with his policies of perestroika and glasnost (openness): the former set of policies meant to restructure the suffering centralized economy of the USSR, while the latter suggested letting go of some (but not all) censorship principles characteristic of the previous Soviet eras. Eventually, the term perestroika became synonymous with the Gorbachev rule and the last six years of the Soviet Union from 1985 to 1991.

Perestroika, its politics and culture, and its ultimate outcome—the collapse of the USSR—were in no way a simple or fully predictable phenomenon. In the three decades that have passed since, many books have been published on the subject, all pointing to the special nature of both this period in the history of the USSR and the haphazard nature of its collapse. The aftersounds of it are still loudly heard in both the post-Soviet, large-scale politics and everyday life alike.

In the beginning of Gorbachev's rule, the Soviet Union showed some signs of possible crisis but no writing on the wall that predicted its imminent collapse.[7] For the general population, even the economic crisis of the late 1980s did not produce an expectation that the Soviet Union was soon going to cease existing.[8] However, Gorbachev's economic reforms, originally meant to revive the system, further compromised the centralized supply chains and resulted in worsening consumer and industrial shortages. With Gorbachev's liberalization of trading policies, where manufacturers gained some independence in deciding how to distribute their products, existing chains of supply got interrupted and the entire centralized economy collapsed like dominos.[9] While shortages were not a new phenomenon to the Soviet public and industry alike, the public discussion surrounding the late-Soviet decrease in life quality was new.

The closest precedent of discourse liberalization that the Soviet Union had before was the Thaw in Khrushchev's 1950s and 1960s. The Thaw ended with Brezhnev's tightening of censorship; so could have perestroika.[10] Yet due to the peculiar combination of circumstances and constellations of actors influencing the last six years of the Soviet Union, the old system fell apart, and on its well-preserved carcass grew the new post-Soviet world with all of its continuities and changes that this book aims to track in the everyday life and architecture of the post-Soviet subjects.

Domestic spatial transformations of the 1990s and the first decade of the 2000s were an inseparable part of the grand-scale social upheavals of the collapse of the USSR, just as changes in the architecture of homes were an inseparable part of individuals becoming post-Soviet and developing a new sense of self.[11] "What does it mean to be post-Soviet?" Madina Tlostanova asks in her book on post-Soviet art and its role in the deconstruction of Soviet colonial modernity.[12] Tlostanova suggests that a post-Soviet individual never fully parted from the communist idea of the radiant future. After the collapse of the Soviet Union, the radiant future simply no longer required communism. But the old Soviet principle of the New Man for the new times continued, requiring post-Soviet individuals to either reinvent themselves or quietly become obsolete at the outskirts of the new reality.[13]

Many theorists have employed Pierre Bourdieu's concepts of habitus and hysteresis to describe the internal and external conflicts faced by post-Soviet individuals. These concepts help to explain the discrepancy (hysteresis) between the existing social dispositions of the individuals (habitus), the way reality changed around them after 1991, and the measures that these individuals undertook to bridge this gap. However, such research often treats Soviet habitus as stable, fixed, and in opposition to the world systems of the new politics and economics.[14] It is a dangerous assumption to make—that habitus (the perception and the reactions of an individual to the social world) stayed the same over the seven decades of the Soviet rule and throughout the vast Soviet geographies. It is hardly possible to equate the habitus, perceptions, and social reactions of an individual in the pre-World War II, Stalin-era Soviet city to the habitus of an urbanite in Brezhnev's 1970s or Gorbachev's perestroika. Therefore, this book rather suggests that the obsession with remodeling was a clash between the changing habitus of the late- and post-Soviet individuals and the massive but stagnant housing infrastructure. It does so by tracing the roots of interest in domestic spatial change back to late perestroika and watching the evolution of the interest in remodeling into a major trend in the 1990s and the first decade of the 2000s.

Becoming post-Soviet did not happen automatically. To become post-Soviet, one had to eradicate Soviet routines, sensibilities, and commodities from their persona, which includes the closest material extension of oneself: attire, modes of transportation, and dwelling. In Erving Goffman's terms performing an identity not only required appearance and manner, but also a "setting": a home, a public place, even a portable scene, such as a civic event that facilitated identity performance.[15] In "Western European countries," Goffman states, "a large number of luxurious settings are available for hire to anyone of the right kind who can afford them."[16] Arguably, a dwelling played an even more important role in an identity of a post-Soviet individual, because there were fewer "luxurious settings" for hire, where one could demonstrate one's success in the new economic and social conditions.[17]

If one did not share the ideas and adopt material cultural elements of the new time, they risked being known as *sovok* or *sovki* (plural)—a pejorative identity term that emerged before 1991 but became particularly widely used after the Soviet Union collapsed.[18] The identity question was always on the agenda in the USSR, the country composed of different historically colonized or formerly independent national subjects. In 1961 Khrushchev declared that the USSR saw the creation of a new community of people of different nationalities having common traits—the Soviet People.[19] According to Khrushchev, these traits included recognizing the USSR as a common motherland, relying on the socialist economy, sharing a social class structure, having a Marxist-Leninist worldview, having the common goal of constructing communism, and sharing spiritual and psychological qualities. The late-Soviet term *sovok* or *sovki* defined the same individuals and traits—reliance on a centralized economy, belief in the Soviet narratives of a carrying government, shared ethical and psychological qualities—as strictly negative.[20] In a nutshell, after 1991, *sovok* was used to describe those who did not want to catch up with reality, moving away from the familiar Soviet ways.

In addition, the proximity of the imaginary and real West—materialized in the form of imported and smuggled Western goods, ideas, rare expats, and frequent labor emigration—played a large role in outlining the post-Soviet identity. For instance, a curious allusion to finding the otherwise unattainable West inside a Soviet domestic space is seen in the early post-Soviet film *Window to Paris (Okno v Parizh)*.[21] In this film the protagonist accidentally locates a window in his communal apartment room that leads to a Parisian roof. In Paris, protagonists attempt to make a quick foreign-currency profit through street performances and petty crime. In the face of the West, they act completely outside of the former Soviet normal (even street performances were illegal in the USSR) and instead in the spirit of the "wild capitalism" unwrapping in the freshly post-Soviet states.

This is not to say that everyone in the post-Soviet cities was ideologically charmed with *everything* Western. In fact, in the decades following the collapse of the USSR, there emerged a powerful and rather widespread nostalgia for the socialist times and resentment for Western-style politics.[22] At the same time, this nostalgia only spread moderately into the world of everyday material objects: while Soviet foods are a major nostalgic subject in the Russian Federation,[23] it is hard to find any evidence of nostalgia for Soviet housing construction, perhaps because the Soviet-built apartment buildings are still present and very much real for a post-Soviet urbanite.

The omnipresent, post-Soviet, home improvement newspeak—*evroremont*—explicitly indicated that a change of home had to be done in the post-Soviet idea of European standards. However, Euro-remodeled domestic interiors were never about precisely copying Western interior design solutions but rather about the new sense of self and a post-socialist emphasis on the new self-respect and the new normal channeled through domestic interiors.[24]

Krisztina Fehérváry writes the following:

> Accounts from the Baltic and Central European states in particular make clear that what I call a "discourse of the normal" indexes a profound adjustment of identity set in motion by the sudden geopolitical shift of these countries from Soviet satellite to aspiring members of a reconfigured "Europe." Those nations and peoples once identified as the most western of the Soviet bloc states suddenly found themselves situated on the undefined *eastern* border of greater Europe, with all the loss of prestige this entailed. Now they were in the unenviable position of having to prove their "westernness" in a new context—to themselves as much as to a European Union reluctant to grant them membership.[25]

While this argument applies well to the Central European states of the former socialist bloc and some of the post-Soviet Eastern European countries, "Westernness" is not a universal explanation to all changes in domestic space, at least not in all post-socialist cities. In fact, lately a switch to the rejection of Westernness has been seen, at least in the political discourse in some post-Soviet states.[26] At the same time, even if Westernness is dropped out of the equation, like in Belarus or more recently in the Russian Federation, the idea of home improvement is still present. Therefore, in the post-Soviet context, the key term to borrow from Fehérváry is normalcy rather than Westernness.

Where did the boundaries of normalcy reside in the USSR, and how have they moved since the USSR collapsed? The meaning of "normal" itself evolved significantly with perestroika and after 1991. In Juliane Fürst's investigation of the late-Soviet notions of normalcy through the lives of Soviet hippies, she registers

that the state's definition of normal largely revolved around political compla-
cency, maintaining studies or a job, and a place of residence.[27] Yet in the early
post-Soviet years, where neither a place of residency nor a job came automatically as the world plunged into what many saw as a perpetual crisis,[28] normalcy
could no longer rest solely on those pillars. Normalcy had to be found elsewhere
than the old Soviet categories. Not only the normal but also the modern, the contemporary, and the cutting edge could no longer be found in anything Soviet;
indeed, the Soviet Union no longer existed, and the socialism was gone even on
paper. In the early post-Soviet years, the widespread nostalgia for the USSR described by Svetlana Boym was yet to develop.[29] Instead of the good old days, the
post-Soviet urbanites strived for modernization.

The post-Soviet remodeling boom signified an emergence of a new spatial freedom (some would say chaos), which is difficult to compare to Western apartment
living or even some post-socialist counterparts, such as the former German Democratic Republic (GDR). Apartment residents vigorously changed their homes, even
in seemingly inflexible structures within prefabricated concrete block and panel
apartments in mass-constructed buildings. In architectural research, such changes
are called user-generated modifications. These changes are surprisingly little studied, despite their extreme importance in the context of growing housing insecurity around the world.[30] The existing literature is scarce and very region specific:
in-depth scholarship exists on Southeast Asian housing, South American housing,
and immigrant housing in the West, but little can be found for housing elsewhere
if it is not related to immigration.[31] In the post-Soviet context, the literature is
limited to several articles on apartment home extensions.[32]

This book's goal is to understand the joint between the collapse of the USSR
and the everyday architecture of urban homes. One issue is immediately high-
lighted: speaking about the collapse of the Soviet Union at large does not provide a meaningful understanding of what that change was like, just as "economic
downturn" in no way suffices to express the extent and diversity of change during the Great Depression. Ever since scholars became interested in writing "history from below," historic focus has shifted from the key political dates and
figures to "the changes in the consumption and communication patterns of the
population, the restructuring of familial and social relationships, the systems
of cultural meanings that governed interactions with ideological authorities, and
evolving practices at home, at the workplace, and at sites of leisure."[33] This shift
in interests also opened a door for increased interdisciplinarity.

Many elements of Soviet and even pre-Soviet times have remained present and
formative in post-Soviet urban everyday life, making it difficult to define what exactly has changed since the dissolution of the Soviet Union. Through sociologist
Jane Zavisca's urban scale lens, "little appears to have changed, at least in the over-

all quality of the housing stock and its distribution"[34] (including dwelling sizes and occupancy numbers), yet the change appears undeniable through the microscale lens of an individual apartment. The everyday life of a family may have changed dramatically due to home modifications. The changes that occurred in the homes and the ways in which these changes took place are important manifestations of the tectonic shifts in perestroika and post-Soviet society. An apartment, in this sense, is a perfect allegory of this change: the outside load-bearing walls have largely remained the same, and even the internal partitions may have remained intact, but the spaces and the way of life have changed dramatically.

In her work on food-related spaces in American homes, Elizabeth Cromley suggests that users of residential buildings should be considered equal to architects in shaping their homes.[35] Unlike architects, users continue shaping buildings throughout their lifecycle and are at the forefront of spatial and architectural transformations at the times of social change. Buildings may stay largely intact in outward appearance, but the homes do not remain the same on the inside. This is the sort of change within the seeming and factual continuity of larger infrastructure that this work hopes to capture and explain.

If social structures are internalized and embodied through daily cultural practices, what better place to study how social structures transform than the home?[36] Looking at the physical and functional organization of a home to investigate the qualities of the society at large and its attitudes toward the private and the public is not new.[37] However, often the visible stability of the superstructure of urban apartment buildings may be mistaken for a sign of the stable and uninterrupted continuity of domestic practices and, hence, the social structures that they embody. That is, of course, not the case: the behaviors of apartment occupants change, and so do their domestic spaces, their functions, spatial rituals, rhythms, and practices. In the case of the former Soviet Union, changes inside the home went along with the changing conditions of labor and consumption (see chapter 1), the post-Soviet retreat of the state from domestic affairs, and the changing demands for individual privacy (see chapter 2), as well as many other changes described in the following chapters.

This study requires rethinking common typological and formal characteristics of post-Soviet apartments, such as apartment buildings belonging to a particular period (type) of housing and the number and function of separate apartment rooms. This approach embraces a great variety of apartment building types comprehensively without extensive focus on differences. Rather, it explores the overwhelming similarities in spatial thinking of apartment dwellers and professional architects alike. Although this approach is used in this work in the case of late- and post-Soviet apartments, shifting focus away from apartment types is relevant far beyond the post-Soviet region.

Many transformations of post-Soviet apartment homes are impossible to analyze using the usual conventions of modern apartment description and naming. Take, for example, the word "bedrooms." The vast changes that have taken place with the post-Soviet emergence of a specialized, monofunctional bedroom are impossible to describe without understanding that "bedrooms"—spaces meant mostly for sleep—did not exist in most Soviet households. Although they were mentioned in Soviet residential design theory and apartment planning documents (for instance, in apartment building series design blueprints), in reality these rooms were mostly multifunctional and were equally used for socializing, domestic work, schoolwork, etc. (see chapter 3). In this way, the established term "bedroom" itself limits the ability to conduct a detailed scrutiny into the late-Soviet housing situation. To avoid this problem, this work replaces conventional room names with terms like "spaces related to sleep" or "spaces related to eating" and focuses on practices instead of room nomenclature.

The repetitive, tactic,[38] and rhythmic[39] spaces of everyday life are the locus of inherent liberty, solutions, and decisions produced by the users rather than by the state, architects, or engineers. Dell Upton, speaking of Henri Lefebvre's sense of power in quotidian life and space, writes: "Everyday life is both a colonized setting of oppression, banality, routine, passivity, and unconsciousness as well as the locus of an ultimate reality and a source of potential liberation."[40] Change—the clash between past structures and present opportunities—produces a condition that is hard to understand through formal naming conventions, even more so in translation. A Soviet and post-Soviet urban apartment does not adhere to the space-defining conventions of an architectural blueprint or the vocabulary of a classic apartment homemaking manual. Domestic practices, on the contrary, show precisely what happened inside these apartment homes without having to delineate the state enforced regimes from the acts of everyday resistance. Finally, abandoning formal nomenclature allows for a more flexible view of apartment architecture and spatial structure: the walls of separate rooms are not seen as an absolute definition of space but rather as just one of the dimensions that determine space use.

Besides abandoning naming conventions, this work offers another twist from a traditional history of residential architecture. It is not limited to the physical characteristics of space, such as walls, doors, windows, façade, and interior solutions, but instead speaks to spatial practices in de Certeau's terms: routines, movements, actions, and other performances[41] that changed along with the collapse of the USSR. However, unlike in de Certeau's writing, this work stays in the field of architectural history and, hence, concentrates heavily on the materiality of apartment homes: the walls, the windows, the doors, and their dimensions, as well as the pieces of furniture that populate them. In this way, this work leans toward the explanation of practice offered by Shove, Pantzar, and Watson: that a practice consists not only of knowledge and meaning but also of "materials—including things, technologies, tangible physical entities, and the stuff of which objects are made."[42]

This work analyzes five domestic practices: remodeling, sleeping, eating, hygiene, and socializing. This set of practices addresses different forms of domestic ephemera, from actions repeated multiple times a day to performances that only take place once every several years, if not decades; some last for minutes while others last for days, months, or years. Despite this great range of temporalities, they are all nonetheless characteristic of almost any domestic space.[43] Hence, they open a possibility to transpose the narrow post-Soviet apartment discussion onto any dwelling place at large.

Everyday History and Scale

"Were there any changes in the approaches to housing design with the beginning of perestroika?" I asked an architect who has been active in apartment building design since the Soviet 1970s. "Changes where?" he responded sarcastically. "In the mentality of people who wanted to enjoy comfortable housing? Or state-level changes in relation to building norms and regulations?"[44]

How does one speak of the changes that took place along a major political rupture? Is simply identifying the change of a ruling ideology or an economic system enough to explain a historic upheaval? There is a methodological question: do we know change according to grand ideological affirmations, or is it through on the ground shifts in the patterns of everyday life? And if it is through the study of everyday life, where exactly are the limits of what composes everyday life? To paraphrase Olga Shevchenko's critique of James Scott, does everyday life consist solely of resistance,[45] or is it rather a balance between compliance, resistance, and opportunity presented on a multiplicity of historical scales?

A reading of the collapse of the USSR solely through the grand political gesture of the end of state socialism obscures the changes and continuities that have constituted the everyday reality of post-Soviet populations. This study does not intend to supplement the traditional grand narrative of the end of state-socialism and its replacement with democratic political systems and neoliberal economics but rather suggests an alternative story of the two decades in question—1985 to the middle of the first decade of the 2000s. This is not a revisionist history; rather, the goal here is to understand the lived experiences of change through their spatial dimension. The apartment home, as it entered the post-Soviet period, is seen as the formative product of socialist state engineering, social knowledge of navigating the communist state, and an internal enclave of personal freedom and difference within a totalitarian society.[46] To paraphrase Egmond and Mason, who suggested to look at the mouse to understand the scale of a mammoth, the faces of both individuals and the state become visible under the microscopic lens of an individual dwelling.[47]

A quotidian interior contains a multiplicity of meanings, and no political narrative remains intact when observed from a standpoint of everyday life.[48] A home may simultaneously carry a narrative of hierarchic power, a counternarrative of resistance, and a multiplicity of other narratives visible at different scales of historical inquiry. And yet, a home is not a thing-in-itself;[49] it does not stand outside the rest of historic context but rather enriches the context with another dimension. Therefore, an apartment home in this work is presented as both a scene and a locus of change, both the predicate and the subject of politics and society, in hope to add a spatial dimension to the everyday life of late-Soviet and post-Soviet cities.

The social conditions that resulted from the collapse of the Soviet Union are currently loosely defined. The existing narratives, such as the transition to market economy or democratic elections, are typically determined through a binary opposition with the previous period: planned economy/market economy, communal property/private property, dictatorship/democracy, and such.[50] These binary categories do not withstand a close scrutiny. For instance, the communal/private property binary fails to describe the sense of ownership that Soviet citizens developed towards their apartments in the later decades of the Soviet rule, despite the state being a formal owner.[51]

The collapse of the USSR is not the only example of when grand binaries prove useless in understanding the trajectories of change and the everyday life conditions that emerge in conjunction. The scope of subjects appropriate for microscale research is enormous; however, looking at quotidian practices and domestic spaces in relation to change over time makes up a particularly fruitful part of the existing research. John Foot provides an eloquent definition of the role of scale in approach to history and, in his case, memory in a Milanese neighborhood: "The particular, the everyday and the ordinary are used to try and explain the general, the extraordinary and the exceptional. The scale of research is reduced to a housing block, individual life stories, families, events and places."[52]

In Foot's case, the study of memory, change, and forgetting in Milan's urban fabric is only possible through oral history and a microscale of inquiry, since economic and urban change have erased the physical traces of past landscapes.[53] Similar to Dolores Hayden's "Invisible Angelenos,"[54] Foot speaks to the invisible experiences in Milan's past and their importance for the understanding of Milan's present palimpsest, unique among all Italian cities.[55] Unlike Foot, centering the inquiry into Milan's forgetting on one neighborhood, Nancy Stieber, an architectural and urban historian, studies a microscale of social interactions inside a reform that led to large-scale housing construction in early-twentieth-century Amsterdam.[56] This approach helps Stieber avoid the discussion of architectural style that, in her own words, "has been ably described" in other studies.[57] This also helps her hint at the controversial role of architects and politicians in urban and social change.[58]

The challenges of binary-reliant, post-Soviet historiography are similar to what French historians address as the Invisible Revolution, a period between 1946 and 1975 when a tremendous amount of social and cultural change took place but little formal change of political course was declared.[59] In a short essay titled "May '68 Did Not Take Place," Gilles Deleuze and Felix Guattari write about the non-normative causes of the iconic 1968 protests in France. The protests were not reducible to a simple set of social reasons,[60] nor did they coincide perfectly with left or right political ideas. These manifestations did not focus on traditional political binaries—the bourgeoisie and the proletariat, or the oppressor and the oppressed—nor were these protests reducible to a social class. Instead of social or economic equality per se, the protesters desired the seemingly impossible: a revolutionary cultural change "as if a society suddenly saw what was intolerable in it and also saw the possibility for something else."[61]

In their disappointment with the outcomes of these protests, Deleuze and Guatarri go as far as stating that "May '68 Did Not Take Place," since the demands and aspirations of the protesting crowds did not cause immediate structural transformation of the state system.[62] However, even if no formal change of regime occurred, Nicole Rudolf argues that subtle changes did take place in what she calls an "Invisible Revolution." Unlike Deleuze and Guattari, Rudolf argues that change should not be tracked in the formal discourse of public politics. According to Rudolf, in French postwar society, change had to be studied inside the urban lived spaces and in modernist housing projects in particular.[63] "Invisible revolution" is a trope much broader than postwar France, perhaps broader than current-day political systems altogether. A revolution does not refer to definitive events, showcased with an overthrown government or a refusal to pay taxes. It rather refers to a sense of changed life, the sense that *everything has changed*, when it is difficult to tell what exactly that "everything" is.[64]

The pitfall is that most of this change is incredibly difficult to see from a planner's viewpoint—a bird's eye over the city with statistical numbers in hand. Moreover, in a post-Soviet city, this change is barely visible even looking at a single building, mostly unchanged except for the patchy balconies poking through uniform residential facades. Besides balconies, not much reveals the diversity of homes found inside a building. To illustrate this diversity, an interviewee for this study, an architect prolific in residential building design, recalled a case when, upon entering an apartment in a building of his own design, he could not find his way through because of the radical changes performed by the apartment's residents.[65] Almost three decades after the collapse of the Soviet Union, even the *Biuro tekhnicheskoi inventarizatsii* (BTI; Bureau of Technical Documentation) is unable to fully comprehend the exact changes that took place inside apartment buildings.[66] That is because to structurally observe change, one must descend to the ground or rather onto the floor of an urban apartment.

Standardization, Domestic Practices, and Imploding the Type

Much of Soviet urban housing was standard, and if it was not standard to begin with, it was gradually standardized to match the many rules that the Soviet state established. Many people are familiar with images of modernist Soviet urban neighborhoods made up of uniform apartment blocks geometrically composed along vast avenues. These apartment blocks were designed, engineered, and constructed to a standard with the maximum possible reduction of panel production variety, and hence construction price, in mind. Of course, most Soviet cities were not limited to the modernist apartment blocks. In many historic centers, such as central Moscow or Kyiv, pre-1917 apartment housing dominated the cityscape all the way until the arrival of the grand housing project in 1955. In Lviv and Saint Petersburg, pre-Soviet housing still composes the largest portion of the housing stock. These urban homes were built long before standardized construction and varied dramatically among themselves depending on the social and economic standing of their occupants, not to mention the historic technology at the time of their construction. And nevertheless, these homes also experienced standardization under Soviet rule, starting with establishing a nine-square-meter standard of housing lived area (*zhilaia ploshchad'*) per person in 1918, finalizing it for the entire USSR in 1922,[67] and ending with the standardized spatial organizations and furniture produced between the 1950s and the collapse of the USSR in 1991. In the 1910s and 1920s, this resulted in the creation of the infamous communal apartments, where rooms or partitioned segments of former rooms were occupied by unrelated families. All urbanites, except for a very small social strata of political or cultural elites, had to adhere to these standards, making Soviet urban apartments a perfect case study in standardized domestic environments.

There are two popular models of categorizing apartment homes: by building type and by themes and chronological progression. The former, illustrated by Gwendolyn Wright's *Building the Dream: A Social History of Housing in America*, has a problem typical to the discussion of the early American apartments and tenements: Wright speaks of the different types of homes separately, almost as counterstatements, with a tenement portrayed as having nothing in common with earlier, fanciful upper-class apartment buildings.[68] Although the economic differences between these homes are undeniable, such an approach obscures the fact that all urban multiunit residential buildings had fundamental commonalities: the dependence on larger infrastructure, the shared transitional spaces, the codependence of residents in keeping their homes safe, etc. Furthermore, it directs the attention of the reader to class difference as definitive to the differences in domestic life, although living in an apartment, rather than a stand-alone home, may be more definitive of the mode of domestic life than class identity alone.

In the subfield of Soviet and post-Soviet studies, the necessity of transcending the type of an urban home has long been present but not consistently formulated. Most existing scholarship uses the categories of two or more of these types of apartment homes: communal apartments,[69] rare Constructivist experiments,[70] Stalin-era buildings,[71] or Khrushchev-era (first-generation) mass-built apartment blocks.[72] Limiting an inquiry to a single type or a relationship between a couple of types might allow for a detailed exploration of a particular architectural and public discourse, yet it obscures the commonality of everyday life mechanisms that are pertinent to all forms of urban homes and domestic architectures. On an urban-scale level, typical studies of the post-Soviet social reality examine a particular neighborhood, microdistrict (*mikroraion*), or other kind of agglomeration. There are only a few powerful exclusions from this pattern on an urban scale of inquiry, the most prominent being Steven Collier's *Post-Soviet Social*,[73] which observes the qualities of post-Soviet infrastructures that are pertinent to all types of urban apartment homes.

In the Soviet Union, a room—a cornerstone of architectural convention—served as a unit of measurement for a home: apartments were labeled as one-room, two-room, three-room, and so on. A room was regarded as anything other than a kitchen, bathroom, auxiliary hallway, or storage space. Yet despite the importance of a room for apartment measurement and definition, domestic functions transcended the physical limits of rooms, putting the importance of a room to question. The formal room nomenclature used in the architectural profession is very easy to follow through the design documents issued for apartment building series—the backbone of mass housing, apartment buildings constructed according to serially designed standardized projects. In a typical blueprint from an apartment series booklet, a two-room apartment was portrayed with a bedroom, living room, kitchen, bathroom (combined or separate; see chapter 5), and an entry space (figure 0.1).

Starting from the second generation of standardized mass housing (1963–1971),[74] Soviet architects consistently drafted monofunctional furniture into the

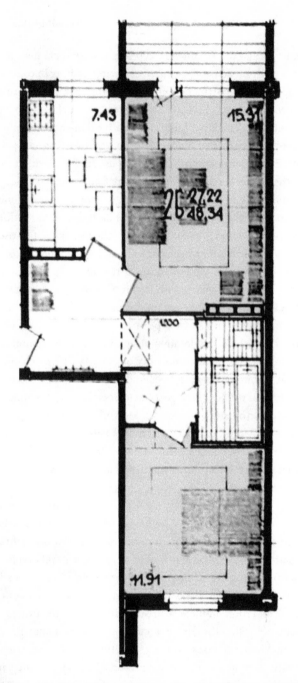

FIGURE 0.1. Apartment in an "84" apartment building series, designed by the governmental design institution Tsentral'nyi nauchno-issledovatel'skii institut eksperemental'nogo proektirovaniia zhilishcha (TsNIIEP zhilishcha) and built starting 1970. Illustration modified from *Seriia 84: Krupnopanel'nye doma i blok-sektsii* (Moscow: TsNIIEP zhilishcha, 1979), 16.

designs of standard apartments, suggesting that each room was to be meant for one particular domestic function: sleeping, eating, socializing, and such. Beyond the professional language of blueprints, the choice to depict monofunctional furniture could have been influenced by a plethora of factors, including the overall drafting aesthetics and conventions. By the 1970s, Soviet architects advocated for the necessity of an isolated individual space for every family member (in other words, at least one room per person) in their professional publications, which if realized would have partially justified the monofunctional furniture in their drawings.[75] Yet, this was virtually impossible, since the number of residents always had to outnumber lived rooms (*zhilye komnaty*) (see chapter 3). A living room during the day had to become someone's bedroom at night. Another room, shown as a bedroom with a double bed in the apartment building series booklet, in reality would have served as a nursery, a sleeping space for a grandparent, and an office while young children were in kindergarten. The functional zones inside the house overlapped and changed over the period of a day, a week, or even a year, particularly for those not blessed with a Soviet country house (*dacha*).[76] The spatial overlaps between functions produced complex daily space uses and choreographies inside these urban homes.

And what is a room after all? According to Soviet standards, a room is a closed space with four walls, windows, and doors. However, those same walls, windows, and doors of the post-Soviet apartments have been significantly changed by residents: moved, removed, new partition walls erected, new openings cut, and old ones blocked, all of this in different configurations and for a variety of functional purposes. How does one find logic in this seemingly chaotic rethinking of apartment homes?

When I first started working on this project, I found myself facing a puzzle: how was I supposed to speak of the changes in domestic spaces in segmented chapters if the physical domestic partitions—walls—and the formal domestic units—rooms—appear to be overstepped in the process of inhabitation? What if a wall inside a home is not a rigid physical or perceptional border but rather can be physically removed or moved or challenged with placement of functional zones and movement flows? What if a room does not contain a precise function but changes its physical outlines and performances based on the needs and desires of apartment occupants? The problem I faced is not unheard of; it has been rich grounds for anthropological and architectural inquiries into vernacular models of domestic living for decades. For instance, Dell Upton determines that in the mid-eighteenth-century Virginia home, room naming may have been assigned prior to the actual function of the space.[77] Lizabeth Cohen, describing an early twentieth-century American working-class home, demonstrates how cooking, dining, labor, and socializing often overlapped in the same space of a kitchen.[78] Elizabeth Cromley suggests questioning the boundaries and limitations of the terms "kitchen" and "dining room" in her work on food spaces in American homes.[79] Lindsay Asquith, summarizing conceptual frameworks for the study of vernacular architecture, points out that "room functions need to be examined in relation to domestic routine and ritual," since simply "the existence of many rooms in the house"[80] does not tell a story in its own right.

In short, this is how I arrived at organizing this work along domestic practices: remodeling, sleeping, eating, hygiene, and socializing. When looking at domestic practices instead of room outlines, the common themes of the post-Soviet change, such as the emergence of private sleeping spaces or the overlap between socializing and eating spaces within the home, appear on the surface. Domestic practices reveal that the patterns of change were similar across incomes, class lines, and apartment types and sizes.[81] The changes that took place in the home were a universal, sociohistoric, post-Soviet tendency rather than a set of isolated idiosyncrasies. This universality of outcomes presents the sought-for link between the microhistoric evidence and the tremendous omnipresent change, as well as the persistent continuities of the post-Soviet era. The apartment dwellers did not erect the physical structure of the apartment building, but they liberally moved walls, transformed balconies, changed room functions, and most importantly, unpredictably populated standard apartments offered to them by the state. The home of a Soviet urbanite, first seen by the authorities as a perfect device for the creation of a proper, "happy and healthy" Soviet citizen,[82] by the late 1980s became a gray zone of desired Western commodities, DIY partition walls, and dusty carpets on the walls to fix temperature and sound isolation problems characteristic of the prefabricated apartments.[83] Something as small as the construction of a new partition to separate and make private a previously walk-through room provides a tangible understanding of attitudes to post-Soviet privacy, where the grand communism/capitalism binary does not.

A critical reader may question the integrity of this approach, considering that this book is about an apartment home: a physical container with seemingly rigid boundaries of walls, especially the load-bearing brick and concrete panel walls of a Soviet apartment. Yet, an apartment home is not solely a built box; it is equally a vehicle for everyday life, "the space both geographical and intellectual," and "the frame and map on which everyday world is reflected and through which an understanding is gained."[84] Walls do not limit a home in this work but outline the framework for thinking about change.

With domestic practices in mind, the chapter structure of this book is as follows. Chapter 1: Remodeling introduces dweller-performed remodeling as a massive, but largely hidden, shift in culture and life. This chapter has a double goal. First, it shows apartment remodeling as an inalienable part of the collapse of the

Soviet Union and the early post-Soviet years. Second, it questions the stereotype that the desire to, and practice of, transforming one's everyday life was primarily related to the widespread apartment privatization that occurred after 1991. Chapter 2 introduces an alternative claim that the roots of demand for apartment remodeling rested deep in Soviet reality and that the basis for supply of remodeling services began while the Soviet system was still standing.

Chapter 2: Sleeping analyzes the everyday practice of sleeping and the ways in which this practice transformed between the beginning of perestroika (1985) and the second post-Soviet decade. This chapter further breaks down the category of privacy, present in every study of domestic space, in order to locate the distinct peculiarities of Soviet and post-Soviet sleep. Unlike, for instance, in the United States, where the number of delineated spaces in a home is measured by the number of "bedrooms," in the Soviet Union a designated bedroom was a rarity rather than a rule. Residents of Soviet apartments slept in multifunctional spaces with standards for acceptable sleep arrangements quite different from those found in American homes of the same era. Chapter 3 tracks the steps in the rise of the distinct bedroom in the late 1980s and early 1990s through media, apartment plans, and construction regulations, as well as the oral histories of the study's interviewees.

Chapter 3: Eating analyzes the transformation of eating and cooking spaces during the same period. The importance of kitchens to clandestine political and cultural life in the Soviet Union between the 1950s and 1990s is well known.[85] Yet domestic eating and cooking per se have been relatively understudied in comparison to the uniquely Soviet political life that took place in the kitchen. Soviet urbanites had a habit of socializing and holding political and philosophical discussions in their kitchens. While this trend first started in intelligentsia circles in the 1960s after the arrival of mass-constructed individual apartments, by the 1980s it became a general societal norm. Perhaps this happened in part because the possibilities for cooking and eating in the last decades of the Soviet Union desperately lacked diversity. Due to the same dull culinary scene, only a few researchers have directed their attention to late-Soviet domestic eating practices, yet the books that were published on the subject, such as Von Bremzen's *Mastering the Art of Soviet Cooking*, gained significant success.[86] This chapter fills the lack of knowledge about the spatial practices of domestic eating and cooking by directing attention to how these practices took place in the late Soviet home and how they transformed along the lines of political change. It does so by looking at the spatial qualities of the small Soviet kitchens, the complex choreographies necessary to navigate cooking, eating, and gathering in these tight spaces, and the ways in which apartment remodeling and layout changes shaped the spatial dynamic of food in the 1990s.

Chapter 4: Cleaning addresses the spaces of hygiene: bathrooms, water closets, and kitchens in late-Soviet and post-Soviet apartments. This chapter highlights the discrepancy between the late-Soviet institutional programming of homes, the aspirations of professional architects, and the desires of homeowners when it came to spaces of hygiene. The chapter also addresses the invisibility of the bathroom in the Soviet world of images and its powerful entry into visual culture, art practices, and socioeconomic anecdotes of the first post-Soviet decade.

Besides pulling together the entire investigation, chapter 5: Socializing speaks about the changes in domestic socialization that took place alongside the collapse of the USSR. Unlike the previous chapters, this chapter is not limited to the urban apartment but expands to the apartment building hallway and its courtyard. Yet like the previous chapters, it does not speak of just one kind of room but instead tracks the shifts in social life from the kitchen to a room, from a living room to the hallway stairs and the courtyard, and back again. Finally, it addresses the surprising resilience of modest multifamily urban housing, particularly important now when housing is once again becoming a central social and political issue, even in economically leading societies.

Geography, Reservations, and Sources

The interviews and most of the fieldwork for this book were done in Kyiv and Lviv, Ukraine, a perfect combination for a study of metropolitan post-Soviet apartment housing. Kyiv has a diverse housing stock: a mix of the Russian Empire–era apartment buildings largely transformed into communal housing with the arrival of the Soviets in 1919, Stalin-era apartment buildings, and mass-built apartment buildings of all generations, as well as new housing built after 1991. Lviv is a city with very different, chiefly pre-Soviet, housing stock, except for several mass-built *mikroraion* neighborhoods; this combination of geographies demonstrates that even in radically different built fabric, post-Soviet urbanites remodeled their apartment homes in a shared, uniquely post-Soviet way.

While the geography of the interviews and archival fieldwork is quite localized, many of the documents and interviews collected apply to geographies much broader than Ukrainian cities. Although the Soviet pursuit of standardization did not result in all urban housing becoming exactly the same, it did facilitate the creation of several very distinct apartment building types, including pre-1917 Revolution apartments, Stalin-era apartments, first-generation apartment blocks (Khrushchev-era), second- and third-generation prefabricated apartment blocks (Brezhnev-era until 1991), and post-Soviet-built apartment blocks.[87] These categories of urban homes were widespread throughout the entire Soviet Union, with some reservations as to the quantitative relationship between these apartment housing types in different regions and modifications of these homes according to regional specifics.[88] For instance, it is safe to say that the majority of the apartment building series designed between the 1950s and 1991 were built in multiple cities and republics. The pre-1917 housing also became standardized through establishing the same room-size norms inside buildings that may have previously differed.

A reservation should be made for Soviet-built housing in former Baltic republics; it is known that mass housing in the Baltic states was built to a better standard than elsewhere in the USSR.[89] This curious exclusion, however, only proves the general rule to be true: apartment housing around the USSR was similar enough for the differences in Baltic mass housing quality to become noticeable on this uniform background.

While the urban Soviet housing funds entered the post-Soviet period in a relatively similar state, further divergences took place after the collapse of the USSR. Besides regional differences in the social composition of apartment dwellers and the resulting differences in their home improvement projects, housing legislature and institutions that oversaw housing varied in different post-Soviet states. This subject is further explained in the discussion of the BTI in chapter 5. Yet despite these variations, all these changes took places on the basis of a shared Soviet infrastructure.

Several types of secondary sources are used in this project: (1) popular magazines and books concerned with domesticity, (2) popular television shows on home remodeling, (3) professional magazines and books on interior design, and (4) films containing or commenting on domestic spaces. All four categories appear to have been transrepublican in Soviet times and largely transnational in the 1990s and the first decade of the 2000s.[90] For example, a home improvement television show named *Kvartirnyi vopros* (Apartment question), produced by the Russian television channel NTV, and many other Russian shows aired in Ukraine and Belarus as well as other post-Soviet states.[91] A German franchise magazine with a section on interior design advice, *Burda Moden,* started being published in the Soviet Union in 1987, while the regional Ukrainian branch of the magazine did not start until 2006.[92] Until then, the Russian version of *Burda Moden* was widely circulated in Ukraine, creating a shared knowledge about domestic interiors between these two post-Soviet republics. In other words, with regional specifics in mind, it is still possible to speak of major similarities across apartment housing in different cities and different former republics, particularly in the first decades after 1991. Therefore, although this book's findings are most relevant to urban housing in Ukrainian metro areas, the trends, milestones, and causation detected are structurally similar to the processes that took place in other metropolitan urban areas across the former Soviet Union.[93]

Were there any traits to Ukrainian urban homes that differed from other post-Soviet metropolitan areas? Yes, and although it would require another book to address these subtle differences and their roots properly, I feel obligated to briefly review one such important large-scale difference.

In different post-Soviet entities, state funding and the amount of control exercised by the city and the state over housing and other urban forms varied. Take, for example, balconies. In many post-Soviet cities, apartment residents drastically modified their balconies, except for cities such as Lviv, where historic building facades were not to be modified by the residents due to the UNESCO-protected status of the entire historic city center. However, the degrees of these modifications varied based on the city and state. For instance, in Kyiv and Moscow alike, residents enclosed balconies in city centers and on the outskirts, but rarely extended the balcony floor past its original size or built additional load-bearing structures (figure 0.2). In Tbilisi, on the contrary, adding load-bearing structures and extending balconies past their original dimensions to create apartment building extensions was commonplace.[94] Of course, these differences were not accidental: in the rigid context of historic Lviv, where laws about the balconies were strict, and strictly enforced, balcony enclosures simply did not happen, while in Tbilisi, where in the 2000s there was little control over balcony encroachments, they did. Thankfully, the phenomenon of post-Soviet balconies is well studied, therefore here I am using it only as a brief illustration of a state-to-state and city-to-city difference.[95]

However, balconies are just a single case of a larger pattern: a variation in the amount of power over existing environments exercised by different post-Soviet states and cities. The most striking case of such difference in state and city administration control comes from the Russian Federation. The Russian capital Moscow is the only post-Soviet city that has successfully demolished the early series of Khrushchev-era mass housing.[96] Although many other cities, including Kyiv, considered this move, there was never enough resources or political power to execute such a massive infrastructural project.[97] In Moscow, unlike Kyiv, the Russian petrostate and private investors provided resources for grand rebuilding projects, while Russia's tightening authoritarian control over urban space, both public and private, overpowered democratic, bureaucratic, and institutional inertia to make these projects happen.

In Kyiv, large-scale urban projects tend to meet popular resistance, especially when residents believe they are being deprived of their rights to their residences or urban space. Ukrainian anti-construction activism is so well known it has attracted academic comparisons with the Ukrainian waves of Soviet monument removals.[98] Often, anticonstruction or antidemolition activists are successful. Without a doubt, had the city started Khrushchev-era housing demolition in any

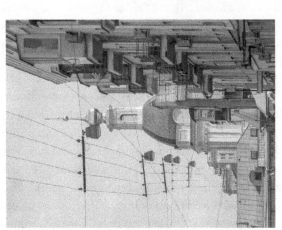

FIGURE 0.2. *Left:* Enclosed loggias in Sykhiv, a bedroom neighborhood of Lviv; *Center:* Enclosed balconies in central Kyiv; *Right:* Enclosed balconies in Moscow. (Photographs by the author.)

Ukrainian metropolitan center, there would have been a major public outcry. That is because of the ownership—formal, spatial, and emotional—that residents have established over their apartments in the years after privatization; it is also because, in the Ukrainian context, this community of individual owners can be strong enough to repel autocratic solutions by the state.

In Moscow, although concerns over deprivatization of housing or unfair neighborhood relocation were voiced, the projects continued without major interruptions.[99] Urban activism, public protests, or other forms of resistance in Russia have become increasingly difficult in recent years, the most famous case being a public campaign to defend Khimki Forest near Moscow from freeway construction. Not only did the campaign to save the forest fail, but one of the central activists had to take refuge in Estonia to avoid prosecution.[100]

In other words, although starting with a mostly similar housing infrastructure and largely shared informational field in the first post-Soviet decades, different post-Soviet republics did develop differences in built environments, due not just to their differing climates, social structures, and regionally available materials, but also to the degree of freedom and private control individuals had over their built environment.

Finally, the geographic reservations of this research reflect the decade and the places where it was conducted. Research in Russia has become increasingly complicated as the Russian Federation gradually solidified as a regime. More importantly, in this postcolonial, yet not postimperial world, it is essential that the Soviet Union does not get studied through Russia alone or become equated to just current republics within the Russian Federation. Limiting research related to the Soviet Union to just Russia not only manufactures an inaccurate view of the Soviet and post-Soviet reality, but also maintains the highly problematic perception of the Russian Federation as the locus of the normative condition for the entire post-Soviet region.

The sociological reservation of this research has to do with important subjects that I chose to mostly omit in this work: gender and sex. Although gender dynamics and sex were and are of central importance to the construction of domestic space in the Soviet Union and in the post-Soviet world, I chose to mostly avoid these subjects as it would have extended this book project indefinitely. In the interest of completing this project, I had to limit its scope to the domestic practices described in the following chapters.

The final reservation has to do with the nature of Soviet architectural and popular writing. On multiple occasions, this book takes time to point out the critical discrepancies between the Soviet formal, architectural, and public media discourse and the reality of urban apartment housing on the ground. Of course, the differences between discourse and reality are not exclusive to Soviet or post-Soviet housing; and yet the scale of those discrepancies reached a particularly impressive degree when it came to Soviet residential architecture. Unrealizable architecture was always a Soviet specialty: from the 1920s Constructivists, who almost exclusively produced "paper architecture," to the classicists' colossus of the Palace of the Soviets, to the 1988 exhibition of the new Soviet "paper architecture" as an aesthetic statement at the Frankfurt Deutsches Architekturmuseum.[101]

The awareness of the differences between discourse and reality is of extreme importance in the subject of housing. Looking at the discourse on its own, without considering actual apartment plans and construction norms and regulations and without talking to apartment residents on the ground, leads to problems such as claiming the existence of open plan interiors in the Soviet standardized housing of the 1960s,[102] which, as this book shows, never existed widely in the reality of most Soviet cities, only in discussion.[103] On the other hand, looking solely at plans, sections, and layouts would be misleading as well, since blueprints are partially silent as to the intentions behind the design.

The fieldwork for this book is a mix of easily available sources that have been previously and effectively used by other scholars, such as late-Soviet and post-Soviet media, and sources that I have reasons to believe have not been previously used for scholarly research, like the Recorder of Deeds-type plans and the oral histories, collected exclusively for the study.

Fieldwork involved collecting several different types of evidence:

1. blueprints of apartment buildings, produced by architectural and planning institutions during the Soviet years and independent architects after 1991
2. blueprints and schematic plans of individual apartments produced by me or the BTI or granted by apartment dwellers
3. Soviet construction standards and regulations
4. interviews with apartment dwellers, architects, construction workers, and engineers
5. late-Soviet and post-Soviet media outlets, including the Soviet magazine *Rabotnitsa*, *Burda Moden* magazine, post-Soviet television shows, and printed and online resources (*Kvartirnyi vopros*, *Idei vashego doma*, and many others).

The use of popular media outlets, *Rabotnitsa* in particular, allowed me to track the specific timeline of public interest in remodeling, something that would be difficult to address otherwise. The choice of *Rabotnitsa* is not random, even though remodeling work was largely perceived as men's or shared labor in the home during the Soviet and early post-Soviet years. A typical compliment for a man was that he had "hands of gold" or could fix anything in the house, yet the domestic sphere was still seen as a "women's kingdom."[104] Besides *Rabotnitsa* being a women's magazine, it was also the most popular women's magazine, steadily published since before the 1917 Revolutions, and a rare publication that actually survived the collapse of the USSR.[105] It is remarkable that this magazine managed to reinvent itself through the entire Soviet history and beyond and maintains some readership until today.

Burda Moden magazine, *Idei vashego doma* magazine and online platform, and the television show *Kvartirnyi vopros* present very different types of popular sources, based on globally successful models, but with a local twist. *Kvartinyi vopros* used a generic global television show format, yet with a local, historically recognizable reference: the idiom "*kvaritrnyi vopros*" (apartment question) was widely used throughout the entire Soviet history as a euphemism for the housing shortage.[106] *Burda Moden* primarily published fashion photographs and sewing patterns, which made it very appealing to the late-Soviet and post-Soviet women used to creating and altering clothes at home. The addition of articles on domestic interiors was a logical extension of manufacturing one's image with one's own hands, whether personal appearance or a dwelling.

To understand the built environments in which the transformations took place, this work extensively uses Soviet and post-Soviet construction regulations—*Stroitel'nye normy i pravila* or *SNiP*. They are a universal legal document that prescribed the dwelling spaces to be built the way they were. SNiP were not unlike the International Building Code (IBC), but were stricter in some aspects, such as the upper limitations of floor area or open-plan dwellings. SNiP were updated when the political or practical need emerged, usually every several years.[107]

Central to this inquiry are architectural plans and other blueprints. When it comes to housing in microscale, except for a number of historic studies, architectural blueprints play a secondary role in everyday-life analysis.[108] At the same time, architectural blueprints present a rich and multifaceted type of research source. The absolute majority of housing was developed or transformed by state institutions, and at least some stage of these transformations was documented. Therefore, an apartment plan and its accompanying documents[109] are a precious source of information on the institutional attitude toward the production of home and, even more importantly, on the controversies inherent to the Soviet state housing agenda. Architectural blueprints help understand a gap that existed between the architectural discourse, the state rhetoric, and the realization of housing projects on the ground. The many architectural competitions handled by Soviet state agencies often compartmentalized and, offering some design freedom, produced numerous apartment housing proposals that may have never been realized but pointed out the problems of the existing housing, often more clearly than the official rhetoric.[110]

Another facet of information in architectural plans opens up with the collapse of the Soviet Union and the emergence of individual apartment design plans and Recorder of Deeds-type blueprints. These plans speak to the two major elements of everyday domestic life in post-Soviet urbanity: the popular image of an apartment home and how this image has evolved in the decades after 1991, as well as the cases of on-the-ground transformation of these domestic spaces.

An architectural plan, hence, is all-encompassing and rich in comparative data. The different types of apartment plans illustrate the Soviet reality, including the state-level orchestration of everyday life through the standardized apartment design, the professional discourse on theoretical problem-solving and practical marketing, and the everyday resistance and change performed on the grassroots level by the apartment dwellers themselves.

And yet, despite their historic richness, plans do not speak. The interviews collected for this book give its research subject a voice. These semi-structured interviews conducted with apartment dwellers, architects, and construction professionals are used as evidence sources and illustrations for the multiple avenues of domestic transformation. They add a final touch to the inquiry on home: without the voices from within the homes, inhabited and under construction, this take on the historic era would not be fair or possible.

Identity

In Mylan and Southerton's take on developing an orderly method for a study of an everyday domestic practice, they note that "there is a tendency within empirical studies towards descriptive accounts of the micro with limited critical analysis of broader social processes."[111] Indeed, this inherent microscale challenge—that of transition between scales—is just as relevant for this book. To understand the larger stakes of this project, it is necessary to look at yet another dimension of cultural practices, that of social identity.

Despite the fascination with the West and the persistence of Soviet infrastructure, post-Soviet urbanites did not produce domestic spaces that resembled their Western counterparts, nor did they recreate the standard Soviet understanding of home but rather developed their own spatial model of apartment living. The spatial transformation of home was a necessary step for an individual to transition from a Soviet to a post-Soviet subject. In the final Soviet and early post-Soviet years, home remodeling became such an important part of social identity that home improvements were mentioned as a class-defining trait by the interviewees in Jennifer Patico's ethnographic study of the transforming notion of the post-Soviet middle class:

> Anya, who was in her twenties, divorced, and living with her mother, talked about herself and her friends as *srednie* [average, in the middle] and said that she thought that these srednie were people who had what they needed but could not often afford traveling abroad or completing significant renovations in their apartments.[112]

Domestic transformation established one's relevance to the post-Soviet reality. This becomes especially striking when looking at the opposite example: those homes that experienced little change since the collapse of the Soviet Union. Such apartments are referred to as *babushatnik*, which can be loosely translated as a "grandma's den." Despite its reference to grandmothers, it is not an endearing term. *Babushatnik* is used to describe an apartment where the owners willingly or involuntarily preserved elements of the former Soviet well-being, such as carpets on the walls and on the floors, a varnished chest of drawers (*komod*), a china set, and old-fashioned souvenirs so graphically described by Svetlana Boym.[113] Despite its clear ties to the lack of renovation and to former rather than present economic prosperity, *babushatnik* does not just define the homes of the poor or elderly. Neither does it characterize the antiquated habitats of former Soviet elites, unwilling to part with out-of-date luxury objects. Instead, it specifically describes an attachment to the old Soviet signifiers of *normal* people or *srednie*—a Soviet version of middle class—which have become irrelevant with the new signifiers of well-being.

Post-Soviet popular culture only knows one solution to the problem of an old-fashioned apartment—a remodeling, either massive or modest, yet often merciless to the signs of the previous epoch. Even when post-Soviet home improvement magazines offer advice on reusing or restoring elements of Soviet domestic interiors, they first and foremost suggest to rethink these pieces through the lens of Scandinavian style or Western mid-century modern.[114]

The transformations of domestic spaces described in the following chapters are a key to understanding the post-Soviet condition and post-Soviet mentality. Whereas in the United States homeownership describes one's economic standing and class identity,[115] in the early post-Soviet decades it was domestic remodeling (*remont*) that positioned an urbanite in post-Soviet societies. The next chapter of this work provides a detailed investigation into late-Soviet and post-Soviet remodeling and elucidates why this domestic practice became popular in the late 1980s and after the collapse of the USSR.

1

REMODELING

> **Citizens of the USSR have a right to housing. This right is provided for by the development and protection of the state and communal housing fund, assistance to cooperative and individual housing constructions, fair distribution of housing area under the public control, provision of housing along the realization of comfortable housing programs, and low apartment and utility fares. The citizens of the USSR must treat the provided housing with care.**
>
> —Excerpt from the Soviet Constitution, 1977

Scholars of the Soviet and post-Soviet fields have a common understanding that the term *remont* (repair, domestic remodeling, renovation) has a meaning quite different from its analogies elsewhere. Yet only a few works investigate the nature of remont, mostly in the form of sociological or ethnographic studies. These studies predominantly analyze the remont boom of the 1990s and the large-scale outcomes and attitudes, and only a few follow the development of remont over time or the reasons it took such a peculiar form. This chapter analyzes the birth of the contemporary understanding of remont through popular sources and legal documents in the years of perestroika reforms and its transformation due to the opening of the labor and commodity markets in the late 1980s and early 1990s. By doing so, this chapter introduces a view of remont other than as a symbolic breakaway from the Soviet past. This chapter speaks to the continuity of domestic transformations from the Soviet to post-Soviet era in the context of a society that may not have been expecting the USSR to collapse but was inherently prepared for it to happen.

What Is Remont?

First, what is remont if not just remodeling? What differentiates remont from an ordinary home makeover in any other time or place?

The roots of the word remont in post-Soviet languages go back to the historic French term *remonte*—the change or the secondary equipment of horses.

According to the *Explanatory Dictionary of the Living Great Russian Language*, by the second half of the nineteenth century, remont was already used to identify repair, mending, and remodeling and only secondarily to refer to its French-inherited meaning.[1] The evolution of the term did not stop in the 1800s; in 1926, the early era of the Soviet Union, remont captured the attention of a Western visitor—the great German Jewish philosopher Walter Benjamin—as one of the most omnipresent words and concepts to be found in post-revolutionary Moscow. Svetlana Boym retrospectively wrote about Benjamin's *Moscow Diaries*:

> In Moscow, Benjamin mastered two words in Russian: remont and *sei-chas*. One characterizes the perpetual transformation of space, a process of endless repair that had neither beginning nor end. Remont may indicate a major construction, or else a mirage, a pretext for doing nothing. The Moscow visitor is familiar with signs that indicate that a store or an office is "closed for remont," most often an indefinite period of time.[2]

Between the 1920s and the 1980s, remont preserved its indefinite nature described by Boym. It also remained a public affair so accurately noticed by Benjamin:

> Shortly before Christmas, there were two children on Tverskaia always sitting in the same spot against the wall of the Museum of the Revolution, covered in rags, whimpering. This would seem to be an expression of infinite misery of these beggars, but it may also be the result of clever organization, for of all the Moscow institutions they alone are reliable, they alone refuse to be budged. Everything else here takes place under a banner of remont.[3]

By the late 1980s and 1990s, the formerly public, never-ending remont became no less omnipresent in private domestic spheres. During the late-Soviet decades, domestic remont, just like any activity requiring commodities and labor, was complicated by commodity deficit and sluggishness of the officially available labor. The story of the Soviet commodity deficit is well known.[4] A Soviet citizen could not simply buy wallpaper due to the absence of variety or the lack of supply altogether. Yet a late-Soviet citizen was often able to encounter those commodities in film or magazines or by visiting other households. The awareness of fast and high-quality remont services did not come out of nowhere; rather this desire developed as a response to the known existence of better-quality services and trendy household interiors. A 1985 article in the Soviet women's magazine *Rabotnitsa* (The woman worker) claimed that remodeling services and consumer goods offered by the state were delivered with a very long time lag and were of low practical and aesthetic quality.[5] This perestroika outcry, belated by more than two decades of gradually developing consumer goods deficit, reflected less on the shortage of goods and labor and more on the growing ability of the individual to hire private construction workers for their apartment remont.

Remont as a culturally significant practice emerged in the USSR long before 1991. In fact, remont as maintenance or endless promise of improvement was so engrained in the Soviet society that the sociologist Ekaterina Gerasimova simply labeled it the "society of remont."[6] Yet, the Soviet remont—do-it-yourself maintenance and the grand Soviet projects of improvement that started to never be finished—differed drastically from the remont desires of the late 1980s and their realizations of the 1990s. A balance between seeing the practice of remont as continuous and denying its Soviet roots is necessary to understand the central place of remont in the post-Soviet life. The remont fever of the late 1980s and 1990s is often discussed in the context of previously state-owned housing privatization and the exposure to the West, which forced people to rethink their lived environments.[7] The major argument in many studies is that Soviet citizens, being only nominally in possession of their state-owned apartments, may have been significantly energized to remodel their homes after they received the right to turn their apartments into private property. However, the emergence of the concept of remont appears to predate the earliest legal precursors of mass housing privatization and even the broad acceptance of the imaginary Western homemaking practices as a definition of quality and affluence. Remont is broader than these immediate consequences of the collapse of the USSR; domestic remont is a form of habitus that developed through the decades of patently problematic housing conditions and lack of means for their improvement or alteration.

Without a doubt, housing privatization and exposure to the Western understanding of domestic spaces are among the most important consequences of the collapse of the USSR. At the same time, no less important is the continuity of the Soviet infrastructure and means of governance that lasted long into the post-Soviet decades. Scholarly works on privatization, Western exposure, and the continuities of the Soviet infrastructure started to appear in the mid-1990s and continue into the present day. Their topics included the socioeconomic effects of privatization, creation of ghettos for the urban poor,[8] and the new understanding of home that may or may not have emerged from privatization.[9] Privatization turned apartment dwellers into homeowners and simultaneously solidified the homelessness of those who did not own housing before 1991.[10] Finally, anthropologists and sociologists published studies concerned with privatization in the context of the state's socialist infrastructures, apartment buildings, and housing management institutions.

The most prominent example of such works is a study by Stephen Collier. Collier argues that despite neoliberal reforms after 1991, the housing infrastructure (such as state-operated communal gas, electricity, and heat networks) persisted, sustaining life in small, post-Soviet towns in the times of economic decline.[11] In other words, while the neoliberal reforms at the corporate level ensured a stable extraction or import of natural gas, the state-owned, communal urban engineering structures continued supplying this gas to the local boiler stations, even if the local apartment population had chronic debt on their energy bills. The socialist infrastructure and the neoliberal political organization were not mutually exclusive. This revelation reinstated the view that many scholars are now taking on the post-Soviet era. Namely, the continuity between the Soviet and post-Soviet times was greater than accounted for by transition theorists. This continuity was especially prominent at the scale and through the lens of everyday life and its structures rather than through large-scale rhetoric of a breakup with the socialist past.[12]

The continuity of everyday practices and structures to no extent denies change. On the contrary, it reinforces knowledge about change by tracing its roots, often before the boiling point of the collapse of the USSR, throughout Soviet history and the politics of everyday life prior to 1991. The ground for the remont boom of the 1990s was laid years prior through multiple shifts in legislation, attitudes, and everyday practices. In the 1990s, the practice of remont exploded and developed into a matter of tremendous social and cultural importance. Remont occupied such a large space in the post-Soviet consciousness that it even gained some notoriety and comedic representations.[13]

In this chapter, remont is first analyzed through the public ideas about apartment housing and remodeling found in late-Soviet and post-Soviet magazines, TV shows, and movies. The analysis of popular sources helps date the increase in interest in apartment remont and track the characteristic issues of Soviet housing that remodeling was aimed to remedy. Second, this chapter addresses an issue of supply required for the practice of remont: access to construction knowledge and materials and the newly emerged late-Soviet and post-Soviet mobility of labor. Demand, somewhat counterintuitively yet necessarily, is addressed last. Urban apartment housing for a long time experienced a lack of maintenance and was often constructed under low-quality standards, leading to a steady increase in demand for better living conditions throughout most of the history of the Soviet Union.[14] From this perspective, the demand did not emerge during the last Soviet and first post-Soviet years, but rather the supply was able to catch up with the demand for the first time since the relatively market-oriented New Economic Policy (1921–1928). Finally, this chapter speaks of the 1980s and 1990s remont as a social practice and a form of habitus. Backed with the continuity of demand and the shifts in supply for remont, the last section shows how these circumstances affected the way of life, the system of social interactions, and the bodily and spatial practices of post-Soviet apartment dwellers.

Remodeling in Popular Sources

The first part of this research traces the narrative of remont in the popular sources of the late-Soviet era. Domestic spaces were rather peripheral to the mainstream media with a powerful exception—*Rabotnitsa* magazine, the major women's magazine read all over the USSR. This focus on *Rabotnitsa* is not random: besides its extreme popularity throughout the USSR and during most of its history, *Rabotnitsa* clearly reflected the changes in the Soviet society through its themes and visuals. In the "country of the victorious socialism," domestic spaces and the domestic sphere were predominantly of interest to women's magazines, *Rabotnitsa* in particular. It started in 1914, as the "women's supplement to *Pravda*," by then a communist propaganda publication.[15] By the 1920s, it portrayed a Soviet woman in the spirit of military communism: with short hair, dressed in a unisex clothing, without any jewelry or makeup. By Stalin's time, *Rabotnitsa* illustrated the return of the traditions, including women portrayed as wives and mothers, not just workers. In the 1960s, it reflected the romanticism of the USSR modernization and the promise of the bright future; in the 1970s, it illustrated the return of the domesticity in place of Khrushchev-era functionalism. Finally, to no surprise, in the 1980s, it took on the questions of remodeling.

Prior to 1985, remont was not a typical topic for major or minor articles even in *Rabotnitsa* with its emphasis on the domestic sphere. However, on the eve of perestroika, it suddenly started publishing articles on remodeling. At first, they were short articles on fixing or constructing pieces of furniture. Soon, articles on remont took over major magazine spreads and acquired large photographs representing fashionable domestic spaces, or in other words, fashionable remont. In 1984, there were several articles about the home in *Rabotnitsa* describing, among other issues, the difficulty faced to receive individual apartment housing for a typical Soviet family.[16] However, throughout all twelve monthly issues that year, not a single article or reader-response letter was written about remont. The situation changed rather dramatically in 1985 and 1986: *Rabotnitsa* published two major articles boldly titled "Zona remonta" (Remont zone)[17] and "Tsena remonta" (The price of remont)[18] dedicated exclusively to remodeling and the troubles of doing it through the municipal institutions taking care of urban infrastructure—Residential Maintenance Offices or ZhEK (*Zhilishno-ekspluatazionnaia kontora*). The articles specifically uncovered the deficiency of construction materials that were supposed to be received from these institutions, the yearlong waiting lists, and the powerlessness of the residents in making remodeling decisions. For instance, "Tsena remonta" called for at least some quality accountability for state-executed remont.

Several general articles on housing in 1987 and 1988 were followed by an explosion of coverage. Between 1989 and 1991, *Rabotnitsa* published seventeen articles on housing and remont with two permanent monthly headings dedicated specifically to these subjects. In 1989, one of them, "Dom v kotorom my zhivem" (The house where we live), dedicated a page to remodeling; another one, "Domashnii kaleidoscop" (Home kaleidoscope), published articles on small home improvements, such as furniture construction. Besides these two permanent rubrics, *Rabotnitsa* published numerous articles on choosing colors, materials, and interior design elements for home remodeling. For instance, an article titled "10 metrov na 100 chelovek" (10 meters for 100 people) gave advice on how to make a small kitchen bigger. It offered two options: "in coordination with an architect you can move walls, expanding the kitchen and reducing the size of a room" or "the wall does not move, but niches are made in it for the shelves, drawers and the fridge and all this furniture is placed flush with the wall.[19] *Rabotnitsa* was not the only popular gendered magazine with articles about remont. *Burda Moden*, an extremely popular magazine, entered the Soviet media scene in the spring of 1987 and at first did not publish articles about home interior or remodeling.[20] However, by winter 1988, *Burda* already had a permanent rubric titled "Our Home" that suggested interior design improvements. Pictures used to illustrate these design ideas were clearly taken from outside the USSR, and the interiors were created with construction materials unavailable to the Soviet reader.[21]

Not only magazines but also many books of the time were dedicated to remont. For instance, *Home Academy Volume 1*, issued in 1990 with the intention to publish more issues in the future. Remont in this book was presented as a private endeavor, also suggesting that patient and skilled apartment dwellers could conduct remodeling on their own without even hiring the newly emerged firms or construction cooperatives.[22] Even those sources that simply informed citizens about homemaking practices without a direct mention of massive remodeling carefully addressed the issue, indicating its importance. In the late 1980s, central architectural and construction publisher *Stroizdat* published translated books on homemaking. A 1988 example of such publications, a book on domestic interiors originally published in Serbo-Croatian, started with a Soviet-added preface: "Contemporary multi-story residence buildings almost completely rule out the possibility of [layout] planning changes (moving partitions, making openings and such). Therefore, only those recommendations should be used that do not require such changes."[23]

This preface strongly affirmed that loadbearing walls and partitions should not be moved, even along the promise of a better apartment organization. A seemingly sound statement, it lost its credibility in the face of all the partitions moved and walls modified in later years. Rather than expressing the reality of Soviet apartment housing, it reinstated the predictable interest of the state and institutionalized architects in keeping things as they were.

Rabotnitsa continued publishing articles on remodeling throughout the early post-Soviet years but was no longer unique in its efforts. Multiple interior design magazines came to post-Soviet markets, this time not to suggest DIY remont techniques but to offer different aesthetic choices for those able to hire professionals to make their remont work. The most notable of these magazines were first published in the 1990s and early 2000s: *Idei vashego doma* (Ideas for your home) in 1995, *Krasivye kvartiry* (Beautiful apartments) in 2001, the Russian version of the *Architectural Digest* in 2002, and many others.

In 1999, *Idei vashego doma* magazine dedicated an entire issue to replanning strategies—moving, demolishing, or constructing walls—for the P-44 apartment housing series.[24] These seventeen- to twenty-five-story panel apartment blocks, first developed in the 1970s, were built throughout former Soviet cities. It also happened to be a rare housing series that kept being built after 1991. Apartment layouts in this series were commonly considered relatively spacious[25] (unlike, for example, the early Khrushchev-era series). Additionally, the series was updated in the 1990s to better respond to contemporary requirements, such as having bigger kitchens. *Idei vashego doma* published its special issue due to the commonality of P-44 buildings and the relative ease of replanning in these panel apartment buildings. And of course, most importantly, the magazine dedicated an entire issue to a particular case of replanning because of the extreme popularity of remont and replanning in the 1990s. This issue, just like many other printed materials at the time, indicated a major trend that took place in post-Soviet remodeling—the displacement of walls and the introduction of the open apartment plan, virtually absent from existing housing.[26]

During the 1990s and early 2000s, multiple remont-centered shows premiered on television. The format for these shows was similar to widely popular American remodeling television shows: homeowners let a team of designers and construction specialists remodel their outdated or unmaintained housing and were later presented with their radically changed, professionally designed dwelling. However, a major difference between the American and the post-Soviet television shows of this kind was that US shows predominantly focused on the most stereotypical unit of US housing, a single-family house, whereas post-Soviet shows first and foremost dealt with an apartment and even more often with just one room. These shows, such as *Kvartirnyi vopros* (Apartment question) beginning in 2001 or *Shkola remonta* (Remodeling school) beginning in 2003, rarely featured replanning since replanning often had to be legally reported and was bureaucratically complex. Instead, they usually approached a given room-sized space with a cosmetic remont strategy and zoned a small room differently to comfortably fit more functions and visually or perceptually expand the space. These shows raised two major housing problems leading to the tremendous popularity of remont: the dilapidated state and small areas of apartment housing interiors.

The omnipresence of remont in the media was a reciprocal phenomenon. On one hand, it indicated the overwhelming public interest in remont; on the other hand, it instigated even broader interest and desire for remont as a necessary marker of access to resources and labor and the ability to keep up with the changing trends.

Supply: Hands, Experience, and Drywall

While the boom of remodeling-related magazine articles and books is a rather clear indication of the topic's popularity, it does not explain why remont became an issue of interest in the first place. The roots of the fashion for remodeling could be found among the shifts in everyday life circumstances, which led to the growing interest and growing possibility of remont.

The first legislation allowing USSR citizens to privatize their apartments came out in 1988.[27] Together with the 1991 collapse of the USSR, it is typically analyzed as the historic threshold effecting the late- and post-Soviet understandings of home.[28] However, even prior to 1991, Soviet society experienced certain shifts that led to the fast increase in interest in home remodeling, as illustrated in the previous section of the chapter. Where there is demand, there should be supply. The late-Soviet supply for apartment remodeling can be broadly divided into two categories: the labor and the construction knowledge.

The first one, skilled labor, was determined by a set of late-Soviet circumstances. On November 19, 1986, the Supreme Soviet passed the law *Ob individualnoi trudovoi deiatel'nosti* (About individual labor activity) which, for the first time since the 1950s, legalized private labor outside of state employment during citizens' free time. This law effectively legalized the preexisting, unofficial construction method nicknamed *shabashka*. *Shabashniki* were construction workers who hired themselves out informally during their vacation time to do quick construction work. This practice existed in the USSR prior to the passing of the private labor law, yet after the law was passed, hiring shabashniki no longer required special knowledge or connections and was no longer looked upon as informal or illegal. The laws concerning private cooperation shifted from less to more restricting a couple of times between 1986 and 1991, but despite these formal norms, the legalization of cooperatives established an official positive precedent for private labor in the USSR. As the formal economy of the USSR gradually collapsed, workers shifted their efforts to informal private jobs, which had earlier had a deficit of skilled or motivated manpower. Apartment remodeling was a sphere where motivated workers were particularly valued.

The inept performance of official institutions—Residential Maintenance Offices or ZhEK—in remodeling services was ubiquitously understood. An apartment owner interviewed for this study, who over the years initiated several remodeling projects, mentioned that her family had to use a public restroom by her house for several weeks because the construction brigade disappeared after dismantling an old toilet but before installing a new one.[29] The rest of the interviewees, when asked about their attempts at remont before perestroika, reported minor changes, such as new wallpaper, and habitually doing superficial renovations nicknamed cosmetic remodeling on their own without any input from the formally responsible institutions. Construction workers, available through the Residential Maintenance Offices in theory, were either unavailable or absurdly unreliable in practice. Considering the incapability of municipal institutions to provide quality remodeling services, the demand for privately employed construction workers was very high. As soon as this demand was met, every Soviet citizen who had enough cash could receive a relatively fast and acceptable-quality remont.

No less important than the legal basis for the labor of private workers is the question of who were these shabashniki. A profound and detailed overview and the history of shabashniki can be found in *Broad Is My Native Land* by Siegelbaum and Moch.[30] In this book, shabashniki are defined as "temporary workers earning money 'off the books' in the late-Soviet period."[31] The heyday of shabashniki happened along with the Great Construction Projects of Communism in the 1960s and 1970s. At the end of the Great Soviet Construction projects and the opening of symbolic Baikal–Amur Mainline in 1984, shabashniki predominantly shifted their labor into the private sphere.[32] Many formerly state-hired construction workers were now able to offer their labor and skills to the informal construction market.

Shabashniki exploited one of the newly emerged types of late-Soviet mobility: the growing formal and informal porousness of the Soviet borders with Socialist Bloc countries and the West. Shabashniki were the carriers of experience and knowledge from outside the late USSR; this knowledge, after entering the Soviet reality, became fashion trends in the understanding of domestic interior remodeling aesthetics. While it is hard to find official statistics on border crossings between the Soviet Union and its neighboring states, border crossings clearly took place, and a large part of it was due to temporary labor migration. To Soviet propaganda, seasonal workers were a foreign element, just like the experiences and knowledge they carried from abroad. Temporary workers migrated following demand for labor, carrying the newly acquired knowledge of new construction methods and materials. The populations of the Soviet border zones could cross borders under a simplified procedure, creating labor traffic between Western Ukraine, Belarus, and Poland; between Finland and Leningrad Oblast;[33] and between Belarus, Russia, and the Baltic states. An illustration of the scale of border crossing can be seen in the introduction to the 1990 Soviet law about the regulations for citizens crossing state borders: "In the context of international cooperation development in humanitarian sphere, the Cabinet of Ministers of the USSR notes that there is a growing number of foreign private and touristic trips conducted by Soviet citizens and visits to the Soviet Union by international citizens. The trips in near border regions of the USSR and the nearing countries have become particularly active."[34]

By 1991, the number of people who, according to polls, wanted to do unskilled work abroad had reached 33 percent of respondents.[35] In 1990, Vladimir Sherbakov, the minister of economy of the USSR and the first vice-prime minister, claimed that thousands of Soviet citizens already worked abroad illegally, in Scandinavia in particular.[36] Returning back home from other countries, these migrant workers carried resources for the reconstruction of their living environments and new knowledge about methods of construction, agriculture, and other industries. Moreover, in 1991, at the time when new construction materials entered the markets of the former Soviet Union, these former shabashniki were already somewhat familiar with these materials and willing to use them for apartment remodeling. To paraphrase Alexei Yurchak, these construction workers were utterly prepared for the collapse of the Soviet Union through their experiences of private labor and construction technologies outside the USSR.[37]

Besides guest labor abroad, expertise with new materials was also brought to the post-Soviet states by importers and producers of construction materials opening operations in the post-Soviet markets. International corporations, such as Knauf Gips, that brought their marketing and production to the post-Soviet countries after 1991 had to provide training and support educational programs in professional educational institutions in order to supply the labor market with workers familiar with their technologies. Knauf Gips developed a framework of collaboration with these institutions in the post-Soviet states that involved instructor training and providing teaching materials, including textbooks that Knauf has been publishing in several post-Soviet countries.[38] At the same time, despite Knauf's best effort, construction workers particularly good at drywall installation are rare in post-Soviet context, because as soon as they become truly good at their job they find higher paying construction jobs in Western countries.[39]

In addition to shabashniki who traveled abroad, local populations and internal migrants were increasingly more involved in the construction industry. The last years of Soviet rule were characterized by a rapid change in the dynamics of job security, income, and respectability. The sharp economic crisis of

1989 to 1991 and the complete demolition of the Soviet centralized economy after 1991 led to the devaluation of income and jobs in previously respectable or at least stably paid professions.[40] The late-Soviet and early post-Soviet military conflicts created large numbers of refugees. One outcome this caused was the internal migration of workers from villages, small mono-industrial towns, and cities to metropolitan centers, where new types of jobs and resources were more readily available than at the periphery. A second related outcome was the shift of the labor force to professions other than their original occupations.[41]

Requalification, another form of mobility besides migration, characterized the late-Soviet working-class occupations. Professions such as coal mining, previously seen as economically and politically prestigious working-class occupations, no longer had much value or stability.[42] A similar process took place in the post-Soviet armies, particularly among army professionals. Mykola N., a current-day owner of a construction business interviewed for this project, reported giving up a military career around 1991 to pursue construction jobs since he did not see any chance of worthy development in the contemporary army. In 1993, he was working as a foreman with construction brigades conducting apartment remodeling in Kyiv, Ukraine. He explained: "When the Soviet Union fell apart, I had to have some job. Since the army was shrinking, I wrote a discharge request. By the will of fate, I ended up here in Kyiv. My relatives were here; mom was also here. My sister's [. . .] husband worked as an architect; during the collapse of the Soviet Union, he started working with firms that entered the market to do *evroremont*." "Evroremont" was a neologism for the remodeling done to new post-Soviet standards in the supposedly Westernized style, typically with the use of imported materials. Mykola N.'s account continues, "This was 1993. He recommended me to his partner, left, and I stayed with this partner . . . That is when I started working with real estate—remodeling and construction." Commissions were "typically remodeling, rarely reconstruction. There were cases of cosmetic remodeling, but also cases of re-planning."[43]

From another perspective, the draft army could have prepared men for entering the construction job market. Another respondent, Ivan G., clarified that he first did construction work while a soldier in a construction battalion from 1976 to 1978. After the army, he did not pursue a construction career until the late 1980s, when he switched jobs from being a driver to doing construction work for government-sponsored and private projects. Ivan mentioned working on a small number of governmental commissions, such as cosmetic remodeling of schools and kindergartens, private domestic construction work, and several private business commissions as early as the late 1980s.[44]

Mykola mentioned that his first apartment remodeling experiences were predominantly commissioned by foreigners who could not find housing acceptable to their standards and, hence, decided to remodel existing desirable housing for themselves.[45] Standards of quality expected by foreigners made a big impression on Mykola and his partner, architect Oleksii R. In the interview, Oleksii mentioned that this first experience was a shock and that the knowledge he gained during his first foreign-commissioned project served him well in his next apartment interior designs.[46]

Professional construction worker Vitalii F. explained that, after 1991, he shifted to privately hired construction labor. Just like Mykola, he explained that many construction jobs in the early 1990s were commissioned by foreigners. Vitalii also discussed several cases of remont in which foreign construction professionals hired local brigades to work on projects commissioned by foreign investors.[47]

By the late 1980s, despite the perestroika reform efforts, the rate of officially accountable construction in the USSR declined. Despite the never-ending housing shortage and the arrival of an additional two hundred thousand troops and their families from their former disposition in Eastern Europe,[48] housing construction rates in 1990 decreased by almost 10 percent, even in comparison to the previous, already-unsuccessful year.[49] At the same time, multiple private enterprises emerged that were capable of securing the means to hire construction workers for their purposes. Construction specialists interviewed for this study, who were active during Soviet and post-Soviet times, reported abandoning government-sponsored construction and shifting to the private sphere, where commissioners happened to have money and a stable supply of jobs.

The collapse of the USSR further secured the position of private labor in the newly emerging post-Soviet economies and opened markets in the former USSR to free trade. The prices skyrocketed, along with an accumulation of consumer goods previously unseen in Soviet consumer reality. Construction materials from abroad entered the former Soviet markets, shocked the population with their quality and functionality, and transformed the mass idea of what was possible in private apartment remodeling.[50] Certain remont methods, such as moving partition walls, had already appeared in mass media during perestroika. Construction materials necessary to move those partition walls or to make openings in load bearing walls, such as metal beams with drywall on the surface, became much more readily available after 1991.

Demand: State of Emergency

Just like with the hibernating consumerism for goods and services that seemingly came out of nowhere in the 1990s, the Soviet people were very well prepared, if not starved, for a chance at making changes to domestic interiors. By the mid-1980s, interiors of Stalin- and Khrushchev-era housing were partially worn out, and many pre-1917 apartment buildings were in a nearly dilapidated state. Thirty years had passed since the Decree of the Central Committee of the Communist Party of the Soviet Union "On Elimination of Excesses in Design and Construction" and the beginning of *khrushchevka* apartment block construction (1954–1957). Also, fifty years had passed since the beginning of the construction of Stalin-era apartment buildings. These buildings and individual apartments had seen a very limited number of changes in that time. Some partition walls in Stalin-era buildings had been transformed to accommodate communal-style, multifamily living, and some cosmetic renovation procedures, such as wallpaper renewal or tile replacement, were done in Khrushchev-era apartments. But that was the typical limit of change taking place in individual apartments until the mid-1980s.

The pre-1917 buildings require a separate explanation. In many post-Soviet languages, there exists a common expression for dilapidated yet still occupied housing: *avariinyi dom*, literally an "emergency house" or, more accurately, "a building in a state of emergency." In American English, the closest synonymous expression is found in architectural practice: "a building in precarious condition." However, unlike the Soviet and post-Soviet analog, this phrase is not frequently used in everyday conversations about housing conditions. The widespread American expression "foreclosed home" carries a similar idiomatic connotation to *avariinyi dom* but does not have any widely used synonyms in Eastern European post-Soviet languages. Svetlana Boym raised an argument of cultural and linguistically untranslatable terms in her 1994 book *Common Places: Mythologies of Everyday Life in Russia*. Boym's "common places" were incomparably more monumental: she spoke of the word *byt*, everyday life with a special Russian sense of stagnation and routine, and *bytie*, the spiritual and philosophical being. "A building in a state of emergency" can be read as a small fraction of the large *byt* category so carefully analyzed by Boym.[51]

"A building in a state of emergency" largely defined the domestic life of the Soviet populations residing in pre-1917 housing in the second half of the twentieth century. The pre-1917 apartment buildings that, prior to the Khrushchev construction boom, composed the largest type of available urban housing consistently deteriorated through the twentieth century. In the 1920s and 1930s, the pre-1917 apartments were massively turned into communal apartments, where a portion of a room, a single room, or a group of rooms were occupied by unrelated tenants and kitchens and bathrooms were used communally. Soviet communal apartments have been relatively well studied in many academic works,[52] art forms,[53] and popular projects.[54] Yet the buildings that contain these communal apartments are often given less attention.

These buildings may or may not have experienced reconstructions after World War II if they happened to be located in the cities affected by war. Many of the buildings, not seriously damaged during the war, only went through cosmetic maintenance. The tenants of these apartments only maintained their personal spaces and only to a degree possible considering the deficit of construction materials. Common areas were typically used with regular cleaning but without other maintenance.

Although the state recognized the problem with poorly maintained housing at the highest level, its efforts to solve the problem were not entirely successful. In 1964, the State Committee of Construction of the USSR issued a decree specifying the terms and timelines of use and repair for different types of housing.[55] Despite this new legal framework for reconstruction and repair, by 1978, the state of housing was still unsatisfactory to the degree that the Cabinet of Ministers of the USSR had to issue another decree prompting housing repair and reconstruction.[56] By that time, repair and reconstruction efforts were no longer just about dilapidated pre-1917 housing but also about fixing construction defects and shortcomings of the new housing built in the previous two decades. This is clearly visible in the Cabinet of Ministers tasking the USSR Gosstroi State Committee in civil and residential construction by 1980 "to introduce into the developed and adjusted series [*tipovye*] of housing projects a section on 'technical exploitation' that will contain instructions on efficient technical maintenance and repair [remont] of the structure and mechanical systems of residential buildings."[57]

Both of these documents abounded with the term "capital reconstruction" (*kapitalnyi remont* or *kapremont* for short). The situation had not changed by 1989, when another decree on the framework and quality of reconstruction came out.[58] Right after the collapse of the Soviet Union in 1991, William Moskoff described the scale of the problem as follows:

> While the housing shortage was not a new problem, it got worse as Perestroika wore on. The predicament was so bad, that in a 1990 nationwide poll of a hundred rural and urban areas housing was rated as the most severe socioeconomic problem in the country. At the end of 1989, some eleven million people were living in dormitories, more than five million were living in what the Soviets regarded as dilapidated housing, and ten percent of all urban families were living in rooms in communal apartments. Almost fifty percent of the population lived in housing with less than nine square meters per person, an amount considered below sanitary standards.[59]

The problem of run-down housing has continued past the Soviet Union; for instance, in 2017, the Ministry of Construction of the Russian Federation stated that 51 percent of apartment housing in Russia required capital reconstruction. This term was used to identify a type of reconstruction that involved repair with possible and typical replacement of the structural parts of the building without changing the function of the building. By the 1970s, a typical method was to demolish everything inside the building skin—historic facades—and replace the historic brick, wooden, or metal load-bearing beams and wooden floors with metal frames and monolith slabs.

When capital reconstruction was approved by the city, the dwellers of the dilapidated buildings were offered two choices: either to move to new apartments offered to them by the city or to temporarily move into the so-called "maneuver fund" housing.[60] Both options had shortcomings: new apartments were located at the outskirts of the city, unlike the old, dilapidated yet very centrally located buildings, and temporary housing was typically represented by dormitory-style apartment buildings with shared kitchens. Additionally, a Soviet-style capital reconstruction could last for years, so those residents who chose temporary dormitories could have been stuck there for a very long time. And yet, no matter how problematic, capital reconstructions offered some kind of change from the deteriorating housing.[61]

Although most acute in the pre-1917 communal apartment buildings, a lack of maintenance, space, and functional space separation led to the majority of the population living in undesirable conditions. The grand Soviet modernization project, the mass construction of functionalist apartment block buildings under Khrushchev and Brezhnev, was not an exception.

Khrushchev-era apartments, the first truly mass solution to the housing crisis, had very small square footage. A typical 1950s American home had three bedrooms, while a typical Soviet apartment had two rooms. Take, for example, National Plan Service catalogue homes. An American single-family, two-bedroom house from the 1952 catalogue had 816 square feet of living area.[62] At the same time, an early Khrushchev-era apartment from the I-434 series built in 1958–1964 had 290 square feet of living area.

A detailed account of the minimalist dimensions of Soviet apartment housing can be found in the two recent books *Communism on Tomorrow Street: Mass Housing and Everyday Life after Stalin*[63] and *Stories of House and Home: Soviet Apartment Life during the Khrushchev Years*.[64] The former started with an investigation into the reasons for Khrushchev-era apartments being so small. In particular, in the very beginning of his khrushchevka study, Steven Harris brought up a letter to the Third All-Union Congress of Architects specifying that life in the standardized apartments was complicated with their small dimensions, making it impossible to normally perform daily functions.[65]

Khrushchevka apartment eat-in kitchens were even more notoriously small than the apartments themselves—4.7 to 7.1 square meters (or 53 to 76 square

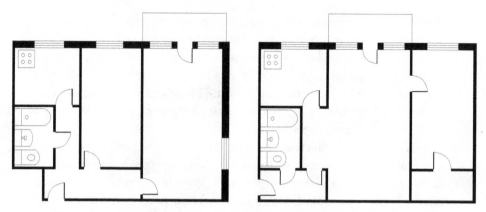

FIGURE 1.1. Plans of two typical early Khrushchev-era apartments.

feet)—while typical kitchens of small 1950s American houses reached 166 square feet (figure 1.1).[66] Already by the 1980s, these kitchens were perceived as largely problematic, which can be seen in a *Rabotnitsa* article suggesting their expansion at the expense of loss of space in the next room.[67] While this was often impossible in the prefab concrete block apartments, the article still insists that improvements were possible even for those "five-square meter" kitchens. The popular dream of a bigger kitchen did not start out of nowhere: by the 1970s, early prefab apartment series with small kitchens and rooms gave way to the "improved plan" apartments with slightly bigger kitchens and rooms. This newer housing was readily available for the residents of older Khrushchev-era apartments to observe, demonstrating that better residential conditions were possible and making them even more desirable. Most studies of Soviet elites specify that regular urbanites were aware of the lifestyles of the *nomenklatura* (bureaucrats) or other petit elites (highly ranked scientists, artists, and military). For example, a 1978 study of Soviet elites specifies that the émigré respondents reported visiting these luxurious political elite dwellings at some point in their lives.[68] Through this social mobility of direct interactions with elites, citizens were able to experience firsthand the possibilities of domestic comfort in better apartment layouts.

In addition to the personal experiences of visiting elite housing, citizens were exposed to the knowledge of better housing through popular culture. The 1981 Soviet blockbuster *Moscow Does Not Believe in Tears* introduced viewers to an elite apartment setting of so-called "generals' apartment houses" on Mosfilmovskaia Street in Moscow.[69] More large domestic spaces that could have easily provoked jealousy in an average khrushchevka dweller were demonstrated to the public in another cult Soviet movie from the 1970s—*The Irony of Fate*.[70] *The Irony of Fate*, a very broadly cited film of the era, also illustrated a major zeitgeist ele-

ment of late-Soviet lifestyles: the broad dissatisfaction with the sameness of consumer goods offered to the public. In *The Irony of Fate*, this sameness is shown
through the two main characters confusing their homes in different cities—
Leningrad and Moscow—due to the fact that their neighborhoods, buildings,
apartments, and even furniture and decorations looked exactly the same. Besides Soviet movies providing the general public with a critical perspective of
their everyday spaces, the late-perestroika TV audience was also exposed to foreign shows, particularly Brazilian and, later, Mexican soap operas, which are
often believed to have had an effect on the ideas of the look and the spatiality of
home.[71] The constructed interiors of these soap opera movie sets exposed the
population to a rather univocal definition of what an affluent house was supposed to look like, among other reasons possibly causing the notorious love of
the early post-Soviet nouveau riche for historicized architectural styles.[72]

Even the official Soviet architectural discourse was saturated with ideas about
better housing conditions. During the 1980s and particularly the second half of
the decade, Gosstroi (abbreviation for the State Construction Committee) held
multiple architectural competitions to develop better types of residential housing,
often on the basis of the Khrushchev-era apartment buildings. A detailed scrutiny
of these competition projects is given in the following chapters. At this point, however, it is important to note that the problem of unsatisfactory housing conditions,
in both old and modern buildings, was recognized at the highest level of the Soviet
ministries. Attempts were made to find solutions for the problematic housing of
the early prefab apartment block series, if not in practice then at least in theory.[73]

Besides the Soviet indigenous demand for remont, it is important to separately
mention the Western expats who entered the Soviet reality in the early 1990s. This
rather small group of people, together with the newly forming post-Soviet elites,
propelled the creation of the first premium construction services and interior design firms, as well as imported furniture and construction material stores. Available housing did not satisfy the standards of these Westerners, but the high salaries
they received were enough to invest in apartment replanning and remodeling.[74]
One of the earliest firms offering such services was Skanflot (a shared initiative of
Aeroflot, Dutch Scanior Design, and local Avangard cooperative). In a 1991 commercial, Scanflot claimed to only work with "large businesses and wealthy entre-
preneurs," specifying a minimal sum and square footage of a commission.[75] Over
the late 1990s and 2000s replannings in regular, nonluxurious homes became so
popular that even the architectural institutions that had designed this housing in
the prior years took interest in resident-performed replannings. So much so that in
2011, Moscow Scientific-Research and Project Institute of Typology and Experimental Design (MNIITEP) released a catalog of possible replanning scenarios
for its most widespread housing series designed during the Soviet years.[76]

Construction and furniture businesses that first came to fruition thanks to Western expats and local nouveau riche also soon opened to the general public in the form of construction material and furniture supermarkets, such as Epitsentr in Kyiv or IKEA in Moscow.[77]

The post-Soviet urban population, long dissatisfied with the commodity and services deficit, eagerly plunged into remont as soon as the necessary qualified labor became available on a private basis and actively continued remodeling in the 1990s with the arrival of foreign construction materials. "Do not take your apartment [layout] for granted!" calls the late-1980s *Rabotnitsa* heading "The House Where We Live," echoing the remont craze of the late-Soviet and the first post-Soviet decades.[78]

Remont as a Domestic and Social Practice

This chapter started with Walter Benjamin's observation of remont as a state and social practice in the beginning of the twentieth century and briefly after the dramatic changes of the 1917 Bolshevik Revolution. It is nothing but logical to end with an observation of remont as a social practice at the end of the twentieth century during perestroika and after the collapse of the USSR.

Once again, late- and post-Soviet remont was nothing like regular remodeling. First, since remont was predominantly undertaken in apartment housing, it inevitably led to cooperation, negotiation, or conflict between the dwellers of the apartment building. Although the same would be true for the rest of apartment housing elsewhere, in the post-Soviet cities conflict was aggravated by the omnipresence of remont. Second, these relationships were often aggravated by the continuity of remont, which may have taken months, years, and, in some extreme and often caricaturized cases, decades.

In the second half of the 1990s and, particularly, after the recovery from the 1998 financial crisis in the Russian Federation that also largely affected the surrounding countries, not just quotidian repair, mending, and repurposing but massive apartment remont became a form of post-Soviet habitus. This habitus was a physical embodiment of the social and economic hopes and insecurities of the first post-Soviet decades, or, in Edward Casey's words, that which "ties the self and the place together."[79]

The population of the post-Soviet countries went through a radical socioeconomic downshift after 1991. Throughout the 1990s, the economies of European post-Soviet countries, still largely dependent on the Russian economy, experienced many ups and downs that were followed by a relative stability between

1999 and 2008. This period of economic safety was the time when remont practice extended past the limits of the upper and upper-middle classes and became
a popular affair among the rest of the urban population. The economic stability
allowed for saving, but the resources were still limited. This led to apartment
dwellers often continuing to live in the apartment during remodeling, whether
they remodeled themselves or hired professional construction workers.

With limited resources, remont became a way of life that lasted for years rather
than a finite period of time.[80] Apartment owner Natalia S. reported that she and
her family stayed in their three-room apartment during the remodeling and replanning of the kitchen and the bathroom, explaining that there was nowhere
else to live.[81] Another respondent, Oksana H., said that their resources were
limited, so they worked on each area of the apartment as soon as they had enough
money to get to it.[82] This meant that remont could virtually last forever, until all
tasks and complications that may have come along the way were done. Even those
residents that were able to live outside of their permanent homes during remodeling reported remont taking a very long time. Maryna D., who purchased a
newly built apartment with her partner in 2000, did not live in the home during
remont. Yet it took an entire year.[83]

Apartment resident Mykola I. recalled that his remont lasted for seven years
and that construction workers "lived here [in the apartment]; they had their own
keys."[84] The family also stayed in the apartment during remodeling and, just like
Oksana's family, moved from room to room along with the moving construction. Mykola further explained, "Imagine, it is 8 in the morning. You are asleep.
Suddenly a man enters your bedroom. He already has a lit cigarette because he
is thinking. He thinks about what work can be done, and he doesn't care that
you are sleeping here."[85] For Mykola, apartment remont lasted until, at some
point in time, he "kicked out" the construction workers.

Curiously, the term remont in many post-Soviet languages defines not only a
process of remodeling but also the state of the domestic space. For instance, one
could say that an apartment has a very high-quality remont, echoing remont being a form of habitus—a stable prism for the perception of reality. The inadequate
housing conditions, the availability of labor and commodities, and the desire to
fit the new reality created the state of permanent remont, when the desire for
renovation appeared to be more powerful than the ability to ever finalize the process. The lasting quality of late- and post-Soviet remodeling, also known as "eternal remont," has inspired several scholars to address it as the perpetual resourceful
mechanisms continuously present prior to and after the collapse of the Soviet
Union.[86]

The never-ending remont is equally in tune with Tatiana Bulakh's observation about the post-Soviet change. Although scholars have long been critical of

the "transition" principle that involved post-Soviet countries growing to resemble Western neoliberal democracies and economies over time, on the ground people may still speak about "becoming Europe" in the very same transition terms, especially when it comes to consumption. Bulakh's Ukrainian respondents in 2014 referred to IKEA and H&M as signifiers of European belonging, because Ukraine did not have branches of these stores at the time.[87] Ironically, both IKEA and H&M were present in Ukraine in 2021, yet the process of "becoming Europe" was hardly complete, as there was always some consumer ideal that was yet to be fulfilled (with unrestricted travel being a part of the world of consumption). Equally, a post-Soviet remodeling, once started, often carried a doom of permanence as some other expense or type of work always emerged in the process.

Besides its infiniteness, apartment remont possessed other qualities of interest: its sensual component, its element of conspicuous consumption, and the social implication of those two factors. Remont was loud, and both early Khrushchev-era apartment series and later panel housing had imperfect sound isolation. While the dwellers of brick buildings were relatively lucky, concrete panels of the apartment housing series transmitted sounds perfectly. This problem is not unique to the USSR and the post-Soviet world; apartment buildings everywhere in the world are notorious for poor sound ecology in comparison to their single-family home counterparts. Yet in the post-Soviet cities where apartment dwellers massively went into remont, it was a highly acoustically toxic activity. Imagine the sound of a drill hitting the wall a couple of floors above you being transmitted by concrete walls into your own home. Now imagine that it is not just one apartment but several apartments that are undergoing remont along your or a neighboring staircase. As soon as this one is done, somebody else is going to pull together their courage and finances and plunge into their round of remodeling. Remont, in this way, became a part of daily life, not only for the owners of the apartment under remodeling but for the entire population of the hallway, staircase, and even the whole apartment block.

The problem of remont noise was reflected in the changes of legislation meant to control acceptable sound levels in residential buildings. Section 24 "Prevention and Elimination of Noise" of the 1969 Soviet law on sanitary norms and healthcare fundamentals is a two-paragraph general statement that it is the responsibility of both citizens and authorities to prevent and eliminate excessive noise.[88] Section 24 of the post-Soviet Ukrainian law on the same subject is a multipage document that specifies that at "protected objects"—apartment housing and other buildings—"holding construction (remont) works . . . accompanied with noise is forbidden on workdays between 9 p.m. and 8 a.m., and at all times on weekends." It continues to specify that "an owner or a renter of the space, which will go under remodeling, must inform the dwellers of all contiguous apartments about the beginning of these works. Under an agreement with all the contiguous apartment dwellers remont and construction works can be also undertaken on holidays and weekends. Noise that occurs during construction works should not exceed the sanitary norms at any time of day."[89]

On the one hand, remont noises still frequently caused conflicts between neighbors, who thought that noise exceeded the norm. On the other hand, apartment remont often led to collaborations between neighbors deciding to perform it simultaneously. One apartment resident, who undertook a replanning and remodeling effort in the middle of the first decade of the 2000s, reported collaborating with their neighbors and doing remont simultaneously, since part of their effort was to privatize and connect the building's attic to their top-floor apartments. There were three apartments on the floor, and the third apartment's owners decided not to participate. Throughout the process, when the two neighboring families shared common construction brigades and legal repercussions, the third neighbor wrote complaints about the remont noise.[90]

Whether the neighbors argued or collaborated and whether it was themselves or others taking on a remont endeavor, remont ended up being heavily present in everyone's life for a long time. The gradually moving remont made some rooms or home functions unavailable or heavily limited. The already modest apartment spaces were even more limited as the residents' possessions and everyday practices had to be relocated away from the area being remodeled. For instance, a three-room apartment undergoing remont in the kitchen and bathroom and using one of the rooms for temporary storage became a two-room apartment with limited kitchen and bathroom functions, while the number of occupants typically remained the same. All of this created semipermanent spatial relationships and altered the way individuals and families performed in those apartments. Remont became something bigger than just a spatial and aesthetic change but rather a new type of living condition that persistently continued into the post-Soviet reality. Remodeling was not something that was just supposed to pass by in a limited period of time. It became a habitus, a special social condition, defined not so much by the finality of remodeling or its final results but by the participation in the continuous remont craze. As the Saint Petersburg countercultural band Leningrad sang in their 2007 song dedicated to remodeling: "Remont has settled in my home."[91] Furthermore, for the protagonist of this song, just like for the millions of post-Soviet urbanites, remont determined not just their home but also their identity. Fehérváry described the juxtaposition of socialist concrete grayness and capitalist color in the Hungarian accounts of displeasure with socialism and demand for capitalist consumption and stylistic freedoms.[92] This work argues that it is not the West-inspired stylistic or aesthetic choices that made a person and a home post-Soviet but rather the shifts in the spatial organization and the cultural practice of domestic remodeling itself that allowed an apartment dweller to leave their sense of Soviet self in the past.

2

SLEEPING

> **Under the Soviet system bedrooms are not permitted.**
>
> —Mikhail Bulgakov, *Zoyka's Apartment*

Sleep, arguably the most important function of a home, is in many cultures associated with a special space—the bedroom. This common understanding, however, has been frequently undermined by the reality of urban living, apartment homes in particular.[1] The late- and post-Soviet spaces for sleep were not an exclusion. In Russian and many other Slavic post-Soviet languages, the word for bedroom is ambiguous: *spalnia* (from the verb *spat'*, to sleep) does not specify whether it is a room or some other sort of space. The fluidity of the word *spalnia* is, of course, coincidental to late-Soviet urban living conditions, yet it accurately defines them. A space for sleep did not have to be a room; this space did not even require a bed; it happened where and when sleep was possible and acceptable. The understanding of a space suitable for sleeping drastically transformed into several trajectories after the collapse of the Soviet Union in 1991. This chapter undertakes the task of tracking the precursors, process, and outcomes of this transformation.

The chapter begins with the story of the late-Soviet and post-Soviet sleeping spaces through the brief account of the urban bedroom's rise and fall in the twentieth century. With the help of an inquiry into the normative floor areas, daily practices, and rhythms, it explains the spaces of sleep typical for late-Soviet urban apartments. This chapter then demonstrates how the desire for private sleeping space became normalized and how private space for sleep turned from dream to reality in the post-Soviet replanning projects.

Soviet housing politics produced a heavily regulated urban household: it had to strictly adhere to the upper limitations of floor area and room numbers per person. While these rules were no longer relevant after 1991, some of the formal tendencies forged under the USSR persisted. Such was the tendency for rooms to be multi- rather than monofunctional. However, the similarities in form (such as the same number of people in the apartment) should not be perceived as an ultimate sign that nothing has changed. Dependent on their economic and social standing, post-Soviet urbanites took different paths in transforming their housing; apartments that used to be very similar radically diverged in their layouts and functional zones with the help of newly built or demolished partitions, different furniture arrangements, and different resident demographics that led to varying uses. Many formally opposite tendencies could be used to bring about similar results. For example, a private sleeping space could have been achieved by either building or demolishing a partition wall. Therefore, this chapter first investigates the preconditions for the rise in the plurality of the post-Soviet approaches to apartment form and then looks at the similarities among different apartment spatial organizations that emerged after 1991.

Sleeping Space in the Twentieth Century

The seeds for many of the housing tendencies that surfaced after the collapse of the Soviet Union in 1991 were planted decades prior to this historic rupture. Soviet apartment housing is a relatively known subject: there exists a substantial amount of scholarly and popular explorations into the nature of the Soviet communal apartments, modernist experiments in the 1920s by Russian Constructivists, and Stalin-era and Khrushchev-era apartment housing.[2] But what did those Soviet apartments evolve from? Prior to 1917, revenue houses represented a large portion of the urban apartment housing. This type of housing was spread all over Europe and the Russian Empire, with apartments found in the Russian Empire cities not being drastically different from those in the West. A modest apartment that would have housed a typical bureaucrat in Saint Petersburg at the end of the nineteenth century consisted of a master's block—an entry space, a living room, an office space, a dining room, a bedroom, and a bathroom—and a servants' block—a small bedroom and a kitchen. Those with lower incomes rented separate rooms or even "corners"—spaces within a room occupied by multiple unrelated people. The situation with corners was particularly typical for Saint Petersburg, the capital of the Russian Empire. A picturesque description of a poor and dilapidated rental room in a prerevolutionary Saint Petersburg can be found in Dostoevsky's description of his protagonist, Raskolnikov, and his housing situation: "It was a tiny cupboard of a room about six paces in length. It had a poverty-stricken appearance with its dusty yellow paper peeling off the walls, and it was so low-pitched that a man of more than average height was ill at ease in it and felt every moment that he would knock his head against the ceiling."[3]

This is what cheap by-room rental housing looked like in prerevolutionary Saint Petersburg, the conditions clearly miserable and not unlike the tenements elsewhere in the world. However, the Soviet communal apartment took shared apartment living to a completely different level. From the very beginning of the Bolshevik rule, Soviet cities were overpopulated due to rapid industrialization, the mass migration of rural populations to cities, and the reluctance of the early Soviet state to allocate money and resources to housing. After coming to power, the Bolsheviks relocated most of the housing resources from the middle and up-per class to the workers, turning the majority of urban apartments into commu-nal living settings, similar to earlier rooms and corners. This requisition of rooms from the rich in favor of the poor became known as compaction (*uplotnenie*). The resulting communal living apartments (*kommunal'nye kvartiry*, or *kommunalki* for short) consisted of unrelated families or individuals occupying separate rooms or partitioned half rooms of the former single-family apartments and sharing amenities: a hallway, a single kitchen, and a bathroom. Although this move may have saved Soviet cities from mass homelessness, it did not provide a sustainable and dignified solution to the housing shortage. Instead, it formalized the crowded housing conditions all the way until the late 1950s and beyond.

Communal apartments were the main type of housing available to Soviet ur-banites until the beginning of the mass housing campaign launched by Khrush-chev in 1957.[4] For the first time in Soviet history, Khrushchev called for providing every family with their own personal apartment.[5] Despite the state policy shift from communal to individual living, the lifestyles and domestic settings con-solidated in the early communal apartments persisted through the rest of the twentieth century and above and beyond the communal apartment type.[6] A typ-ical 1960s three-member family domestic setting in communal apartments is described in Yuri Trifonov's short story "Exchange":

> [His] daughter slept behind the folding screen in the corner. Her desk, where she did her homework at night, was also there. Dmitriev made her a bookshelf, put it above the desk and conducted an electric wire for a desk lamp. He put together a special room behind the screen, "sol-itary unit" [*odinochka*], as they [jokingly] called it in the family. Dmi-triev and Lena slept on a wide Czechoslovakia-made couch that they were lucky to buy three years ago and that since then has caused jeal-ousy of their acquaintances. The couch stood by the window and was separated from the "solitary unit" with a decoratively carved oak cup-

board; a grotesque object that Lena inherited from her grandmother and that Dmitriev frequently suggested to sell. Lena agreed, but his mother-in-law was against it.[7]

While set in a communal apartment, a similar overlay of domestic functions would have persisted into a one- or two-room private apartment that this family would have been assigned according to Soviet regulations.[8] In a home described by Trifonov, functions could not have been spatially separated since the home of the family of three was limited to one room. Similar to many types of domestic spaces throughout human history—a yurt, a hut, or a rented apartment room in an industrializing city—the home stayed unprescribed and changeable, limited only by the pressure of the outside world and the floor area inside its walls.

A family like the one from "Exchange" was meant to move to a new personal apartment in a modular *khrushchevka* house,[9] where they would no longer have been limited to one room but would have enjoyed the luxury of two rooms and private amenities: kitchen, bathroom, and some storage space.[10] Khrushchevkas, without a doubt, greatly improved the conditions of life of the Soviet urbanites; yet the fluid use of space characteristic of their prior communal apartment existence remained.

Numbers and Bureaucracy

The story of the Soviet sleeping space continues with numbers. "The citizens of the USSR have a right for housing," stated article 44 of the Soviet Constitution in 1977.[11] A simple and seemingly straightforward statement on paper, in practice it took the form of a mathematical problem.

The major principle in Soviet housing distribution grew from the early days of housing requisition after the 1917 Bolshevik Revolution. According to Bolshevik logic, housing resources had to be allocated by the state. Starting from its early days and throughout the rest of Soviet history, housing allocation by the state remained the predominant way to get housing. In August 1918, the All-Russian Central Executive Committee finalized the legalization of apartment or room requisition by canceling private property on real estate in cities.[12] According to Lenin, an apartment was subject to compaction "if the number of rooms in this apartment equaled or outnumbered the number of persons."[13] In 1919 the People's Commissariat of Healthcare developed sanitary norms of ten square meters of housing for each adult with an additional five square meters for each two- to twelve-year-old child.[14] This norm shifted within a range of a couple of square meters throughout the Soviet history, but the logic of a limited floor area per person remained the same.

By Brezhnev's times, the Housing Code of the Russian Federative SSR specified that an adult citizen had a right to seven (1970s) to nine (1980s) square meters
of housing and that an adult citizen was only eligible for state-initiated relocation
if they were limited to less than five square meters of area in their already existing
housing.[15] In addition, Soviet authorities followed a rule derived from Lenin's
statement on rooms: an apartment was allocated to a family based on a $k = n - 1$
formula, where k[16] represented the number of rooms and n represented the number of people to live in the apartment. A room in this case is any separate livable
space other than the kitchen, bathroom, and entryway that was separated with
walls and had windows. For instance, based on this simple formula, a family of
three—two parents and a child—would have received a two-room apartment. A
family of four—a grandparent, two parents, and a child, or two parents and two
children—had a right to a three-room home. If a similar formula was used to
describe the typical plan of a post-World War II American single-family home, it
would look like $k = n + 1$, where 1 would represent the designated living room.

Architect and author Vladimir Papernyi, a former dweller of a Soviet apartment, describes this quality of Soviet housing in his book *Kul'tura Dva*: "In this
[Lenin's] formula . . . there essentially is everything that is later going to create
such an acute condition of a communal apartment, since this formula fixes an
impossibility for each person to have a separate room."[17] Papernyi supports his
point with a famous and archetypal quote from Mikhail Bulgakov's 1920s novel
Heart of a Dog, where an apartment dweller—respectable medical professor
Philip Philippovich—is approached by the newly assigned communist House
Committee:

> ". . . this is precisely what we have come to talk to you about—the din-
> ing room and the examination room. The general meeting asks you vol-
> untarily and by way of labor discipline to give up your dining room.
> Nobody has a dining room in Moscow."
> "Not even Isadora Duncan," the woman cried in a ringing voice.[18]
> . . .
> "And the examination room too," continued Shvonder. "The exam-
> ination room can perfectly well be combined with the office."
> "Uhum," said Philip Philippovich in a strange voice. "And where am
> I to take my meals?"
> "In the bedroom," the four answered in chorus.
> The purple of Philip Philippovich's face assumed a grayish tinge.
> "Eat in the bedroom," he said in a slightly choked voice, "read in the
> examination room, and examine patients in the dining room. It is very
> possible that Isadora Duncan does just this . . . But I am not Isadora

Duncan! . . ." he barked out suddenly, and the purple of his face turned yellow. "I shall dine in the dining room, and operate in the surgery!"[19]

Although fictional Philip Philippovich wins the fight over rooms as far as the Soviet 1920s go, the nonfictional former and contemporary proletarians and elites of the Soviet Union soon found themselves stripped of precisely what is questioned in Bulgakov's passage: room identity. While the concept of a communal apartment soon proved to be problematic, and an official program for a separate apartment for every family was launched in the 1950s,[20] apartment rooms largely did not regain their identity until the collapse of the Soviet Union or to this day. Moreover, the meaning of a room itself, as a unit of lived space, became compromised through the Soviet approach. The Soviets introduced a new form of thinking about housing conditions: not by rooms, not even by corners, like before the 1917 Bolshevik Revolution, but by the number of square meters. This type of thinking virtually disregarded walls and did not speak of the necessity of the housing to perform certain functions but rather only of the floor area offered to every Soviet citizen. Just one room of a communal apartment could now have hosted most of the domestic functions at once, sometimes even including cooking and hygiene. A room, as a container for separate functions or old forms of bourgeois privacy, was no longer to be found.

In the Soviet Union, Sanitary Norms and Regulations (*Sanitarnye normy i pravila*, or *SNiP* for short) were a set of documents equivalent to the Building Code. They defined the upper and lower area limits for each apartment of the forthcoming apartment block. These norms were typically developed by the Central Research and Design Institute for Residential and Public Buildings (TsNI-IEP zhilishcha), approved by the State Committee for Construction of the USSR (Gosstroi) and published by Construction Publishing (Stroiizdat), and primarily circulated among architecture and construction professionals and bureaucrats. They meticulously defined the way Soviet housing had to be designed, constructed, and used.[21] The absolute majority of Soviet housing, other than housing built for top elites, was built according to social norms and could not go below or over the limits established by the Sanitary Norms and Regulations.

The Soviet *SNiP* differentiated between the so-called living area (*zhilaia ploshad'*)—floor area of the rooms, excluding kitchen, bathroom, toilet room (if any), and hallways—and effective area (*poleznaia ploshad'*)—floor area of the entire apartment.[22] The limits of the living area for a typical urban housing unit during different time periods were as shown in table 2.1.

In addition, in 1985 and 1989, *SNiP* specified that an area of a room had to be no less than eight square meters. This regulation number grew throughout the Soviet history, originally starting at six square meters in 1962.

TABLE 2.1. Upper and lower limitation for apartment floor areas in square meters according to SNiPs of different years.

YEAR SNIP WAS ADJUSTED	ONE-ROOM APARTMENT (STUDIO WITH A SEPARATE KITCHEN)		TWO-ROOM APARTMENT (ONE BEDROOM)		THREE-ROOM APARTMENT (TWO BEDROOMS)		FOUR-ROOM APARTMENT (THREE BEDROOMS)		FIVE-ROOM APARTMENT (FOUR BEDROOMS)		SIX-ROOM APARTMENT (FIVE BEDROOMS)	
	Min	Max	Min	Max	Min	Max	Min	Max	Min	Max	Min	Max
1971 (1978 edition)	12	36	23	48	36	63	46	74	56	91		
1985		36		53		65		77		95		
1989		36		53		65		77		95		108

Starting from Khrushchev's 1955 manifesto "On Elimination of Excesses in Design and Construction," frugality and construction went hand in hand. Apartment buildings were no longer supposed to make an impression but rather house as many families as possible in modest but private apartments. Since housing design and construction had to be frugal, real-life apartment floor areas rarely reached the upper limits defined by the Sanitary Norms and Regulations and stayed closer to the lower ones. Since housing was predominantly designed in series—sets of plans, sections, details, and material specifications used repeatedly for construction in different locations—it is possible to identify typical floor areas and apartment layouts. A typical Khrushchev-era apartment from one of the popular series (1–335, 1–434, 1–464, or 1–480) reached thirty-one to thirty-three square meters for a one-room home, forty-six to forty-eight square meters for a two-room home, and fifty-six to fifty-eight square meters for a three-room home.

More than ever before, in the 1950s and 1960s, residential design became determined by mathematical equations. A 1966 edited volume on mass housing development in the Ukrainian SSR identified that apartments were to be developed with an average floor area of S, where S was determined by two variables: an average family composition n and an average square footage per person H. The average number of family members for Ukraine was determined at 3,4 persons (as of 1959), while an average for Uzbek SSR was established at 4,1 persons. This statistical data was followed by a calculation of cubic air volume per an adult necessary for healthy living and light homework. Heavy with detailed statistics, this overview nevertheless ended in a near-qualitative conclusion: a one-room apartment was a good fit for two people, a two-room apartment could fit three, a three-room apartment would suit four to five people, and six and more people deserved five rooms.[23]

Brezhnev's famous formula "economy has to be frugal," first presented at the 1981 26th Congress of the Communist Party of the Soviet Union, signified the continuation of earlier Khrushchev thriftiness for floor area and materials into the 1970s and 1980s. Since the problems with the tiny spaces of early modular apartments were already recognized, the 1970s apartment series were built with only a slight increase in the overall floor area but with a tangible increase in quality of life due to slightly bigger kitchens, higher ceilings, and better temperature and soundproofing. The tendency to enlarge kitchens, ceiling heights, and overall floor area continued through the 1980s. However, the logic behind the distribution of apartments along the $k = n - 1$ formula did not change. The size of rooms grew, but the functional use remained the same due to the same number of rooms being offered to families of the same composition.[24]

Keeping in mind that the number of rooms had to equal the number of occupants minus one, a typical Soviet family had a manner of household spatial organization rather different from that of the Western European or US situation. The number of functions in a typical household—sleeping (bedroom), eating (kitchen), entertainment and rest (living room), homework or household work such as sewing (workspace)—inevitably outnumbered the number of available rooms. In practice, this meant that no room could ever have one single function. A room that hosted sleeping at night would host entertainment and represent the functions of a living room during the day. Although such a situation was not exclusive to the late Soviet Union, unlike in most other cities around the world, it was a prescribed norm covering the entire population, except for the extreme elites.

In the late 1970s and 1980s, Gosstroi hosted multiple architectural competitions for the first-generation (Khrushchev-era) mass housing modernization solutions and new types of urban apartments. These conceptual competitions showed expanded floor areas, bigger rooms, and less utilitarian plans. They casually included double beds—a characteristic sign of a monofunctional room—but they still followed the $k = n - 1$ rule. For instance, a two-room (not two-bedroom) apartment had one room shown as a bedroom with a double bed and another room shown as a living room with a sectional couch, yet the same apartment was supposed to be suitable for three people (figure 2.1).[25] If such an apartment were ever built, those three occupants would have a couple of different options: to sleep in one room all together, which would make a double bed virtually impossible, or to have one or two people sleep in the walk-through room.

The walk-through room typically preserved its social and entertainment functions: the TV and the couch, as well as the glass cabinet with occasion tableware or bookshelves.[26] The person(s) allocated in this quasi-walk-through living room would have to unpack their bedding at night and hide or cover it in the morning for the daytime social, rest, and domestic work functions. Their clothes would need to be stored elsewhere or a wardrobe would need to be placed in the living room. Most importantly, everybody needing to get to the kitchen or bathroom at night would have to pass by their sleeping area. The rhythms and space of the household would need to be orchestrated in accordance with the sleep of the person staying in the walk-through room. Similar to Trifonov's characters from "Exchange," an occupant of the far room in a walk-through apartment had to first check whether the person in the walk-through room was asleep and then quietly sneak to wherever they were going without turning on the light.

The functional overlap within a small room (about sixteen square meters) forced the Soviet furniture industry to produce convertible or adjustable furniture for sleep, rest, entertainment, and social functions. The rise of the furniture industry in the USSR followed the end of World War II, Stalin's death in 1952, and the shift to mass "compact" housing.[27] Small domestic spaces in a mass-built apartment block required furniture smaller than that of the pre-war period, while the overlap of functions required this furniture to be multifunc-tional. This meant smaller dimensions and lighter materials: a piece of furni-ture that could have been easily taken up the stairs of the five-story Khrushchev-era buildings with no elevators.

A typical panel apartment from 1–464 series (first introduced in the late 1950s and built until the late 1970s) had two rooms—one was 3.2 meters (10.4 feet) wide, and the other was 2.6 meters (8.5 feet) wide. The latter room was isolated with no through traffic, seemingly well-suited for a bedroom. However, the di-mensions and layout of this room did not allow for a comfortable placement of a double bed. If the 2.6-meter-wide room had contained a 1.8- to 2-meter-wide bed, an apartment dweller would be left with only several dozen centimeters to walk around it. A wall closet on one end of the room and a door on another end made it impossible to put a double bed into the room's dead end and climb onto it without walking around. In other words, a regular double bed, as we think of it today, simply would not have fit. Although this situation changed with the later apartment series, the convertible furniture was already acquired, and the num-ber of family members per room typically did not decrease.

A perfect piece of compact apartment furniture could also perform more than one function—such as sleep, entertainment, and socialization. This is why con-vertible couches or day beds became Soviet consumer ideals. The characters of Trifonov's short story "Exchange" claim their Czechoslovakian convertible couch as the subject of their acquaintances' jealousy despite its squeakiness.[28] The So-viet PBS-style film *The Time of the Great Housewarming*, dedicated to the suc-cesses of mass housing construction in the 1950s and meant to promote panel apartment living, demonstrates a species of furniture earlier unseen in the So-viet domestic interiors: a single folding bed, similar to a horizontal Murphy bed familiar to Americans.[29] A folding bed, however, lost in popularity to a convert-ible couch or a day bed, possibly because it was a part of a sectional piece that not every Soviet family could afford or find among the limited supply of Soviet stores. A 1972 Soviet brochure authored by Boris Merzhanov—head of a studio in TsNIIEP zhilishcha, a professor, and a major authority in Soviet residential architecture—suggests an interior for a "common" room of an apartment.[30] The common room would host the sleep of a couple: "the two sleeping spots—two couches placed at an angle—create a well isolated zone for rest." An illustration for this setting shows a television set in front of one of the couches that helps clarify Merzhanov's "rest" as a space that will be used not only for sleep but also for socialization (figure 2.2). The abundance of convertible or multifunctional furniture in the late-Soviet home inspired material culture scholar Victor Bu-chli to speak about it as a new mode of everyday life, a new *byt*,[31] enforced by the state as an attempt to fight the petite bourgeois Stalin-era domestic aesthetics.

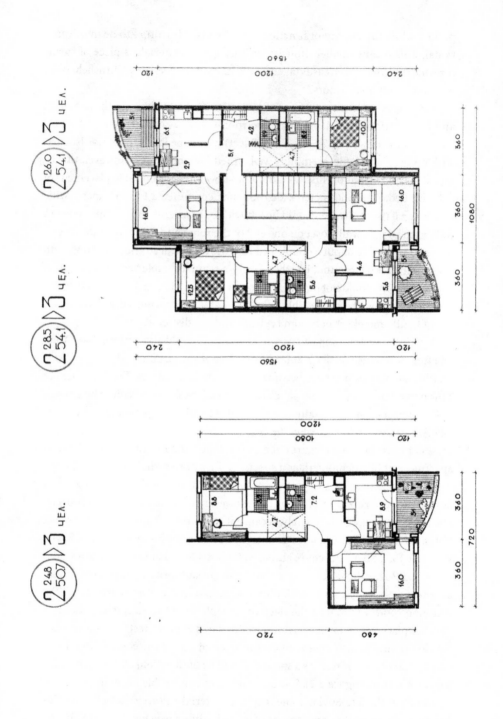

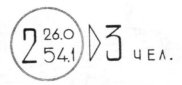

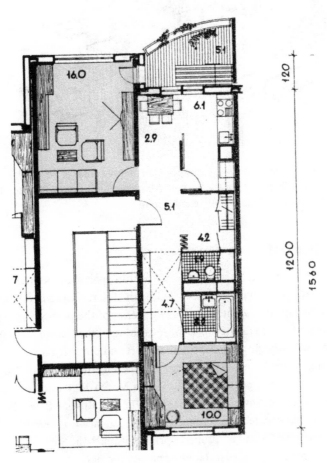

FIGURE 2.1. Published architectural projects from the "Modernization and Reconstruction of the Early Series Apartment Housing" contest catalogue, Gosstroi, 1987.

FIGURE 2.2. An illustration from Boris Merzhanov's *Inter'er zhilishcha* (Residential interior) illustrating the use of multifunctional or convertible furniture (1970). (Courtesy of Znanie Publishing House.)

The Rise of the Bedroom

After 1991, a new domestic space emerged within apartment homes: a separate bedroom that primarily hosted sleep. While the interest in remodeling clearly started in the late 1980s, the physical emergence of the post-Soviet bedroom could be traced to two later events: the beginning of the housing privatization campaign and the beginning of drywall import and production.

Let us start with privatization. The first legislation establishing unlimited private property rights appeared in the USSR in March 1990 and continued appearing in the former Soviet republics into 1991.[32] The Russian Soviet Federative Socialist Republic enacted a new property law on January 1, 1991.[33] The same law also contained a statement on property privatization.[34] The Supreme Council of the Ukrainian Soviet Socialist Republic passed the new "About Property" law in April 1991.[35] Similar laws were passed by the lawmaking institutions of the other republics. The umbrella law of the USSR and the local laws enacted in separate republics all introduced private property and general mechanisms for privatization of property, as well as the legal right to sell or buy private property and use private property for profit. This ultimately meant that the $k = n - 1$ rule became obsolete. The citizens of the still-standing USSR could now formally privatize and, hence, buy housing with the number of rooms based only on their desires, needs, and financial abilities.

The entire population of the USSR and the heir states did not immediately race into the business of privatizing, buying, and selling housing. But the possibility produced fundamentally new housing opportunities never seen before. In addition to selling or buying housing, people could now rent or lease apartments. Most importantly for this study, a family's apartment could have enough rooms to separate room functions.

In reality, room segregation did not happen immediately, nor did it happen in every apartment. Despite the former Soviet societies going through extreme economic hardship due to the crash of the centralized economy and rapid inflation, the post-Soviet urban environment became saturated with money. Post-Soviet nouveau riche quickly put together capitals that by an order of magnitude outnumbered the resources of the rest of the society.[36] Unlike the money of the previous regime, which had to be earned consistently in small increments over large periods of time and had very limited buying power, this new money in sufficient amounts could buy anything. This led to what may be called, for the sake of the argument, a post-Soviet-style gentrification. People whose income and life quality lowered dramatically in the 1990s could sell their apartments to those whose income dramatically grew. There was very little new construction in the first post-Soviet years. Instead, as shown in the previous chapter, many construction professionals shifted to remodeling existing apartments. In the early 1990s in particular, those were the apartments either purchased by foreigners or nouveau riche or purchased for the purpose of renting them out after improving their condition.

During the Soviet era, prior to the 1990–1991 shift in property laws, simply buying an apartment was a nearly impossible task. A person in need of housing during the late-Soviet decades had two ways to go: to apply for state housing and stay in a housing line for years or decades, or to become a member of a housing cooperative, invest money and effort into construction, and hopefully become an apartment resident within a couple years. Cooperatives, however, had their own problems, including high prices, the risk of losing a spot in a state housing line, and, when the apartment was finally rendered habitable, the necessity to receive permission from neighbors to trade apartments with another apartment dweller. After 1991, a person who had one way or another accumulated the necessary amount of money could simply buy an apartment from its previous owner and dramatically change their living conditions at will.

Therefore, the connection between privatization and a separate bedroom is simple: if one desired to have a separate bedroom and had enough resources, one could simply buy a bigger apartment. The role of construction materials, and drywall in particular, is a bit less straightforward. As described in the previous chapter, new materials and technologies entered the post-Soviet market, making previously impossible remodeling moves realistic. One such case is the construction of new partition walls, and the material essential to making this construction quick and precise—drywall.

Unlike some other materials, drywall was actually produced in the Soviet Union under the name of gypsum sheets (*gipsovye listy*) or dry stucco (*sukhaia shtukaturka*). As early as the late 1950s and 1960s, gypsum sheets appeared in the Sanitary Norms and Regulations[37] and Soviet technical standards (*Gosudarstvennye standarty* or *GOST*).[38] Gypsum sheets persisted in GOSTs in the 1970s and 1980s, indicating that this material was actively used in construction along with the usual partition material—gypsum concrete.[39] However, due to how products were distributed within the giant centralized economy of the USSR, many places never saw drywall in the construction on the ground, as the produced goods were allocated somewhere else in the country. Furthermore, gypsum sheets and gypsum concrete never entered the consumer market. At the same time, there was no easily accessible alternative sheet material for wall construction; everything accessible was rather inconvenient, like the Soviet method of wall construction called *dranka*: a form of sheathing in which a wall was constructed out of raw wood boards, then covered with a smaller diagonal grid of wooden planks and stuccoed over. A *dranka* partition wall obviously was hard and time-consuming to execute, especially for an individual inexperienced in construction. A *dranka* partition wall also rarely ever looked perfectly flat, no matter how much one tried. In the 1990s, different drywall manufacturers first started importing drywall to the former USSR and then began production in the post-Soviet countries. In the mid- and late-1990s, the German corporation Knauf Gips opened three factories in the Russian Federation, one factory in Ukraine, one factory in Moldova, and one factory in Kazakhstan.[40] Over these first post-Soviet years, drywall became extremely popular in residential and other construction.

Due to the availability of new materials and construction labor for hire, apartment dwellers could easily remove walls and erect new ones, substantially changing the preexisting layouts of their apartments. This type of remodeling, referred to as replanning (*pereplanirovka*), could go in several seemingly opposite yet inherently related directions. Those directions can be illustrated with the case of a typical two-room Khrushchev-era apartment from the 1–447 apartment series (ca. mid-1950s to mid-1960s) (figure 2.3). The layout of the apartment is characteristic of all khrushchevkas—a tiny three-square-meter vestibule with doors to the bathroom and to a walk-through room. The walk-through room leads to the kitchen and another separate room.

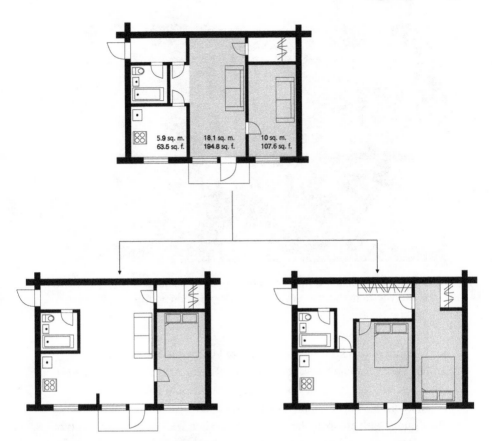

FIGURE 2.3. Typical Khrushchev-era apartment plan transformations from Soviet to post-Soviet versions. (Drawing by the author.)

An apartment like that was originally meant for three people. The demographics of the residents could have ranged from a core family (two adults and a child) to several generations (such as a mother, a grandmother, and a child or an adult couple with one of their parents). After 1991, the dwellers of this apartment no longer had to be three. Let us look at several scenarios that happened to this apartment type and its bedroom with the advent of replanning and change in residential mobility.

If the apartment population decreased to one or two adults, they could have chosen to remove a wall between the kitchen and the walk-through room to expand the small kitchen area (typically 5.6–6.0 square meters) (figure 2.3). This change could have allowed the second, untouched room to accommodate sleep, while the rest of the overlapping functions could have been moved to the now open-plan living room/dining room/kitchen.

FIGURE 2.4.   A room in a typical Khrushchev-era apartment, with furniture and layout preserved from the late-Soviet years. (Photograph courtesy of Yulia Savchenko.)

Replanning of this kind regularly appeared in media. For instance, an article in *Idei vashego doma* (Ideas for your home) from 2003 titled "In a khrushchevka" sets an example of a single young professional who removed all the internal, non-load-bearing walls in a two-room Khrushchev-era apartment to create a studio with an open plan.[41] In 2005, kitchen wall removal for one type of two-room 1–335 series apartment appeared twice in *Idei vashego doma* (figure 2.5).[42] Besides magazines, books on replanning offer their own general advice: "To get a large space for hosting guests, you can disassemble the wall between the existing kitchen, the small and the large room. Dining alone or with the family is more pleasant, when in a spacious rather than a jammed room."[43]

This type of replanning is also illustrated in an interview with Hanna F. conducted as a part of this research.[44] Her sister's family of two adults and one young child replanned their two-room 1960s apartment in 1998. Originally, the apartment had an entry space with doors to all available spaces: two separate rooms and the kitchen, bathroom, and toilet. Since the kitchen was considered small, they decided to demolish the wall between the kitchen and the adjacent room. After the renovation, the newly created large space was used as a living room and a kid's room. The other isolated room became a bedroom. In this case, a bedroom was used for rest and occasional homework. Hanna stated: "They are a family that did not watch television. Perhaps they had a TV at that point, but most likely it was in that room that was joined to the kitchen. But the bedroom

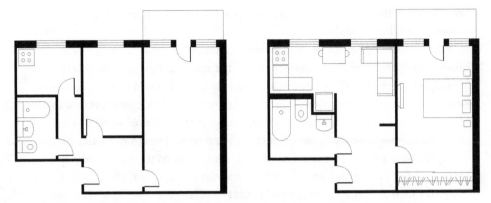

FIGURE 2.5. Before and after apartment plans redrawn from *Idei vashego doma* magazine in "Prevrashcheniia khrushchevki" (Khrushchevka transformation) in 2005.

was just the bedroom, because he [the husband] either slept or rested there or he worked there on his computer. In general, this was the parent's zone."[45]

Yet even in this case, when one room was dedicated predominantly to the function of sleep, there were ways to quickly transform it upon necessity: "They had convertible furniture. They had one more convertible couch and they had a convertible bed built in to a closet. You know, one of those beds that you can lift and hide away. It used to be always folded out, but in case of necessity it could have been hidden away, so the room could have been transformed into a living room."[46]

Another type of khrushchevka replanning involved creating a new wall and a small corridor to isolate the former walk-through room (figure 2.3). Although this solution required sacrificing some space of the walk-through room, it also allowed for both rooms to gain separate entries. This type of replanning is characteristic of multiple-generation or multiple-family occupancy of two-room apartments. During this research, only one respondent reported doing this type of replanning in his two-room apartment. In his case, the apartment was occupied by two adults (himself and his mother), and both were willing to sacrifice some of the already modest floor area to achieve more privacy through the construction of a new wall.[47]

Although such a case only came up once during the interview process, Recorder of Deeds engineers in Kyiv claimed that this type of replanning was among the most widespread in Khrushchev-era apartments (figure 2.3). Engineers, who recorded apartment layout changes, particularly noted that transformations like this were done to create private spaces for households composed of several core families.[48] At the expense of the former-Soviet walk-through room, occupants of those apartments created separate spaces with more privacy for separate families or adults.

The choreographies of these apartments changed dramatically. Figure 2.5 shows an example of this transformation: the room that used to be a walk-through room is cut off with the help of a newly created corridor that now has entrances to both rooms. This meant that the room was no longer accessible to the extended family or friends in the same easy manner it used to be when it doubled as a social space. In an original layout, a walk-through room like that was previously perceived predominantly as a living room rather than somebody's bedroom, even if it hosted somebody's sleep at night.[49] However, when it lost its walk-through quality, it became equal to the rest of the rooms in the apartment: the undetermined rooms, where functions were allocated arbitrarily, according to the number of family members and their needs. If an apartment was occupied by two or three generations and more than one core family, such replanning would have created separate family microcosms in each isolated room, with both sleep and socialization functions present in each of these rooms separately for separate core families.[50] The same can be said about the second, non-walk-through room. Although the wall and the door separating this room from the rest of the apartment space have always been there, they have not previously isolated the room from the entirety of the apartment population or even guests.[51] When the spatial functions no longer overlapped throughout the apartment but rather doubled in each private room, there was no longer a need for the rest of the apartment population to access this far room (figures 2.3, 2.5).

The world of material objects in these apartments also changed in a couple of distinct ways. The two most notable distinctions in the materiality of post-Soviet bedrooms followed commodity consumption models: the "poverty culture" of re-use and maintenance and the consumption economy of the newly rising commodity market.[52] Commodity deficit and the very narrow choice of available goods caused Soviet urbanites to repair and reuse rather than throw away old or broken things. At the same time, the limited yet powerful introduction to imported capitalist and socialist bloc–manufactured goods induced a consumerist culture, different in form yet similar in nature to the consumerism of capitalist societies.[53] Within the same average household, some pieces of furniture could have been repaired for decades, yet other pieces could have been vigorously hunted down (*dostavat'*) from the limited sales, through bribing, or through the informal economy.[54] The 1991 introduction of the free market and unlimited commodity import invigorated and complicated naïve Soviet consumerism with the wide choice of product options. But most importantly, the border between poverty and consumerist cultures became much more evident. Repaired furniture became widely seen as a sign of low economic standing.[55] On the other hand, relatively affordable new furniture became readily available through international retailers such as IKEA[56] and JYSK[57] or emerging local manufacturers and sellers. Repaired and new furniture could still coexist in one household if the dwellers had limited resources or found repairing old furniture appealing for aesthetic, sentimental, or hobby reasons. This meant that the international furniture types, such as a full bed or kitchen cabinet sets, entered post-Soviet households but did not completely replace convertible couches or single beds. Just like with the placement of sleep in an apartment, there was no one single route of physical transformation. At the same time, the sleeping furniture was now orchestrated according to the needs and resources of a household rather than according to the scenarios constructed by the apartment allocation policies.

Objects other than furniture populating post-Soviet apartments also changed. Soviet-made objects were not replaced by globally produced ones, but the social purpose of these objects changed a lot. The multifunctional Soviet spaces that also hosted sleep were populated with conspicuous setups and objects: the carefully orchestrated tableware sets, travel souvenirs, books, decorative figurines, and gadgets meant to signify the social position of the apartment dweller(s).[58] These objects virtually followed the model formulated by David Stea for Mexico City dwellings in the 1990s. Stea writes that since all spaces of a middle-class home, other than spaces occupied by servants, were permeable for all members of the extended family, there were very few private objects.[59] Instead, most objects to be found were to represent the social status of the core family.[60] In a Soviet apartment, in a completely different social and spatial setting, the material culture consequences of the permeable room thresholds appeared similar: little to no private objects were left on display, and the nature of these private objects was highly dependent on social norms. The individual separation of space after replanning let the personal objects populate private rooms, be it an apartment turned into an open-plan single bedroom or a walk-through room apartment turned into several private rooms with equal functions.

Space, Rhythms, Collective, and Private Sleep

Most importantly, what kind of implications did these changes have for a post-Soviet sleeping space? In place of the old spatial performances and rhythms of an average Soviet apartment, there emerged several new types of spatial organizations and dwelling routines. According to their new income, apartment dwellers were either able to isolate sleep from the rest of domestic functions by locating it in a separate room or complicate a spatial overlap by stuffing even more functions and people into one separate, former walk-through room. On a surface level these two ends of a typical apartment-transformation spectrum look opposite to each other. However, under a closer look they are not that different in their motivation and conceptual outcomes. Both sleeping space scenarios revolve around the concept of privacy.

A Soviet apartment changed every night and every morning to accommodate sleep, in the absence of places designated to be for sleep only. After the collapse of the Soviet Union and the popularization of apartment replanning, as well as the introduction of new property laws, there emerged a number of households where the apartment dwellers were able to designate a separate space only to sleeping—a bedroom in a familiar, Western sense of the word. This room, empty during the day, only became populated during the night. It also provided a space perfectly separated from the representative part of an apartment: no longer did this room have to be transformed in order to host guests. A bedroom brought a sense of privacy rarely present in Soviet apartments—a space with entrance limited to only one or two bedroom occupants rather than anybody permanently or temporarily occupying the apartment space. For the first time in their lives, many post-Soviet adults could control their own private living space and construct their own daily rhythms independent of the other apartment dwellers.

Due to the end of governmental housing supply and the growing income inequality, frequently multiple related nuclear families lived in the same apartment.[61] When a new wall was built to separate entrances into two adjacent rooms, the dwellers of these rooms lost the former shared socialization and representational space—their daytime living room and nighttime quasi-bedroom. Instead, they gained more privacy within their own personal rooms. No longer did they have to walk past somebody sleeping at night to get to the far room; no longer did the occupant of the walk-through room have to hide elsewhere to gain the privacy of a closed door. The room was now isolated in the same way the other one was from the very beginning, and the occupants of different rooms appeared equal in their spatial settings.

An interview with two generations of the same family, who now live separately and differently, addresses the construction of their sleeping space and illustrates the plurality of sleep space models that emerged after the collapse of the USSR. Oksana H. is in her mid-fifties and is a current-day resident of a four-room apartment in an apartment series building (ca. late 1990s). She shares her experiences of bedroom settings throughout her life before her present housing situation (moved in the first decade of the 2000s). Currently, she lives with her husband and younger son; her older daughter has moved out of her parents' place and has an apartment of her own.

Oksana recalls that before this current apartment, she "only had my private bedroom once, when my brother was in the army, and I still stayed with my parents for some time. It was literally a half a year. That was the only time when I had a personal bedroom." She states that what matters most to her "is not even bedroom per se. As I sew at home, I need a space to set a sewing machine. When we [two adults and two children] lived in the dormitory in one room, the sewing machine was in the kitchen. It was impossible to move in there [due to the lack of space]. Now when there is a room, I can at least place the sewing machine and not have to disassemble it. It is always standing there, and I can sit down and sew [anytime]. I don't have to pack it and hide it anywhere." "So, your bedroom is not just a bedroom, but also a workspace?" I ask. "Yes, an office. Children have it the same way too—everything is in their rooms."[62] Her daughter is in her early thirties and lives with her partner in a two-room apartment. She has a different setting: "Our bedroom is just a bedroom. We sometimes come home at different times. Because of this our workplace is in the living room; while one of us is asleep another one can keep working."[63]

If the spaces for sleep have been transformed in multiple ways since 1991, what can be concluded about the nature of these transformations? Despite the multiple strategies and the growing material and economic stratification of post-Soviet apartment dwellers, there is something all of these transformations, instigated by both poverty and wealth, had in common. The two most important categories shared by all transformed sleep spaces are their newly emerged privacy and the changed everyday rhythms.

The spatial privacy part is simple. Whether post-Soviet apartment dwellers succeeded in gaining more privately occupied sleep space by constructing new walls or removing old walls and acquiring full beds, the intent was always the same: to gain a space of one's own, where sleep would happen on one's own terms. Several studies of everyday life before the mass housing era agree: sleep of the Soviet citizen was not a private affair.[64] Unlike the bourgeois bedroom, where a sleeper's body was separated from the rest of society with walls and doors, a Soviet sleeper's body was seen, heard, and regulated by the other members of society. The bourgeois shame attached to nighttime sleep that Norbert Elias described in his book *The Civilizing Process* fell victim to the earliest Soviet attempts to eradicate everything old, capitalist, and bourgeois-proper.[65] The fight on shame in the first Soviet decade sometimes took bizarre and extreme forms, like the radical nudist "Down with the Shame!" Society active in the mid-1920s. The society's activities included naked marches through the streets of Soviet cities, Moscow in particular, to encourage communists to abandon bourgeois shame of the naked body. Its activities were not met with much enthusiasm by the general public or by the state.[66]

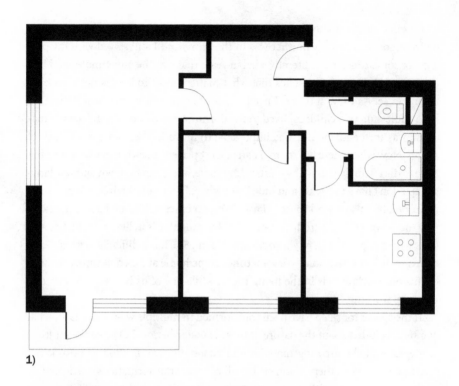

1)

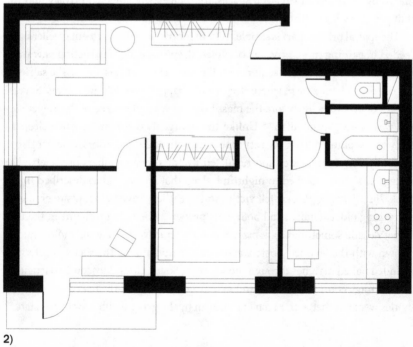

2)

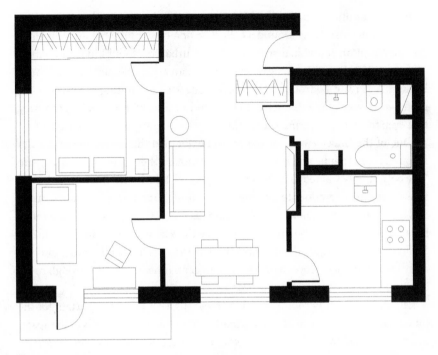

3)

FIGURE 2.6.   1) A plan of a two-room apartment (I-515/5 series) before remodeling and replanning; 2) and 3) Plans of the same apartment replanned to have two isolated bedrooms and a separate living room space. Both of these replanning options indicate a separation between nighttime and daytime spaces. Both suggest direct access to each bedroom from a shared space. (Redrawn from Ruslan Kirnichanskiy, "Pereplanirovka: Modernizatsiia dvukhkomnatnoi kvartiry v khrushchevke I-515/5," *Houzz*, September 3, 2015, https://www.houzz.ru/ideabooks/52262255/list/pereplanirovka-modernizatsiya-dvuhkomnatnoy-kvartiry-v-hrushchevke-1-515-5.)

Removing clothing may have been too much for the early communist state, but removing the isolation of a bedroom was a universal state strategy, as the Soviet backbone proletariat class was not unused to the "corners" in rental apartments and barracks. Sleep had to be undertaken as a collective act and had to be ideologically correct, thus performed in spaces where no private misbehavior could escape the socialist public view.[67] The Stalin-era collective sleep of a communal apartment fell out of favor in the late 1950s; yet the sleep of an individual in mass-built apartments still did not become private. Sleep rather shifted from a collective to a core family group, where members were still to participate in building socialism, if not in the entire state then within each given apartment.[68]

Perestroika and the fall of the USSR changed this dynamic with spatial imagination no longer rotating around a collective or a core family but an individual. The dream of an individual space led Soviet urbanites to all kinds of contrivances. In 1992, *Rabotnitsa* magazine published an article eloquently titled "Your Dream: A Private Bedroom." The article suggested separating a corner of the room with a specially constructed podium and a frame with a curtain, promising that even in a small apartment a dream of a private bedroom can come true.[69]

One of the interviewees for the project explained the separation of a walk-through room that he and his mother undertook in their two-room apartment: "We both simply wanted to have our own space."[70] Like in this interviewee's case, a new wall and a new door to a former walk-through room may have not secured this then young adult a home separate from his parents, but it did provide a much broader ability to manipulate his own space the way he wanted to. In addition, it allowed him to adjust the daily rhythms within his individual room and the rest of the apartment since there was no longer an inhabited walk-through room between him and the shared utilities.

The change in daily rhythms and choreographies is no less important for the understanding of apartment transformation than the physical walls of the apartment. Henri Lefebvre offers a framework for thinking about rhythms in *Rhythmanalysis*. In the post-Spatial Turn disciplines, already dominated by Lefebvre's principle of social construction of space, rhythmanalysis is frequently applied to understand the ways in which "the so-called natural rhythms"—the rhythms of the human organs, circadian rhythms, daily and seasonal repetitions in nature—"change for multiple, technological, socio-economic reasons."[71] According to Lefebvre, capital and capitalism have in many ways modeled everyday rhythms of an individual. While in agreement with Lefebvre, this study shows that the socialist regime has modeled everyday rhythms of its subject no less than the capitalist one.[72] The sleep-wake rhythm of a Soviet apartment dweller locked in a $k = n - 1$ rule appeared codependent on the rest of the apartment collective. Only if the entire population of the apartment agreed to respect the sleep of the occupant(s) of the walk-through room could that sleep take place in comfortable circumstances. Even beyond personal relationships and agreements, different apartment dwellers may have had different requirements to their everyday rhythms: a younger generation would have left and returned early, adults would have left early and returned late, while the retired older population would have no need to wake up early or stay out late if not for the overlapping presence and nonmatching rhythms of the other two generations. The younger generation would have often been allocated to the private rather than walk-through room(s), so that adults and the older generation could enjoy some after-hours entertainment such as watching television while the younger generation was already asleep in an isolated room. The spatial functions of sleep, entertainment, nursing, socialization, and the daily rhythms of different family members overlapped, forcing the necessity of collective agreements and action.

Post-Soviet rhythms and sleep changed dramatically. Whether a young adult was able to afford an individual apartment or a family of two was allocated in a separate room, the post-Soviet apartment dwellers removed their sleeping space from the daily routine of social functions formerly happening in the same space that had hosted sleep at night (figure 2.6). The space of a separate room no longer had to be competed for; the television and other forms of entertainment now existed privately in separate rooms or in the still-shared spaces, such as the kitchen or a designated living room in bigger apartments. But even more importantly, there was no longer any traffic through the spaces of post-Soviet sleep and no group accord necessary for healthy sleep to be sustained. Individual sleep shifted from the realm of collective to the realm of private, with the daily rhythms no longer defined by the $k = n - 1$ rule but solely by the desire of an individual apartment dweller to privately orchestrate their sleep.

EATING

Crowded, but not aggrieved [*V tesnote, da ne v obide*].

—Russian saying

"The kitchen was 8 [square] meters. When we brought in the furniture, I had a choice: either to have a fridge or a table. After the stove and the sink were put in place, both a fridge and a table would not have fit simultaneously," recalled Oksana H. while showing me the original layout of her Soviet-planned apartment before she remodeled it in 2001.[1] We were seated at the dining table in her living room, looking into her kitchen through a portal in the wall. The dining area is a continuation of the kitchen area. The rest of the living room is taken up by a separate den, as it is often called in American homes—couches, armchairs, and a coffee table. Although Oksana's original kitchen layout was already three square meters (thirty-two square feet) bigger than the smallest Soviet-built apartment kitchens, her concern was that it would be impossible for her family of four to comfortably cook, store food, eat, and spend time together confined to those eight square meters (eighty-six square feet).

In 2001, Oksana wanted everything having to do with food—cooking, storage, dining, and socializing over a meal or tea—to fit into the kitchen. She was willing to move the kitchen walls rather than change her expectations for the space. That is why as soon as her family was able to move into their new apartment, they started replanning the layout of their new home. They adjusted their food spaces to their vision, even though they did not have enough resources to do it all at once and had to take months to accomplish the entire project. As Elizabeth Cromley, expert in quotidian spaces, puts it, the "food axis" of a home—spaces related to cooking, food storage, and eating—"change with time, region and climate, ethnicity, gender, class, and household economics."[2] Inspired by the many post-Soviet urbanites who sacrificed their orderly lives for months and sometimes even years of remodeling, chapter 4 tracks how these apartment dwellers formed their understanding of food spaces within late-Soviet homes and how this sense changed on the eve of and after that historic rupture—the collapse of the USSR in 1991.

To speak about the gradual changes in food spaces effectively, this chapter is structured under three themes: the late-Soviet domestic food spaces and practices, the late Soviet and post-Soviet remodeling boom, and the transformation of domestic food-related architecture along the collapse of the USSR in 1991. Kitchens, especially the small Stalin and Khrushchev-era kitchens largely disregarded in the world of the official Soviet homemaking, were the first in line to be remodeled by eager urbanites. First, this chapter explains the peculiarity of late-Soviet eating spaces, determined on the one hand by the institutional construction of a proper Soviet home and on the other by the grassroots, everyday practices occurring tangentially to, or even against, the effort of the state.[3] Second, this chapter speaks of the increasing interest in domestic remodeling in the late 1980s and the full-blown remodeling boom in the 1990s to provide context for the physical transformations that took place in these food-related spaces. Finally, this study addresses the transformations themselves: both the physical and ephemeral changes that took place in apartment homes, influencing everyday life for post-Soviet urbanites.

From Solid to Collapsible Tables

The majority of Soviet and post-Soviet urbanites had access to a kitchen in their dwelling. Throughout Soviet history, a few types of urban housing had no kitchen access, such as barracks (baraki, a type of communal housing not necessarily equipped with kitchen or hygienic facilities) and communal apartments that were established in previously nonresidential buildings. But most communal and individual dwellings had a kitchen available. At the same time, the majority of Soviet homes had no dining room.[4] With a small number of exceptions, such as early Constructivist experimental apartment buildings, Soviet urbanites cooked their food in the kitchen.[5] The question of where food was consumed requires a more complex explanation and a brief historic retrospective. To identify where late-Soviet apartment dwellers ate in the absence of a dining room, it is first necessary to differentiate between the types of late-Soviet urban housing, with communal and individual housing being the largest categories. In communal housing, cooking spaces—kitchens—were shared between multiple unrelated individuals and families. Individual apartment dwellings had their own separate kitchens. Existing dining rooms in urban homes fell victim to compaction—*uplotnenie* described in the previous chapter. At the same time, newly built apartments were distributed by the state following the $k = n - 1$ formula that required the number of residents (n) to outnumber lived rooms (k) by 1, making a separate dining room virtually impossible in any type of housing.[6]

A typical kitchen in a communal apartment contained several stoves, a workstation, and some storage. While a communal kitchen could have accommodated seating, food was rarely consumed in this shared space.[7] Apartment dwellers perceived a kitchen as a utilitarian labor space rather than the cozy hearth of a home.[8] Communal apartments were a social experiment; unrelated families and individuals from different social groups were placed in one apartment to live together. Conflicts were frequent; theft or even intentional ruining of food were not unheard of.[9] Excessive use of the shared spaces was perceived as antisocial. Alcoholics drinking in the communal kitchen or sleeping in the communal corridor or neighbors taking over the bathroom for too long were typical examples of antisocial behavior.[10]

A communal kitchen could become almost anything but rarely a place for eating. Rather than being eaten *in situ*, the prepared food would be taken and spread into rooms.[11] The food was then consumed at a large, almost corpulent table, particularly iconic for the communal Stalin-era (1922–1952) apartments.[12] A family room in a communal apartment, or in an individual apartment built prior to the late 1950s, was typically big enough to fit a large table. All kinds of domestic practices took place at those large round or rectangular tables, such as meals, homework, and ironing. In the staged journalistic photographs of the mid-century USSR, workers were often portrayed at home with their families, celebrating, enjoying tea, reading the newspaper, or doing some sort of work at such tables; these tables came to symbolize domestic comfort and well-deserved rest (figure 3.1).

No less important than everyday practices *shown* in the Soviet mid-century images are the practices and spaces *not shown*: utilitarian spaces, kitchen included, remained invisible to the photo and film camera. This circumstance was not due to the specific communal kitchen inconveniences, but rather due to the general understanding of a kitchen as a utilitarian workspace, in all types of apartment housing. Food practices of a mid-century Soviet urban apartment, therefore, existed somewhere in between what Sarah Bonnemaison defines as the "traditional patterns of cooking, eating and living in a single room"[13] and a former bourgeois apartment kitchen, which used to be a space of servant labor and living and became the space of housewife's labor after the 1917 Bolshevik Revolution.[14]

It is only with the arrival of the prefabricated mass housing and the accompanying furniture production that kitchens surmounted their utilitarian past and became used not only for cooking but also for consuming food. Khrush-

FIGURE 3.1.   *Left*: A cooperative worker unable to stay away from home for long doing her work at her home table. Soviet Information Bureau Photograph Collection, photographed between 1945 and 1949. "Soviet producers' cooperatives" folder. Davis Center for Russian and Eurasian Studies Collection, H.C. Fung Library, Harvard University. *Right*: Preparation for the Victory Day celebration, photographed between 1945 and 1954. Soviet Information Bureau Photograph Collection. "Soviet family on VG-Day." folder. Davis Center for Russian and Eurasian Studies Collection, H.C. Fung Library, Harvard University.

chev's course toward an individual apartment for every family implied a separate set of auxiliary spaces—such as kitchens, bathrooms, and storage—for every apartment. However, instead of simply transferring the old practices of cooking and eating into their new apartments, the Soviet urbanites had to largely adjust to their new spatial organization.[15] The theoretical model of a home chosen by the Soviet architects, engineers, and politicians was not unlike its Russian Constructivist and Western, specifically German, functionalist counterparts. A model Khrushchev-era (1953–1964) kitchen in many ways resembled the Frankfurt kitchen:[16] its organization was supposed to be as efficient as possible to alleviate the burden of everyday domestic labor. The modernist qualities of the new Soviet residential design "included the use of reinforced concrete; the harmonization of internal spaces, as well as of interiors with natural landscape; a striving for a sense of openness; and the conformity of form to function in terms of structure, furnishing, and décor."[17]

At the same time, a major difference existed between the Soviet prefabricated housing and examples in other countries, starting in 1958 and practically starting with the second generation of prefabricated housing (1963–1971):[18] Sanitary Norms and Regulations strictly prohibited open kitchen design due to the safety restrictions for gas stoves.[19] Therefore, the modernist striving for openness may have persisted in concept but only made it into a few examples of first-generation prefabricated housing on the ground. Khrushchev's housing campaign strove to be, among other things, economical.[20] Together with the continuing norm of housing area per person (nine square meters or ninety-seven square feet from 1918 to 1983 and twelve square meters or 129 square feet from 1983 to 1991 in the Russian Soviet Federative Socialist Republic)[21] and the spacing between the concrete slabs at 3.2 meters (10.5 feet), these apartments were quite small. This meant that a Stalin-era all-purpose large table would no longer fit comfortably in the new small rooms. Besides, these small rooms already hosted a number of functions (such as sleeping, homework, and watching television) for a number of residents that mandatorily outnumbered the number of rooms. Space for family meals was no longer to be found in the lived rooms and had to relocate somewhere else.

The spatial layout and performance of a kitchen changed dramatically in the late 1950s: individual kitchens with a dining table and chairs, used for preparation as well as food consumption, replaced the earlier utilitarian workstations of communal kitchens. Daily meals relocated to the kitchen despite the tightness of these newly reimagined spaces. Under the 1958 change in the Soviet building codes, the lowest overall permissible area of an apartment dropped down to sixteen square meters (172 square feet) of residential area,[22] and kitchens went from a minimum of seven square meters (seventy-five square feet) down to 4.5 square meters (forty-eight square feet).[23] Due to this same tightness, the large table was entirely left behind and replaced with a small table instead. Oftentimes these new kitchen tables were collapsible to fit the new, limited space.[24]

The Soviet furniture industry, sluggish like the rest of the Soviet consumer goods sector, switched its design standards and sped up furniture production with the introduction of prefabricated apartment homes. Since the new apartments were small, they were very furniture-conscious: a 1956 architectural contest specified that furniture and fixtures for the standard apartments in the new three-, four-, or five-story apartment buildings must include a 90-by-90 cm (35.4-by-35.4 in) kitchen table, a sink built into a small cabinet, a stove, a mounted cabinet above the table, and some shelves or a cabinet above the sink.[25]

The famous 1959 Kitchen Debate between Khrushchev and President Richard Nixon fueled publication of many domestic manuals and technology instructions and drove even more interest in the formerly utilitarian space of the kitchen.[26] Although demand for domestic technology in the USSR grew faster than the level of its production, kitchen technology, and refrigerators in particular, now became visible to the public eye.[27] With the arrival of these new furniture designs and domestic technology strategically developed for the new, smaller apartments, a kitchen became systematically present in the world of Soviet images.[28] For example, *Bol'shaia sovetskaia entsyklopediia* (Great Soviet encyclopedia) illustrates a kitchen with a photograph from a showroom with new examples of modern furniture, meant to transition the problematic communal apartment life of a Soviet person into the modern sterile and civilized interiors of the new, individual apartments.

The new apartments would also provide impetus to the never-ending project of women's liberation from "kitchen slavery."[29] Although this image clearly indicates the functionalist aesthetic of these new kitchens, it does not do justice to real kitchen interiors of the time that were actually smaller and limited to a set of furniture and fixtures described in the competition call above: a table, a few stools, a sink, and two or three separate cabinets at most (figure 3.2).[30] A full set of kitchen fixtures, furniture, and a large dining area could not have fit into the early mass-built housing kitchens, often between 4.5 and 6.8 square meters (between forty-eight and seventy-three square feet) as in the widespread K-7 apartment building series, originally built between 1958 and 1969.[31]

Despite the modest size of the Soviet kitchens constructed in the 1950s and 1960s, urbanites still consumed their daily meals at the kitchen table. Soviet research in the 1980s indicates the following: "During weekdays 100% of single people and couples ate in the kitchen and so did 80% of families with three-, four- and more family members. During weekends almost ¾ of the overall number of interviewed families also ate in the kitchen. Eating in the family room [*obshchaia komnata*] has episodical character and happens mostly during holidays and while having guests."[32]

Food Spaces of the Late Soviet Home

In this way, a kitchen was no longer an auxiliary space meant only for meal preparation but was a desirable place to be. In the last three Soviet decades—the 1960s through 1980s—eating and spending time in the kitchen became the unquestionable norm. Unlike the communal apartment kitchens of the 1950s, the small kitchens of the new modernist housing were widely showcased in film. Only a decade after the virtual absence of kitchens in Lev Kulidzhanov's film *Dom v kotorom ia zhivu* (The house I live in, 1957), the 1966 Marlen Khutsiev's film *Iiul'skii dozhd'* (*July rain*) illustrated the ongoing shift in the status of a kitchen and the transition of eating and social functions away from the room and into this

FIGURE 3.2.   "Kitchen fixtures" illustration from Boris Merzhanov's book *Inter'er zhilisha* (Moskva: Znanie, 1970).

formerly auxiliary kitchen space.[33] Around the time the characters in *July rain* gather and play guitar in the kitchen, the protagonists of another widely popular movie *Operatsiia Y i drugie prikliucheniia Shurika* (Operation Y and Shurik's other adventures) (1965) still dine in the room.[34] Less than a decade later, the same *Operation Y* protagonist under the command of the same director eats in the kitchen in *Ivan Vasil'evich meniaet professiiu* (Ivan Vasil'evich: Back to the future) (1973).[35]

In 1984, *Rabotnitsa* illustrated that a guest's visits were taken seriously by saying that in this guest's presence the family dined in the lived room, not in the kitchen as usual.[36] Another *Rabotnitsa* article titled "10 metrov na 100 chelovek" (10 meters for 100 people) claimed the following: "Even if a family lives in a large apartment that has a living room, still they only gather there 3–4 times a year when they have guests." "Having guests" in this case entailed formal celebratory occasions, such as birthdays and big holidays. Everyday space use was presented differently: "At other times we all spend our nights at the cozy kitchen where a TV never goes dark, never-ending conversations with friends are held, sometimes until morning, and dekaliters of tea are consumed . . . Perhaps our housing conditions—the minimal square footage—gave birth to this tradition: the hearth of the apartment is the kitchen. Here we like to write, read, draft, knit, and even do homework.[37]

In the last three decades of the USSR, the social functions of the kitchen became elevated to what Svetlana Boym described as "kitchen culture": a trend that started among the Soviet intelligentsia in the 1960s to informally gather in the kitchens and "occasionally" eat.[38] By the 1980s, kitchen culture took over the rest of Soviet society; *Rabotnitsa* puts it that a kitchen "has to combine two functions: [that] of a kitchen block and [of] a living room."[39]

The move away from the utilitarian kitchen progressed further with the Brezhnev-era (1964–1982) resurrection of a belief in domestic comfort. Domestic advice manuals of this period suggested decorating kitchens with sentimental memorabilia rather than just functional objects like in the minimalist Khrushchev-era interiors.[40] Kitchens were now called to become "aesthetically expressive and distinctive,"[41] a vision that bloomed with the great variety and abundance of kitchen modifications in the 1990s.

Inside the home, the everyday and occasional foods were separated not only in their symbolic meaning but also in terms of the place of their consumption. In late Soviet apartments, casual, everyday eating took place in the kitchen. Formal dining with extended family or an extended group of friends on a special occasion always took place in one of the lived rooms. Formal dining with an extended circle required a large table; no regular Soviet family could afford to keep a large table like that in one of their lived rooms or the kitchen at all times since it would have consumed all the available space. Instead, urbanites would have a collapsible table in one of the rooms that would only be fully unfolded on a couple of important occasions a year and whenever domestic work, like sewing, required a large work surface. The gateleg tables that came to replace the round tables of the communal apartments were nicknamed "table-books" for their ability to unfold and were a highly desirable piece of domestic furniture.[42]

Moreover, many Soviet celebrations were tied to television, such as the traditional annual watching of a Soviet New Year's Eve show *Goluboi ogonek* (Blue light). Since a typical late-Soviet family only had one television set (and a dream to someday have another in the kitchen), the room where formal eating took place would also be the room with the television.[43] This way it was possible to watch holiday shows without leaving the dining table.

In the absence of affordable restaurants or quality casual dining places, celebrations were held at home. During those gatherings, special foods were consumed that were prepared in the kitchen but bore too much meaning to be consumed in an everyday setting.[44] By late perestroika (i.e., late 1980s), many foods were difficult or impossible to buy. These foods were nicknamed *deficit*. Deficit, as a noun, referred to goods that were no longer easily available in stores on an everyday basis due to production and distribution problems with the planned economy. To hunt down a deficit, one had to either stand in long lines to get it on some rare occasion when it randomly appeared in stores or buy it overpriced through carefully cultivated personal connections with store employees. Depending on the region, different foods could be deficit, but typically deficit meant quality meats and meat products.[45] And, of course, families had complex or expensive recipes that were only used for special celebrations. During different time periods and for different social strata, these recipes ranged from luxuries or ethnic and regional foods, such as red or black caviar, gefilte fish, and haroseth,[46] to the affordable Soviet celebratory classics, such as Olivier salad.[47] The deficit foods, luxury foods, or imported versions of familiar foods (such as Pepsi Cola instead of regular Soviet soda water with syrup) would only be consumed with guests at the unfolded large table typically in the biggest room of an apartment (figure 3.3).

Sometimes extra chairs or extra stools were borrowed from neighbors to accommodate large parties. At other times, apartment dwellers with extended families or large friend groups used two- to three-meter-long wooden planks to make benches out of stools for celebratory occasions.[48] Although celebratory eating happened in the living room, the social gathering may have later relocated to the kitchen if there were smokers in the group. Post-meal socialization was more comfortable in the kitchen, with its resourceful use of space, as opposed to the large, overly formal white-clothed table in one of the lived rooms.[49]

The tradition of the celebratory feasts in apartment homes, particularly those held for the favorite Soviet holiday—New Year's Eve—outlived the Soviet Union itself. Jennifer Jordan states: "food becomes incorporated into our personal memories, identities, and daily practices and also into the collective identities of communities, diasporas, and nations."[50] Despite the emergence of many public places that offered New Year's Eve parties, post-Soviet urbanites continued gathering at home, and spending hours eating food, drinking, and talking by the "holiday table."[51]

In the first half of the twentieth century, food may have been prepared in the kitchen, but eating permeated and penetrated all the rooms of the Soviet apartments on an everyday basis. In the second half of the twentieth century, though, the situation turned the other way around; social functions took over the originally food-centered space to a degree that eating and food preparation became nearly supplementary in the social space of a kitchen. At the same time, it is crucial to remember that many of these kitchens were rather small, if not tiny, with

FIGURE 3.3. A New Year's celebration at a table unfolded in the biggest room of an apartment, late 1990s. (Copyright of the author.)

a typical Khrushchev-era apartment kitchen not exceeding seven square meters (seventy-five square feet), and the so-called improved plan apartment's[52] kitchen starting at eight square meters (eighty-six square feet).[53] "Improved plan apartments" is an umbrella term used to define apartment series buildings where apartments had bigger floor areas, separate kitchens, and more storage space than the early prefabricated series. In terms of architectural series, improved plan apartments typically refer to the second generation of prefabricated apartment building construction starting in 1963.

How did the small dimensions of Soviet kitchens affect the cooking and eating practices of the post-Soviet urbanites, after the prescribed upper limit for the kitchen area was no longer effective? How did the Soviet spatial practices transform after the state that facilitated their creation ceased to exist? To answer these questions, it is necessary to look at the late- and post-Soviet practices of kitchen remodeling.

Post-Soviet Kitchen

The late-perestroika and early post-Soviet eating spaces exemplified a paradox. Chapter 1 "Remodeling" demonstrated that despite the shortage economy and

the decline in overall social prosperity, perestroika and post-Soviet reforms enabled access to private labor, private production, and imported goods. Despite
the fascination with the West and everything Western, Soviet urbanites did not
produce food spaces that closely resembled their Western counterparts but rather
created their own spatial model of eating, cooking, and storage. Inside an urban home, this predicated the period's leitmotif: remodeling and apartment replanning, with kitchens being first in line to change.

Kitchens, perhaps more than any other part of the Soviet mass-constructed
prefabricated apartments, are cited to be small and inconvenient.[54] *Rabotnitsa*
magazine was among the earliest Soviet sources to suggest a radical revision of a
kitchen. The article "10 metrov na 100 chelovek" (10 meters for 100 people) offered
the following solution: "in coordination with an architect you can move walls,
expanding the kitchen and reducing the size of a room. Third option: the wall does
not move, but niches are made in it for the shelves, drawers and the fridge and all
this furniture is placed flush with the wall."[55]

The issues with kitchens were not a secret to those responsible for the design of
the Soviet apartment homes—Soviet architects, planners, and engineers. And
yet, the changes clearly anticipated by the public and the architects were impossible to implement within the context of a centralized Soviet economy. For instance, until the last days of the Soviet Union, prefabricated panels remained a
basic unit for residential construction; monolith concrete construction remained
rare and had to be approved by the highest authorities on a case-by-case basis.[56]
In the standardized prefabricated panel apartment buildings, the technology and
the law did not allow for much variation.[57] All rooms and spaces were typically
constructed as rectangular boxes and bearing in mind the constraints of the
spans and the spacing of the load-bearing panels. Innovation came in the form of
a new apartment series with bigger or differently organized prefabricated panels.
Between the beginning of mass prefabricated housing construction in the 1950s
and its end after 1991, the dimensions of the prefabricated panels grew, and so did
the floor area of apartment kitchens.[58] The 1970s and 1980s had seen the rise of
the so-called improved plan apartments, when the span between the load-bearing
panels went from around 2.6 meters in the late 1950s to 3.6 meters in the late
1980s.[59] The building code minimum requirements for the kitchen areas went up
accordingly from 4.5 square meters in 1958 to eight square meters in 1989.

With mass prefabricated housing construction, the architectural profession
separated into two distinct branches. On the one hand were architects and engineers who developed the prefabricated apartment buildings meant for mass
construction, and on the other were those who worked on individual projects,
including individually designed apartment buildings. Architects who worked in
individual construction faced the same problems with small dimensions predi-

cated by the building code, but they approached them differently. As one of the respondents for this research put it, he "only ever looked at the building codes (*Sanitarnye normy i pravila*) to find a way around their limitations."[60] Because of the building code minimums, architects only had a chance to design the composition and form of apartment layouts, not their dimensions. However, by the late-Soviet period, architects commonly believed that formal dimensional requirements were problematic and could barely host all the functions that had to be located in a kitchen. Therefore, architects would invent tricks to enlarge these small spaces. For instance, a respondent for this study explained that he used to attach storage areas directly to kitchens during the planning stage and would never actually construct those storage areas after the plans were approved by the State Committee of Construction.[61] As a result, an additional ten to fifteen square feet would be added to the kitchen area, and that could be enough space to comfortably fit a refrigerator so that the residents of the apartment would not need to stand up and move their stools out of the way every time they needed to get something from the fridge.

By the 1980s, the last decade of Soviet rule, kitchens frequently were not only small but also desperately outdated, still resembling their utilitarian predecessors from the early 1950s. Despite the Soviet 1950s–1960s campaign for new kitchen cabinet sets for small prefabricated apartment buildings, not everyone was able to find or afford them. Well-made, diverse furniture was among the major Soviet shortages, and even those who were able to buy kitchen cabinets during the peak of their production in the 1960s witnessed those cabinets gradually lose their glamour during the subsequent two decades of daily use.

Under Gorbachev's reforms (1988–1991) that liberalized the labor code and paved the way for individual production of goods, cooperatives changed the rules of the furniture world by creating custom kitchen cabinets from available materials. Then, in the early 1990s, locally produced materials were replaced with custom-ordered imported elements assembled by local specialists.[62] By the late 1990s, kitchen furniture stores were abundant in larger post-Soviet cities and frequently offered remodeling or interior design services in addition to the furniture itself.[63] The Soviet kitchens that lacked individuality in the 1980s became, in the 1990s, a battlefield for individual solutions meant to impress, similar to how book and souvenir collections were used as a sign of social status during Soviet times.[64] The favorite[65] and the most universally used[66] part of the Soviet household became filled with the senses and symbols of the new post-socialist well-being (figure 3.4).

Since the collapse of the Soviet Union, food-related spaces, and kitchens in particular, have experienced a wide range of transformations as if to spite the strict Soviet laws. While kitchens were the hearth of the Soviet urban home and a

FIGURE 3.4. A 1990s kitchen setup. (Copyright of the author.)

hub for counter-Soviet thinking, they were also—ironically—the most regulated part of a Soviet apartment.[67] A kitchen had to have a window and a door, particularly because the majority of the Soviet apartment homes had gas stoves.[68] For the same reason, between 1958 and 1971, almost no kitchen (other than rare kitchenettes with electric stoves) could be combined with any other room in the house and had to have a door rather than a portal.[69] To reiterate, a kitchen was supposed to be bigger in an apartment with more rooms, quietly addressing the fact that meals were to be consumed in the kitchen, even in a large family.[70] At the same time, a kitchen was not to exceed a building code's upper limitation for state-owned and assigned (and hence, social) housing; having two kitchens in the same apartment was simply unthinkable, although many apartments were meant to be populated by multiple generations.[71] However, after 1991, kitchen restrictions in the Soviet-era *Sanitary Norms and Regulations* no longer made sense.

The early post-Soviet eating spaces followed two different avenues of transformation with virtually the same spatial outcome at the end. The first avenue, available to those with enough financial resources and the courage to start a massive remodeling job in their dwelling, was to remove a wall between the isolated Soviet kitchen and the adjacent room to create a version of an open plan, with the help of a dining table, other furniture, or semi-partition walls. The second option was to create additional partitions in the lived rooms. This option may not have affected the walls of the kitchens but would have dramatically shifted the spatial dynamics (figure 3.5).

FIGURE 3.5.   1–447 series apartment plan transformations from Soviet (*top*) to post-Soviet (*two on the bottom*) period. In apartment 1, cooking and daily eating take place in the kitchen, while occasional eating takes place in the room that assumes most living room functions. In apartment 2, the spaces for eating and cooking merge, producing a dining zone that may be used for both daily and occasional eating. In apartment 3, the room that used to assume living room functions gains more privacy through the construction of a new wall. In this case, formal dining may relocate to the kitchen, which is adjusted to host more guests under more formal circumstances. (Drawings by the author.)

Because of the notorious tightness of Soviet kitchens, partially objective and partially constructed through the business of these spaces, kitchens received a lot of attention after the Soviet Union collapsed. The ghost of the Cold War and the Kitchen Debate—a dream of a convenient and spacious American-style kitchen—kept haunting the Soviet, post-Soviet, and post-socialist homes long after the confrontation was over and the Soviet Union itself was gone.[72]

Krisztina Fehérváry gives an account of the post-socialist Hungarian tendency to construct American open-plan kitchens in newly built homes and privatized apartments.[73] A similar tendency toward the open plan and the language of the Westernized interiors could be found in all post-Soviet and post-Warsaw Bloc countries. Yet, Fehérváry's article contained an important moment that should not be disregarded when talking about Americanized kitchens and their overall Westernization. She wrote that "the newly built suburban family house was fast becoming the most important indicator of middle-class status nationwide" even in cities, where central-city living had been considered prestigious for decades.[74] Unlike many cities of the former Socialist Bloc, most post-Soviet megacities did not have a consistent tendency toward suburbanization and construction of new, individually designed housing from scratch.[75] With the exception of Baltic urban populations[76] and Moscow elites,[77] post-Soviet urbanites improvised with the available housing stock instead of constructing Western kitchens from scratch with no spatial restrictions. In these circumstances, the newly constructed kitchens barely resembled their supposedly Western prototypes and did not reproduce the Western model of home dining. Similar to the rest of the post-Soviet spheres of life, rather than transitioning to the Western models, urbanites created a model of their own, the post-Soviet cooking and dining areas becoming their own space with their own set of spatial practices.

Irene Cieraad convincingly argues that in the United States an open-plan kitchen was a reaction to the enclosed Fordist efficiency kitchens and the resulting alienation of women in these spaces.[78] However, in post-Soviet apartments, demolition of a wall between the kitchen and an adjacent room, hence opening the plan of the apartment, was usually not a response to the spatial retrenchment of the early mass-built apartments. Rather than being driven by the necessity to open the space of the kitchen to the rest of the house and simplify domestic logistics as in the case of the American kitchens,[79] the opening of the post-Soviet kitchen was a desperate attempt by the residents to enlarge the space for cooking, food storage, and eating, sacrificing the lived space of the other rooms if necessary.

This attitude was best illustrated in the *Rabotnitsa* article on kitchen remodeling that suggested three ways to improve a small kitchen situation: to move utility lines to the adjacent room, enlarging the kitchen and making the room smaller; to move the wall of the kitchen further into the adjacent room; or to make niches for kitchen cabinets in the wall and then solve "the problems" in the room that may have resulted from such transformation.[80] Since this article was published in 1989, it did not suggest removing a wall completely, a move rather unimaginable in the Soviet-era overpopulated apartments. However, the basic idea, to fix the problem with the kitchen at the expense of another room, was already well established.

After 1991, replanning with the goal to enlarge a kitchen was usually accomplished through a partition removal. Furthermore, it was a move toward the "modernization" of an apartment and the lifestyle of its inhabitants. The last four decades of the Soviet rule in the architectural realm can be decidedly identified as the absolute, complete rule of modernist architectural ideals: function and utility over decoration, codification of the many principles stated in the Athens Charter of 1933, as well as the formal reliance on science and industrial prefabrication as the main architectural and construction principles. Nevertheless, through the post-Soviet remodeling and rethinking apartment layouts, post-Soviet urbanites "modernized" their modernist homes. The removal of the wall between the kitchen and the living room and the creation of an open-plan living room was a central move in this modernization.

For instance, a book titled *Re-planning, Remodeling and Apartment Design* (2006) summarizes: "Vast majority of Russians, according to the statistics, still live in mass-built apartments. And the most mass built out the mass built are *khrushchovkas* [first and second-generation apartment series]: a small kitchen, closet-like rooms, low ceilings. However, professional architects and designers argue that even this, particularly re-planning and innovation-resistant housing can be perfected, made more modern and comfortable." The book then suggests how to improve such apartments: "The most wide-spread method is to demolish several internal partitions and create one large space, meaning adjoining several (two or more) rooms into one."[81]

This type of replanning is illustrated in a home of two adults and one young child described by Hanna F. Her sister's family replanned their two-room 1960s apartment in 1998. Originally, the apartment had an entry space with doors to all available spaces: two lived rooms, a kitchen, and two doors to the bathroom and the toilet. Since the family liked to spend their time in the small kitchen space, they decided to demolish the wall between the kitchen and the next room: "We put a big fridge in the niche that used to be the kitchen entrance . . . dining table went around where that partition between a bedroom and the kitchen used to be, and what used to be a bedroom became . . . a family and entertainment zone."[82] In other words, after the renovation, the newly created large space was used as a kitchen, living room, and child's room (figure 3.6).

Not all apartment residents could demolish the wall between the kitchen and the adjacent room even if they wanted to, simply because the wall may have appeared to be load-bearing.[83] Not all apartment residents chose to do so even if they could; yet, when the Soviet urbanites had economic resources to reconstruct their space in any way, they usually established a dining zone that created different spatial uses from those of the Soviet period. The most subtle example is found in larger apartments, where the walls of the kitchen remained intact, yet

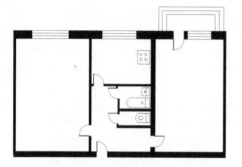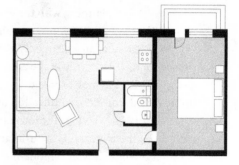

FIGURE 3.6. A two-room apartment plan drawn based on an interview with a resident's relative, Hannah F. (Drawing by the author.)

there appeared a separate living room (which would not become a sleeping space at night) with a designated dining area and a permanently placed dining table and a separate den (figure 3.7).[84]

Another scenario for keeping the kitchen walls was even more subtle, yet more transformative to the everyday practices of the apartment occupants. In those apartments where several generations of families lived together, residents could erect a new wall isolating the former walk-through room for further privacy of one of the adults or families. Typically, residents would create a hallway separating the shrunken former walk-through room and creating separate entrances to both spaces.[85] Besides providing more privacy for sleep, this also meant that the social functions of the walk-through room were now relocated to the kitchen more so than ever before (figure 3.7).

This case of remodeling can be illustrated with the kitchen furniture trend, which was widespread right before and after 1991. Instead of regular movable chairs and stools, apartment residents started acquiring kitchen benches and micro-sofas to create what the post-Soviet population called a soft corner (*miagkiy ugolok*)—a couch-like bench in the kitchen (figure 3.8). These kitchen bench-couches were not produced by the Soviet state furniture industry. The technical standards (*GOST*) employed by the Soviet furniture industry did not contain any regulations or mentions of a kitchen bench, although they contained regulations for the rest of domestic furniture meant for sitting, including kitchen stools.[86] The last 1967–1972 edition of the *Great Soviet encyclopedia* never mentions the soft corners, although it does mention a long list of close relatives: sofas, daybeds, ottomans, couches, chairs, and stools.[87] Soviet designers intended the kitchen seating to happen on chairs or stools, and no elements of living room furniture were to be introduced into this space, still largely seen as utilitarian from the perspective of the state and its planning institutions. However, by the end of the 1980s, soft corners became an extremely popular trend. A 1989 *Rabotnitsa* article

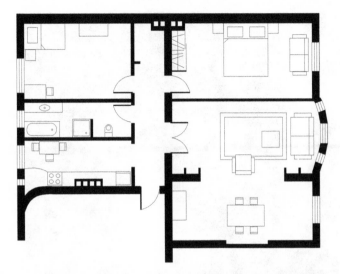

FIGURE 3.7.   Remodeling plan of a four-room apartment suggested by *Idei vashego doma* introducing a dining space separate from the kitchen. (Modified by the author from *Idei vashego doma* online platform article, https://www.ivd .ru/pereplanirovki/custom_house/custom_flat/1100).

on kitchen interiors indicated that they were a contemporary "mass craze," now produced by privately organized cooperatives and appearing for sale.[88] This spatially fixed sitting area was not only to provide additional comfort for everyday eating[89] but also to adjust the kitchen space to occasional formal gatherings, establishing a micro-living room inside the kitchen.[90] In fact, apartment residents were frequently willing to relocate food storage and refrigerators away from the kitchen and into the hallway to free a bit of space for a soft corner in the kitchen. The trend went so far that the soft corners, similar to the living room couches, were sometimes used for sleeping at night, illustrating that post-Soviet sleep still occasionally encroached into any living room–like space in the house, even if it was the kitchen. An interviewee for this study, praising the layout and the size of the kitchen in her improved plan apartment, concluded that the kitchens were so big that some neighbors "put couches in their kitchens and . . . slept on them."[91]

Like most of the respondents for this study, the owner of a five-room apartment, Mykola H., invited me straight to the kitchen when I came in to interview him. His large kitchen consisted of three overlapping zones: a cooking zone, a large dining table with six chairs, and a couch facing a widescreen television. Mykola, who purchased this apartment in the mid-1990s, explained that although different family members preferred different rooms, the kitchen was the most populated space in his home and was where all family and extended

FIGURE 3.8.   A kitchen bench (*miagkiy ugolok*) purchased as a luxury item in the late 1980s. (Photograph courtesy of Anna Egorova.)

gatherings took place, like "when children and grandchildren get back from Kyiv, for instance, for New Year's." Indeed, although remodeling in this apartment ended in the early 2000s, the rest of the apartment was less inhabited: the furniture was minimal, and some rooms appeared to be rarely used. Mykola explained that even during gatherings, both friends and family barely made it "to those living rooms out there [in the apartment]."[92]

Similarly, a large multifunctional kitchen remained a favorite place for another apartment resident, Iryna M. When she first visited the apartment with her father as a child, her "father and Uncle Misha [apartment owner] would sit in the kitchen and play backgammon. They would lock the kitchen door and smoke there. Uncle Misha did not turn on the heating; he would just light one stove burner and warm up from it."[93] As she grew up and moved to the apartment she used to visit, she continued to spend time and invite guests to the kitchen. When asked where she spent time with guests, she said, "Always in the kitchen. Sometimes we do go to [one of] the rooms; it is comfortable there too with a coffee table and a couch. But it is really always in the kitchen, and in summer we sometimes spend time on the balcony."[94] While the previous apartment resident only had chairs for seating in the kitchen, current resident Iryna brought in a couch and a long bench, finalizing the function of the kitchen as a social space.

These two examples illustrate a contemporary use of kitchens in large apartments, but the same is true for small ones. A resident of a one-room apartment, Mariia K., started a major kitchen remodeling because when she moved into her apartment, her kitchen was "the most used" and the most "worn out" of the apartment spaces. Mariia explains: "Because I have a one-room apartment, and the other room is my sleeping space, I spend a lot of time here [in the kitchen] and so do my guests. I wanted it [the kitchen] to look pleasant."[95] After remodeling the kitchen, Mariia switched from a Soviet-inherited rectangular table to a compact round table that is convenient for arranging dinner parties or drinks. Besides remodeling the cooking area, Mariia rezoned her kitchen. "Back then [before remodeling], when I had guests, they all nestled where they could: on the windowsill, a couple of people on one chair, or they sat on the countertop when there were a lot of people."[96] The new round table was placed into a corner where, due to its shape and placement, it comfortably sat more people, and the fridge moved back to where the table was and was no longer the first thing guests faced when they entered the kitchen.

The Favorite Place in a Home

In 2010, Elizabeth Cromley observed that after a century of division between food storage, preparation, and consumption, in the second half of the twentieth century, American homes have reunited these food practices in a "hearth of the home": a kitchen and a family room combined.[97] The wall between the family room and the kitchen came down; Cromley's review of homemaking media indicated the preference for a cooking island that allowed the cook(s) to socialize with the rest of a home's population instead of the blind wall of a Frankfurt kitchen, which separated the labor of cooking from the rest of the domestic functions. Cromley's observation was fundamental: the wall was no longer there. There was, however, something else that went beyond whether the wall existed— the functions of cooking, eating, and food storage themselves.

The Soviet and post-Soviet apartments' limited space and the many sociospatial transformations around the collapse of the USSR show that the wall may, but does not have to, come down in order for the architecture and the spatial uses of a home to change. With the boundary between casual and formal dining blurred, the formerly separate food spaces came to overlap. The post-Soviet urbanites demonstrated a tendency formally similar to the one described by Cromley: to combine a kitchen with a living room.[98] The difference was that instead of demolishing a wall, they often simply moved the living room functions into the existing kitchen.

Despite the limitations of prefabricated construction and because of the newly emerged freedom to spatially modify one's home, a post-Soviet apartment finalized an already-existing vector toward removing spatial use bias: even sleeping on the couch placed in the kitchen no longer seemed to be oxymoronic nor scandalous. After the collapse of the Soviet Union and the elimination of censorship, the kitchen largely lost its role as a political club. Nevertheless, it did not lose the status of a "favorite place" in the post-Soviet home.[99] Instead, the kitchen gained a new dimension: a favorite place to improve and transform according to individual desires and needs.

Several years ago, Moscow authorities started tearing down early Khrushchev-era prefabricated buildings with the 4.5-square-meter (forty-eight-square-foot) kitchens. The official agenda of the city is that these buildings are morally and physically obsolete, meaning that they no longer fit the contemporary requirements for housing, and they especially fall short of new kitchen standards.[100] Ironically, the contemporary food-related practices of the post-Soviet apartment dwellers are flesh and blood of these compact Soviet apartments. These buildings left an imprint on the spatial imagination of generations of Soviet and post-Soviet urbanites, just like these apartment dwellers left their marks—hollowed out and demolished walls and constructed partitions—on the body of the grand Soviet mass housing project.

CLEANING

> **The Communist Party of the Soviet Union sets a goal to resolve the sharpest problem in increasing the wellbeing of the Soviet people—the housing problem. During the first decade the housing shortage will be eliminated. Those families that currently live in overpopulated or bad housing will receive new apartments. As the result of the second decade every family, including newlyweds, will have a comfortable apartment, conforming to the requirements of hygiene and cultural *byt*.**
>
> —Communist Party of the Soviet Union, XXII Congress, 1961

Apartment sanitary blocks—either combined (bathtub, sink, and toilet in the same room) or separate (bathtub and sink in one room and toilet in another)—were rarely present in the late-Soviet visual culture, practically invisible, unlike iconic kitchens and lived rooms. In communal apartments, sanitary blocks were a common territory; as a result, dealing with their maintenance was perceived as a burden.[1] Yet even in private apartments, the bathroom appeared to be second in line of maintenance priority after the kitchen.[2] Elements of that hierarchy lasted until nowadays: "I am now done with the kitchen, so I'll get to the bathroom as soon as I save enough money," explains a one-room apartment owner, proudly presenting her new kitchen *remont*.[3]

Fehérváry expresses a similar observation to line up kitchens and bathrooms, both formerly utilitarian spaces, in the broader post-socialist context: "In the postsocialist era, kitchens and bathrooms have been singled out for transformation by residents, a trend reflected in special issues of home improvement/interior decor publications."[4]

The interest in and visibility of bathrooms right before and after 1991 is particularly noticeable in contrast with their Soviet inferiority. While a kitchen firmly secured its place in the Soviet imagery in the 1960s, a bathroom and a toilet room mostly stayed out of sight until the last years of the Soviet Union.

This chapter not only explains the spatial transformations of bathrooms and toilet rooms throughout the late-Soviet and post-Soviet years but also tracks the introduction of bathrooms to the world of images and the accompanying commodification of these spaces of hygiene. At the end, this chapter suggests the shift of the post-Soviet bathrooms from the realm of utilitarian auxiliary spaces of an apartment (such as a closet) into the status of representational spaces, not unlike the status that kitchens gained several decades earlier.

The rare images of Soviet bathrooms—exceptions that prove the rule to be true—are found in comedic episodes of Soviet film, *The Irony of Fate* and *Afonia* in particular.[5] In *Ironiia sud'by* (*The Irony of Fate*, 1975), drunk and heartbroken antagonist Ippolit showers in the bathtub, without taking off his coat and fur hat. In *Afonia* (1975), plasterer Kolia gets drunk and falls asleep in the bathtub. In both of these cases, the bathroom is a site of abnormal behaviors and embarrassment for the characters. Another rare exception is the bathroom episode in the film *Moskva slezam ne verit* (*Moscow Doesn't Believe in Tears*, 1979). This latter film is a unique cinematic artifact that anticipated perestroika and the post-Soviet reality through speaking of desires: material, social, and romantic.[6] Here the bathroom is shown as a clean, bright, pleasant space in a comfortable modern apartment of the main protagonist, a member of the Soviet elite.[7]

While late-Soviet spaces of hygiene were missing from the world of images, in the 1950s and 1960s they were omnipresent in the formal discourse on apartment housing. Varga-Harris provides numerous examples of individual bathrooms being used as an example of Soviet achievements in the home-building industry: an individual bathroom is presented as a sign of new happy times and a farewell to the constraints of life in a communal apartment.[8] And yet in all of these examples, a bathroom is nothing but a rhetorical device: there are no concrete qualities to this bathroom other than its belonging to an individual apartment. There is no concrete description of a convenient sanitary block: whether it should be small or big, what it should contain, how it should be finished, and whether the pipes should be leak proof. Instead, this rhetoric focuses on individual access; it is not that the bathroom is supposed to be qualitatively different, it is that the communal apartment neighbors would no longer be there to limit and orchestrate the access to hygiene facilities.

Similar to the enthusiastic rhetoric of the 1960s, institutionally published manuals on domestic interiors, even in the last decades of the USSR, only mention sanitary blocks very briefly and without illustrations of toilets, instead concentrating on the choice of finishing materials for the bathroom: tiles, oilcloth, and such.[9] Even *Rabotnitsa*, which published several major articles on remodeling during perestroika, did not mention bathrooms. There were many articles on the interiors for sleep, kitchens, children's rooms, and hallways, but there was not a single one on bathrooms, which suggests that until the 1990s bathrooms and toilet rooms were simply considered utilitarian spaces with no particular aesthetic requirements and choices other than cleanliness. If one were to make up an idea of Soviet and post-Soviet bathrooms based solely on mass media imagery, it would have looked like bathrooms barely existed prior to the rise of remodeling magazines in the 1990s.

There is a precise, traceable moment when the Soviet toilet came out of the shadows and became a subject for public gaze and discussion: in 1992 Ilia and Emilia Kabakov presented their installation *The Toilet* at the *Documenta* art exhibition in Germany.[10] A Soviet toilet suddenly transformed from an inconspicuous part of Soviet everyday life into a metaphor for perestroika and the collapse of the USSR. At *Documenta*, the Kabakovs presented an installation of a public, not private, restroom. This public restroom familiar to every Soviet citizen consisted of several stalls with no doors and an unexpected twist: upon entering the toilet a viewer realized that the toilet was rendered habitable and became a commonplace Soviet household with a couch, a table with a recently finished meal, and a reproduction of a classic painting on the wall.

The nightmare of the Soviet toilet and a fear of any hygienic space, which grew out of Soviet communal apartments and scary public restrooms, has taught Soviet citizens to squint their eyes upon entry. A dim, weak light hanging from an unattainably tall ceiling of a toilet in a communal apartment[11] or the single lightbulb of *The Toilet* were there to emphasize: a public restroom was not a place to look at. And yet, *The Toilet* as an art installation subverted this basic principle: this toilet became a place and a subject for gaze. The disgusting Soviet public bathroom, which according to Boym caused a desire to "close one's eyes," entered the visible sphere of the Soviet home.[12] Besides, just like the rare Soviet public restroom, it remained a place to look for: *The Toilet* pavilion accumulated lines, just like its insufficiently placed prototypes did in the Soviet public places.

While a typical reading of the Kabakovs' installation implies that it is the home that has been established in the toilet, this chapter takes inspiration in a metaphorical reading: that of a toilet entering a home. Indeed, the 1991 collapse of the Soviet Union seemed to have opened the lens of the former Soviet vision to the private spaces of hygiene. In the 1990s, images of bathrooms first appeared in mass media in relation to remodeling. The plentiful advertisements of tiles and fixtures, as well as luxurious stores that sold imported bathroom fixtures, entered the post-Soviet reality.[13] According to Boym, the sanitary block, which for centuries has been a civilizing threshold between Eastern Europe and the West, blurred en route from Soviet to post-Soviet hygiene:

> The toilet, of course, is an important stopping point for the discussion of Russia and the West. Travelers to Russia and Eastern Europe, from the Enlightenment to our day, have commented on the changing quality of personal hygiene as a marker of the stage of the civilizing process. The "threshold of civilization" was often defined by the quality of

toilets. Perestroika started, in many cases, with perestroika of public and private toilets. Even Prince Charles pledged to donate a public toilet to the Pushkin Institute in Petersburg.[14]

Just like the rest of a post-Soviet apartment, the spaces of hygiene adapted to the new times, new understanding of cleanliness, and new aesthetic ideas. Unlike the previous period, post-Soviet spaces of hygiene obtained a new social quality that was not previously recognized by the Soviet media—they demonstrated status and economic standing, no less than the rest of the apartment. The introduction of sanitary blocks into the world of domestic interior aesthetics in the 1990s may have been similar in nature to the establishment of kitchens in the Soviet imagery of the 1960s, when kitchens stopped being perceived as solely utilitarian and outside aesthetic judgement (see chapter 3). The bathroom and the toilet room shifted from a domestic unshowable to the last frontier in the celebration of extreme wealth: post-Soviet nouveau riche were anecdotally claimed to admire golden toilets,[15] equally as a cash overflow extravaganza of the early 1990s and a subversive commentary on the previous absence of the toilet from the public imagery. If a toilet was not made of solid gold, it had to at least have a golden rim, like in an apartment for a "respectable" person, as shown in the 1994 inaugural Russian issue of *Salon inter'er* design magazine.[16]

Combined or Separate?

On a practical level, the spatiality of late Soviet domestic hygiene boiled down to three categories: 1) not having a personal bathroom when living in a communal apartment, 2) having a bathtub and toilet in one room, or 3) having the bathtub and toilet in separate rooms.[17] Together, the hygienic spaces of an apartment were typically addressed as *sanitarnyi uzel* or *sanuzel,* which best translates as a sanitary block. When toilet and bathtub were placed in separate spaces, those rooms were called a toilet (or toilet room) (*tualet*) and a bathroom (*vannaia*) respectively.

The communal apartment dwellers were the least lucky as they never had easy access to the domestic hygiene facilities. Because multiple families lived in the same apartment that typically only had one bathroom and one toilet room, getting to use the bathroom was always a matter of lines, time limits, cleaning disputes, and splitting utility bills. The troubles of the communal apartment residents with hygiene were many, and they are vividly discussed in scholarly literature. Svetlana Boym, Christine Varga-Harris, Ekaterina Gerasimova, and Steven Harris all indicate the lack of access to bathrooms in communal apartments due to overcrowding, the lack of maintenance because of their shared status, and the complex schemes of use. For example, in many communal apartments every family or single resident had to have their own individual bathroom light switch and toilet seat to use.[18] The spaces of hygiene in an individual late-Soviet and post-Soviet apartment received much less attention; therefore, those spaces are the ones that this chapter will discuss in detail.

In the apartments built after the 1957 decree "About the Development of Residential Construction in the USSR" and the 1958 update of the building code, bathrooms no longer had gas water heaters. The gas heaters had originally dictated a larger cubic volume of the bathrooms, and since they were no longer there, a sanitary block safely fell under the official course towards minimization of apartment floor area.[19] Although the 1958 building code indicates that "apartments no bigger than 45 square meters can be developed with combined sanitary blocks,"[20] the same building code specifies that the apartments are to be designed "economically"—with a minimal area—and hence combined bathrooms, unless required otherwise.[21] Indeed, in the first decades of prefabricated housing construction, smaller one- and two-room apartments were often built with combined bathrooms.[22] This did not change until the third generation of prefabricated housing (starting 1971), when some series introduced a separate bathroom and toilet room to two-room apartments.[23] At the same time, sanitary blocks with a separate bathroom and toilet room were seen as more convenient and desirable.[24] Overall, despite the loud mention of comfort in the 1961 Communist Party program, the early series apartment design was not about comfortable use. Instead, it was about uninterrupted access to hygienic facilities, which communal apartments, particularly the ones in the pre-1917 buildings, could not provide.[25]

However, with the evolution of prefabricated housing types and the increase in floor area norms in the 1970s and 1980s, the discourse began shifting from simply having access to hygienic facilities to the quality of the facilities provided in individual apartments.[26] In the late Soviet years, there prevailed a belief that a separate bathroom and toilet block was a much better planning solution than a combined one.[27] A public preference for separate bathroom and lavatories is evident not only in conversations with apartment dwellers but also in the prestige gradation of different types of housing throughout the late-Soviet years. Elements of collective initiative were introduced to housing construction in the 1970s, with cooperatives and institutions receiving a certain amount of freedom in apartment planning. While architects designing for cooperatives were still limited by the upper limits of the building codes, unlike in social housing they no longer had to closely follow the lower limits. Although the later building codes suggested constructing combined bathrooms in smaller one- or two-room apartments, cooperative and institutional apartment building residents were often lucky to secure separate bathrooms and toilet rooms even in one or two-room apartments.[28]

A preference for a separate bathroom and toilet room continued dominating apartment dweller moods after 1991, yet the value of the separate sanitary block had been enhanced with a new meaning. This new meaning did not have to do with the increased comfort of using a toilet room and a bathroom separately in an apartment with more than one resident. Instead, it was about the possibility of demolishing a partition wall between the toilet room and the bathroom and gaining more useful space, since a separate sanitary block had bigger floor area than a combined one.[29] But let us continue in order and first look at the way architects understood the situation with the late-Soviet bathrooms.

Architectural Fantasies and Reality

Soviet literature on residential architecture often enthusiastically discussed innovations and improvements that were never implemented in reality as if they were already present on the ground.[30] The case of the late-Soviet and post-Soviet spaces of hygiene is a perfect illustration of this gap between the formal architectural and homemaking discourses and the practical reality of apartment dwellers. Just like any part of the Soviet apartment household, spaces of hygiene—bathrooms, toilets, and less hygiene-dominated kitchens—went through some dramatic transformations after 1991. The precursors of these transformations were reflected in the professional architectural discourse. Yet the estimates of the existing situation and the solutions formally voiced by architects in the late-1970s and 1980s were rather far from the reality of existing housing and apartment dwellers' needs.

One architectural dream that never got realized in the late Soviet Union was a dream of multiple separate sanitary blocks.[31] An illustration of the multiple sanitary block rhetoric can be found in Boris Merzhanov's 1974 homemaking manual targeted toward "architects, designers, and a broad circle of readers."[32] In his book, Merzhanov uses a number of examples to illustrate a domestic spatial organization of hygienic facilities that he considers desirable. First, he suggests an example of a four-room apartment in 111–78 and 111–83 prefabricated panel apartment building series with two completely separate sanitary blocks, resulting in two toilets being placed in one apartment (figure 4.1). According to Merzhanov, the introduction of two separate toilets was to make the apartment "more comfortable for performing personal hygiene procedures for all family members."[33] A trustful reader may assume that 111–78 and 111–83 series four-room apartments were indeed always built with two sanitary blocks, equaling two lavatories and two bathrooms. At the same time, a formal booklet on 111–83

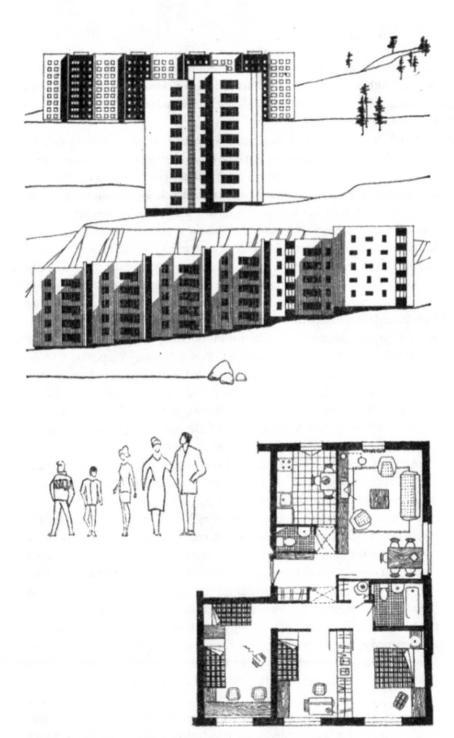

FIGURE 4.1. 111–78 series according to Boris Merzhanov's book *Sovremennaia kvartira* (1974). (Drawing modified by the author.)

series presented plans with only one bathroom in four- and five-room apartments.[34] Although regional variations of these series may have indeed included two sanitary blocks, this was certainly not a universal rule for every building in this series ever built.

Merzhanov again exemplifies progressive Soviet apartment planning with the apartments designed in the so-called New *byt* apartment buildings: experimental projects of residential buildings with public services—laundry, cooking, and/or childcare—planned into the apartment block. In such buildings, separate apartments were not supposed to have full kitchens but just kitchenettes meant for minimal use. The space freed with the absence of a full kitchen was to be taken by a second sanitary block in an apartment as small as three rooms.[35] At the time of the publication, one such building was already constructed in Moscow's Novye Cheremushki neighborhood. According to the original design concept, it was supposed to house regular families that were willing to change their lifestyle and reduce the amount of domestic labor.[36] However, Merzhanov, as if on purpose, forgets to mention that the building was never constructed or populated according to the original design. Even prior to its completion, its public services and areas were significantly reduced. More importantly, right after completion, the building was assigned to the Moscow State University and became a dormitory, therefore eliminating the original concept of more than one sanitary block for an individual apartment.[37] Despite all Merzhanov's examples, very few prefabricated standard apartments had more than one bathroom and one toilet room.[38] Individually designed buildings, a minority in the world of Soviet housing, also followed the rule of one sanitary block, even in large apartments meant to host five or more people (figure 4.2).

One very small category of Soviet housing had acquired multiple sanitary blocks before 1991. Only the housing for extremely high-status elites—military generals, major Communist Party figures, university rectors, and such—could evade most regulations and overcome the austerity principle of Soviet construction. Such apartment buildings were always designed individually and never in series, and many design decisions were made in coordination with the future residents. In an interview for this study, an architect who worked on individually designed apartment buildings in the last Soviet decades and after the Soviet Union collapsed explained the need for multiple sanitary blocks with multiple generations—multiple core families—living in the same apartment.[39] According to him, even if an elite apartment was large, simply having a substantial amount of space for sleep or rest was not enough for truly comfortable living. In order to become comfortable, these apartments required another sanitary block. Otherwise, even a large and luxurious elite apartment became not unlike a communal apartment, with its morning and evening lines to the bathroom and

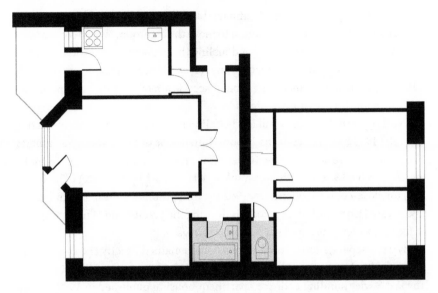

FIGURE 4.2. An example of an individually designed apartment building with four-room apartments containing one sanitary block (blueprints issued in 1989). (Redrawn from Kyivproekt archives, folder #098833.AR-2. Drawing modified by the author.)

toilet room.[40] Such buildings were extremely rare and proved the general rule of one bathroom block per apartment home to be true.

Therefore, despite the alternative reality of the professional architectural discourse, it would be incorrect to assume that Soviet architects and architectural writers were simply delusional. Rather, in a widespread Soviet manner, they projected what they knew was desirable onto the existing housing situation. A perfect case of such projections can be found in design competition catalogues suggesting reconstruction and improvements for early series, such as the competition organized by State Committee of Construction in 1987. The first prize project suggests arranging a combined sanitary block and a separate toilet room in apartments for five occupants.[41] The second prize design offers the exact same solution for five-person apartments.[42] The third prize design suggests that two toilets should be placed in an apartment for four people, which had never been realized in the Soviet mass-housing construction before.[43] The outcomes of the competition are a clear statement on the hygiene issue: according to architects, large apartments were to be equipped with two toilets in a country where this has not yet happened on a considerable scale.

The unanimity of designers in 1987 is far more impressive when considering that the opinions were not as univocal only six years prior. In 1981, some projects suggested having one separated sanitary block in apartments for six or more people; some offered a strange solution to move the bathroom away from the toilet room in large apartments, while not doubling their functions anywhere else; and yet a third kind suggested introducing one full combined sanitary block (bathtub, toilet, and sink) and another toilet room placed separately in a different part of an apartment for three or more residents.[44]

While overall floor areas and kitchen dimensions grew consistently starting from the 1958 building code, bathroom dimensions did not. The 1958 Sanitary Norms prescribed separate lavatories to have minimal dimensions of 0.8 by 1.2 meters (2.6 by 3.9 feet) with high-tank toilets and 0.8 by 1.5 meters (2.6 by 4.9 feet) for close-coupled toilets.[45] By 1962 the dimensions for the high-tank toilets disappeared from the building code, indicating the gradual end of using this type of fixture, which was popularly known as Niagara.[46]

By 1971 separate toilet room dimensions remained exactly the same. Bathrooms had to have minimal dimensions of 1.73 by 1.5 meters (5.6 by 4.9 feet).[47] The last Soviet building code for apartment housing published in 1989 no longer mentioned separate toilet rooms but simply indicated that the minimal dimensions for a bathroom were to be 0.8 by 1.2 meters, which is exactly the same as in 1958.[48] In other words, in the last three decades of the Soviet Union, virtually no changes happened in the floor area of sanitary blocks.

Post-Soviet Architects

After 1991, two processes took place simultaneously: while architects were finally able to realize their vision and design multiple hygiene blocks within the same apartment, residents of the existing apartments resourcefully transformed, partitioned, and combined their existing sanitary blocks and hygienic practices to gain more usable space for new functions and equipment.

Since most housing built after 1991 was no longer allocated by the state,[49] the upper limits of floor area and amenities suggested by the Sanitary Norms and Regulations or other documents developed in the post-Soviet states no longer applied to the majority of the new apartment buildings being built.[50] This meant that the plans, floor areas, and space compositions predominantly depended on the investor and the market, with only the minimal requirements defined by the legislature. In a large apartment, an architect could finally introduce as many bathrooms as they desired, only dependent on the future marketability of such an apartment home. Moreover, when factories that produced prefabricated apartment building series took the initiative to adjust to the new market conditions, they modified their series to fit the new post-Soviet demands by introducing another bathroom block to larger apartments. One such example is a set of post-Soviet modifications for one of the most widespread apartment series—P-44.[51] In the 1990s and the first decade of the 2000s, several derivative series, such as P-44T and P-44M, were developed to substitute the "morally obsolete" original.[52] Unlike its previous version, newly developed P-44M had two separate sanitary blocks in four-room apartments.

P-44 was just one example of a characteristic phenomenon: despite the collapse of the ruling system, many elements of the Soviet infrastructure remained and continued functioning after 1991, but not without changes. This was particularly true for the factories and organizations that specialized in producing prefabricated panels for housing construction. Stroitel'noe Upravleniie No.155, a former Soviet construction institution that became an independent organization after 1991, developed the new prefabricated series I-155 with two sanitary blocks in both three- and four-room apartments.[53] The Moscow Scientific-Research and Project Institute of Typology and Experimental Design (*Moskovskii nauchno-issledovatel'skii i proektnyi institut tipologii, eksperemental'nogo proektirovaniia*, or MNIITEP) developed yet another series where three- and four-room apartments had two separate sanitary blocks.

In individually designed apartment buildings after 1991, the decision on the number of bathrooms in new housing was often left to the prospective owners (figure 4.3). Cast-in-place concrete construction became a dominant method for apartment housing construction.[54] Cast-in-place concrete buildings were frequently commissioned without partitions and amenities in an expectation that the new owners would like to implement their own vision.[55] This was unlike the earlier developed approach to prefabricated buildings, which were sometimes still built as an economical option; such buildings always had walls already in place.

Although the introduction of multiple bathrooms in new construction was a major trend after 1991, architectural microtrends are also worth mentioning. One such microtrend originated from Western expats, who became abundant in large post-Soviet cities. After the collapse of the Soviet Union, foreigners entered post-Soviet cities mostly in hopes of making business on the wreckage of socialism.[56] These foreigners needed temporary, semi-temporary, or permanent accommodations. Although hotels meant particularly for foreign travelers were constructed and sustained at higher standards (such as hotels administered by the state joint-stock company Inturist), the functioning of those was also affected by the calamity of the 1990s. And even then, a hotel could only provide a temporary solution.

These foreigners took interest in the post-Soviet real estate market and were among the first clients to create a demand for organized, professional remodeling labor, able to change existing apartments according to Western standards of living (see chapter 1). Construction professionals and architects, who entered the

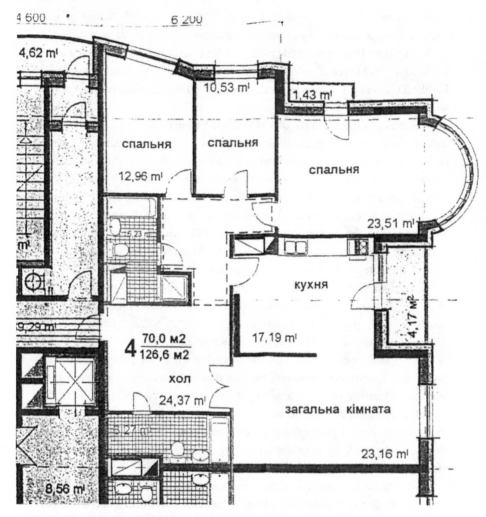

FIGURE 4.3. Individually designed post-Soviet apartment building home with two bathrooms, blueprints developed in 2002. From Kyivproekt archives, folder #330201-AP. (Drawing modified by the author.)

rapidly invigorated apartment remodeling market as early as 1992, recall that one of the major problems cited by foreign clients were kitchens and bathrooms, the latter being even more important than the former.[57] Because of small footprints and remote locations outside historic cities, mass-built apartment blocks were of no interest to Western expats. Instead, they purchased apartments in historic or Stalin-era buildings. These apartments had larger floor areas, yet the state of bathroom interiors and appliances left much to be desired. In addition, Western European clientele simply had requests different from Soviet standards. For instance, almost no Soviet housing was equipped with bidets. Although bidets can be found on some design stage blueprints for the third generation of prefabricated housing series (1971–1985), those same bidets never appeared on the Recorder of Deeds plans, which means that they were rarely installed in reality.[58] Water supply and drain elements for bidets were not shown in project documentation either.[59] Several architects interviewed for this study indicated bidets to be among the exotic requests Western clients made for their apartment remodeling.[60]

Although illustrative of what early post-Soviet bathrooms had, and what they did not have, this microtrend never spread to the majority of post-Soviet urban housing. Architects, interior designers, and construction workers took a lot of knowledge from these early commissions into their further practice, but bidets did not become overwhelmingly popular and are rather rare in post-Soviet apartments to this day. The reason bidets did not become a popular bathroom solution was that the majority of late- and post-Soviet bathrooms were simply too small to fit them.

Post-Soviet Bathroom Remont

During the same formative post-Soviet years when architects introduced the second set of sanitary blocks to new apartments, regular apartment residents combined their separate toilet room and bathroom blocks together to gain some more usable space for the newly available domestic object of desire: a stationary washing machine.

The collapse of the Soviet Union drove the extinction of some hygienic practices and enabled the emergence of others. A notable practice that came to an end was boiling laundry in the kitchen. Soviet women, the population predominantly responsible for laundry, used to boil durable white laundry in large pots on the kitchen stove as a way of removing stains and sanitizing fabric.[61] This practice fell victim to the spread of washing machines and the introduction of effective laundry detergents. In the first decade of the 2000s, post-Soviet television was populated with the anti–laundry boiling commercials of Tide laundry detergent: a popular television personality traveled from household to household comparing the brightness of laundry when boiled and washed with Tide. After the inevitable victory of Tide, he notoriously threatened the audience: "Are you still boiling [laundry]? Then we are coming for you!"[62] Despite the extinction of laundry boiling techniques, laundry processes did not completely abandon kitchens: now the question was about where to put a washing machine.

In the 1950s, when the first prefabricated series apartment buildings were constructed to house a wide range of the Soviet urban population, many Soviet people did not have washing machines.[63] The 1960s official rhetoric was saturated with the subject of domestic machinery that was to liberate women from their domestic workloads. The tone of this rhetoric, inseparable from the Cold War competition with the United States, assumed that not all women had been liberated yet because not every household had the necessary machines, washing machines in particular.[64] In the following decades, the Soviet industry produced a substantial number of washing machines, yet most of them were of a type quite different from currently common washers and required a completely different spatial set up.

Prior to the 1980s, Soviet industry only produced wringer washing machines or top-loading activator washing machines.[65] These structures were portable, did not match the level of the kitchen countertop, and could not serve as an extra usable counter surface in the bathroom due to their intricate geometries or top-loading construction. This meant that in an apartment, washing machines occupied leftover space; they were not built in and were stored in the bathroom[66] or elsewhere in the apartment until it was time to use them. At laundry time these washing machines were mounted on top of the bathtub (figure 4.4). In the 1980s, Soviet industry first started producing automatic washing machines named Vyatka. The number of households that owned washing machines grew to 78 percent.[67] These machines were very similar to the front-loading automatic machines available today. They were large, heavy, and stationary. And they required a space of their own in the late-Soviet and post-Soviet home—the space that was desperately lacking in the sanitary blocks of mass-built apartments.

A front-loading washing machine quickly became a necessary attribute of a post-Soviet household.[68] Therefore, the space for a washing machine had to be found somewhere, no matter how small the apartment. This problem divided apartment dwellers into several categories. Those who were lucky enough to live in Stalin-era apartment buildings could simply fit their washing machine into the extra space that they had in their bathrooms due to the bigger bathroom floor area. The last Soviet building code prior to the Khrushchev-era shift to extra-frugal housing construction determined the minimum sanitary block size as 0.9 by 1.4 meters with the caveat of being at least twelve cubic meters if there was a gas water heater. Since a residential story was not supposed to be less than three meters tall,[69] this meant that the floor area of such a bathroom would be at least four square meters. This would have provided enough space for placing a washing machine in the bathroom, and if not, it could have always been placed in the kitchen that the code determined to be no less than seven square meters or seventy-five square feet—a large, comfortable kitchen by Soviet standards. Additionally, placing washing machines in kitchens became particularly popular with the new availability of modular furniture after 1991. The washer could now be built into the row of kitchen cabinets and other appliances underneath the

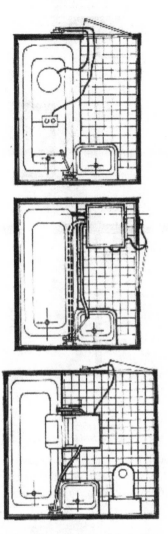

FIGURE 4.4. "Mounting washing machines" in bathrooms of different configurations. An illustration from a 1988 Soviet book on contemporary apartment interiors. R. N. Blashkevich, *Inter'ier sovremennoi kvartiry* (Moscow: Stroizdat, 1988), 95.

kitchen-counter surface. And yet, this convenient solution was only easy in apartments with larger kitchens, not in the first generation of mass-built apartment blocks.

The 1958 building code, the first document to fully reflect the changes in the official housing planning policies, dropped the minimum volume for bathrooms with gas water heaters down to 7.5 cubic meters, placing the minimal bathroom

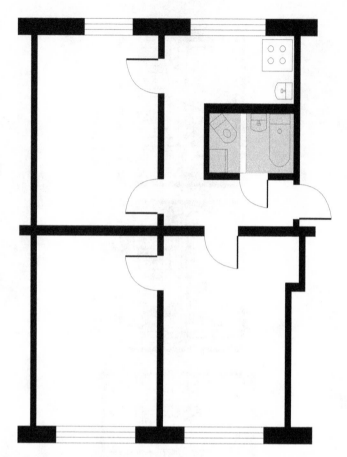

FIGURE 4.5.   A plan drawn by the author based on Recorder of Deeds documents of a Khrushchev-era apartment after removing a wall between the toilet room and the bathroom to fit a washing machine.

floor area at a little higher than three square meters.[70] These three square meters were not enough to fit a washing machine. Such apartments, equipped with three-square-meter bathrooms, were typically also the ones that had extremely small kitchens; therefore, a washing machine could not fit there comfortably either. And yet, many residents of these first-generation khrushchevkas found a solution: if the sanitary block consisted of a separate bathroom and toilet room, the dwellers of these apartments could demolish a wall between the toilet and the bathroom and remove one of the swinging doors from when it was two separate rooms, gaining the necessary 0.3 square meters to fit the washing machine. To no surprise, this type of re-planning is quoted to be among the most popular transformations that took place in prefabricated apartment housing (figure 4.5).[71]

FIGURE 4.6.   A combined sanitary block in Kyiv containing a bathtub, a sink, a toilet, a bidet, and a washing machine. (Photograph courtesy of Anastasiya Ivanova.)

The newly available hygienic options of the post-Soviet era called for more space, and the space was found at the cost of a partition wall between the bathroom and the toilet room.

After 1991, apartment dwellers and architects alike called for more space dedicated to hygiene in an apartment home. The Soviet spaces of hygiene were no longer enough to fit all the requirements of the new time, be it the luxurious bidet and Jacuzzi of the Western expats or local nouveau riche or the economically priced washing machines of khrushchevka residents. Furthermore, a bathroom became a visible part of a home, with the spaces of hygiene as much a subject for aesthetic transformation and judgement as the rest of the post-Soviet apartment.

Just as kitchens massively transitioned from utilitarian to representational spaces beginning in the Khrushchev era and ending in the Brezhnev era, the spaces of hygiene transitioned after the collapse of the Soviet Union. Instead of bleak spaces meant to produce a healthy yet modest Soviet person, these new spaces of hygiene became a place of comfort and self-appreciation. The bathroom was now to become, using Jennifer Patico's terms, "respectable."[72] It became a place of conspicuous consumption, where bathroom equipment, hygienic products, and even the number of bathroom blocks emphasized social standing. Fehérváry addressed luxurious post-socialist bathrooms as the elements of "idealized lives—and selves—long imagined to exist elsewhere," particularly in the West.[73] Beyond the dreams of the imaginary West and the practicality of new appliances, a renovated bathroom quickly became necessary to conform to the standards of the new times that forced even less well-off post-Soviet urbanites to remodel the bathrooms in their small apartments. Since "hygiene is a strong signifier of respectability," spaces of hygiene must satisfy societal standards for where cleanliness is produced.[74] The terrifying bathrooms of the communal apartments and the utilitarian yet aging bathrooms of the Soviet prefabricated blocks inevitably gave way in popular imagination to the consumption-centered bathrooms fit to sustain respectable post-Soviet identities.

SOCIALIZING

Housing is always more than just housing.

—David Madden and Peter Marcuse, *In Defense of Housing: The Politics of Crisis*

In his 1961 Congress of the Communist Party speech, Khrushchev announced that building communism was supposed to be finished in twenty years.[1] Communism never quite got built, but the Soviet state did succeed in constructing millions of housing units, if not communist then modernist in form and spirit, and in dramatically modernizing the domestic life of urban citizens.[2] Just like with the rest of the modernist housing experiments, this one also did not go exactly as planned.

A modern, "functional" interior is "destructured, fragmented into its various functions."[3] The revolutionary-scale, twentieth-century effort to rethink and restructure domestic space materialized in the quintessential modernist home—an apartment block. Yet a home still did not abide by the meticulously structured scenarios established by its creators. The home transcended the preexisting conventions of a dining room or a bedroom, of a room altogether, of privacy, of a family. In fact, it often transcended the limits of an apartment itself as the functions contained inside a home spilled out past its walls and into the in-between spaces of hallways, attics, basements, courtyards, and streets that surrounded a single residential unit.

This chapter aims to outline the spaces of socialization in the late- and post-Soviet apartment, the semiprivate or semipublic spaces that surrounded it, and the limits of control exerted by the state and the residents onto their extended homes.

The Absentee State

During the Soviet era, housing and the home were an area of primary state concern and, hence, unprecedented state control. Of course, there was also the arms race and the space program, but those were matters of international prestige. Internally, housing was one of the most critical issues to the Soviet state from its very beginning in 1917, with the placement of working-class families in former bourgeois apartments. The issue continued through Khrushchev's housing campaign starting in 1957 and all the way to the return of the housing crisis[4] and the modest attempts of housing privatization during the belated perestroika reforms of the late 1980s. The collapse of the USSR in 1991 created a completely new reality—a reality where the newly independent states were concerned with regional conflicts, hyperinflation, collapsed production, and belated salaries. Housing, a former priority and pride, had to step back.

Control and concern over the housing conditions and the domestic life of post-Soviet citizens became virtually nonexistent in the first years after 1991. Post-Soviet states did undertake property reforms; however, it is important not to overestimate their role in the reformation of ordinary residential spaces.[5] The participation of the state in matters of housing virtually stopped with the privatization campaign and unsuccessful attempts to introduce Western housing market models.[6] The self-removal of the state from matters of housing in the former USSR is particularly visible in comparison to a different post-socialist country: the former German Democratic Republic (GDR), where after unification generous state investments were made into modernizing socialist-built apartment blocks, as well as new housing construction.[7] Furthermore, instead of a privatization campaign, the German state provided tax credits for single-family home construction. In the former East Germany, these tax credits, coupled with the loss of industrial jobs and increased rents, resulted in extremely high vacancy rates in multi-unit housing, even in major cities.[8] This situation, however, is rather unique for the unification of Germany and is unlike anything that happened in the post-Soviet metropolitan cities.

In the former-Soviet cities, changes first and foremost came from the private individuals and private investors rather than the state. Perhaps even more telling than the lack of working initiatives is that many housing construction regulations simply did not change on paper throughout the 1990s.[9] The ones that did change were heavily based on the old Soviet Sanitary Norms and Regulations.[10] The housing reality, on the contrary, changed dramatically: the old building norms were established to suit state-owned social housing, where the most important parameter was the upper value of apartment dimensions and areas. After the Soviet Union, these upper limits became meaningless since the absolute majority of housing being built was no longer social housing allocated by the state. This is not to say that compact apartments stopped being built, but their construction was now determined by a projected customer demand. Bigger apartments were being built for a different customer base.

What mattered more than the property reforms was the disappearance of institutional supervision over the transformations undertaken in individual apartments. This unexpected (but quite quickly accepted) freedom led to a curious paradox. Prior to the late-1980s, moving partitions and altering walls in apartments was not a popular, widespread practice due to the many reasons described in chapter 2. However, in the 1990s, it became extremely widespread, sometimes in grotesque forms. State institutions rarely intervened until something went terribly wrong, like in the case of a historic apartment building that partially collapsed on a central street of Kyiv in 2003, thankfully not killing anyone. Back then, newspapers attributed this collapse to the massive replanning done to transform one of its stories into a hotel on the second floor of this six-story building.[11]

In many post-Soviet states, a centralized system of documentation for such changes was not introduced right away. For instance, in Ukraine this system did not become formalized until 1997.[12] An architect interviewed for this study recalled that back in the early 1990s, no organization had monopoly over the registration of apartment layout changes, and several organizations could offer such services.[13] This lack of monopoly on replanning registration meant that the registration may have been done rather cheaply and in the spirit of the Soviet and post-Soviet informal economy: without engineer- or architect-approved blueprints, based solely on the experience of construction workers. Additionally, this meant that before 1997, amid the institutional confusion, an apartment owner could do anything they wanted inside their home and sometimes even sell it without having to report the changes to anyone at all. In different post-Soviet states, replanning recording was monopolized by existing or new institutions in different years. However, in most megacities, registration procedures were established no later than the first decade of the 2000s, and the process of recording apartment changes has been centralized since.

In the Soviet Union, control over the state and the preservation of housing funds was performed by the Bureau of Technical Inventory (*Biuro tekhnicheskoi inventarizatsii* or BTI), analogous to the Recorder of Deeds. Prior to 1985, the BTI routinely took care of urban and rural housing and nonresidential structures; it also planned maintenance and registered property rights for these buildings. During Soviet times, the latter appeared to be a relatively simple task since, even after the introduction of housing privatization in the late 1980s, 70 percent of the urban housing stock was still owned by the state or state institutions.[14] The mass privatization and the form of real estate market that appeared after the collapse of the USSR expectedly overwhelmed and hindered the work of the BTI, creating a breeding ground for long waiting times and corruption. With time, this complex procedure gave way to simplified documentation and databases, but not until the first two decades of the 2000s.[15] At the same time, despite the privatization of individual apartment units, the shared structure of every apartment building remained the responsibility of state-governed Housing Maintenance Offices (*Zhilishchno-ekspluatatsionnaia kontora* or ZhEK).[16]

This extreme freedom to execute individual apartment remodeling without supervision from any authority and no serious legal effects did not last long but produced a substantial number of urban legends and accidents. While this study did not particularly concentrate on urban folklore, such stories unavoidably came up in the interviews with apartment dwellers, architects, and construction workers alike. To avoid mentioning those would not do justice to the spirit of the era, so it is worth citing one.

A current-day apartment owner, who earned extra money as handy worker when he was a college student in the 1990s, recalled a case of a client who accumulated several apartment properties and in 1997 decided to remodel them to attract higher-class renters. The apartment owner requested that part of the outside load-bearing wall be demolished between the kitchen and the balcony to make the kitchen feel bigger. The builders refused, explaining that the wall was supporting the roof and that a metal beam would be necessary to fortify the wall if its portion was to be taken out. The apartment owner then found discarded tram rails in the courtyard next door and insisted that construction workers install those instead of the beams, which she considered to be too expensive. "They were extremely heavy. We pulled them all the way up to the fifth floor. How, I do not know."[17] To install the first one, the apartment owner had to invite all male family and friends to help the construction workers lift it up to the top of the wall opening. To pay for their services, she threw a major feast. The second beam was never installed, as the apartment was sold before another opening that required a beam was cut. The workers refused to pull it back down from the fifth floor, citing its extreme weight and leaving the new owners to deal with a tram rail in their newly acquired home.

This story was not in any way an isolated incident: makeshift solutions to major apartment remodeling were widespread. Presently, it is impossible to know how many of the existing apartments were changed throughout the Soviet and post-Soviet years since only a portion of the changes were formally registered with the BTI. Apartment owners who did not foresee a need to sell their property or otherwise change its ownership in the near future often did not report the changes that they made, particularly if those changes went completely against the established rules. An interviewee for this study, together with her husband, combined two apartments on the same floor of a prefabricated panel apartment building: "We did it all by ourselves. We only have the engineer's conclusion from Gosstroi (Ministry of Regional and Ministry for Regional Development, Building and Housing of Ukraine)." This bureaucratic conclusion indicated that the plan to combine two apartments was structurally sound. The interviewee continued: "We were not officially married then. And there was some weird regulation that one family could only buy one apartment [in the building]. So as the owners of two separate apartments, we have not changed anything [in the paperwork] because in our county back then it would have been very difficult, if not impossible. And then all of it became irrelevant because we had no plans of selling it."[18]

Another interviewee simply explained partition removal in the 1990s as follows: "We did not need to get any permissions; back then everybody did everything themselves."[19]

In practice, if a replanned apartment was not being sold or inherited, or if neighbors did not extensively complain about the noise and procedures of remodeling, authorities did not monitor what was going on in individual apartments. However, if remodeling resulted in damage to the overall apartment building structure, particularly when accompanied with human victims, it could result in an administrative or a criminal court case. Yet many cases of extreme building damage did not come from individual apartment remodeling but rather from commercial space remodeling on the first floors of apartment buildings.[20] This had to do with an inherent quality of apartment housing—because the load of the rest of the structure was largest on the first-floor walls, massive layout transformations on the first floor could do the most damage to the entire building. Transformations inside individual apartments on upper floors, on the contrary, produced minimal damage to the overall structure.

Socializing in the Home

Apartment layouts, of course, were not the only realm of life where the previous systems of control were eliminated or suspended due to the collapse of the Soviet state. The political and social lives of post-Soviet subjects experienced a similar removal of all former restrictions. Previously impossible public protests became a norm, private trade took over the city streets, the use of public space by youth subculture groups became less persecuted, and most importantly for this work, the forms of socialization in the home and semiprivate spaces changed.

These changes came in two seemingly opposing physical forms in the 1990s and the first decade of the 2000s. On the one hand, the residents of post-Soviet apartments replaced their old wooden or *dermatin*-sheathed (a Soviet type of faux leather) doors with the metal ones, and then even bulletproof metal doors, seemingly turning their apartments into impregnable fortresses. On the other hand, the liminal, semiprivate spaces of courtyards, hallways, basements, and sometimes even attics and roofs of these same apartment buildings became improvised social spaces for many members of the post-Soviet societies.

Anecdotally, many scholars of the Soviet and post-Soviet periods have told me they felt the introduction of heavy apartment doors was a sign of the apartment spaces becoming more private, where the understanding of private is in line with the logic of privatization: alienated from the state and individually controlled. However, the situation was more nuanced and includes both a loss of control over semiprivate space and an attempt to regain control over the security of private spaces and private belongings—a sense of security that was compromised after the collapse of the USSR. The following paragraphs describe and exemplify these two simultaneous processes, as well as the restoring force that determined the spatial practices in those spaces in the early post-Soviet decades. But before turning to the complex dynamic between the public and private spaces of a post-Soviet apartment building, let us first establish a definition of spaces of socialization inside an apartment.

The space of socialization in the home has in many ways already been outlined in the previous chapters. Through the boundaries and overlaps of the other practices—sleep, eating, and hygiene—the spaces of socialization become tangible, if not apparent. That is no accident. Sleep, cooking and dining, and hygiene frequently occupied the primary role in a domestic setting, while socialization may have happened parallel to eating at the dinner table or during the day in the same space that would host sleep at night. In fact, the term "living room" did not emerge as a name for a room with a specialized function. In eighteenth-century American working-class homes, "living room" defined the space "in which cooking, eating, and socializing combined with income-producing work and even sleeping."[21] However, in the twentieth century, particularly with the post–World War II reemergence of modernist design principles, a space dedicated solely to socialization and leisure started being seen as a matter of social well-being. In the United States, a definitive idea of a place for domestic socialization and leisure came with the establishment of the postwar family room in single homes.[22] A similar shift took place in postwar Great Britain, where the 1960s return of modernist design and the introduction of central heating resulted in an open plan "democratic" living room in the state-built public housing.[23] Although such a specialized living room was a product of modernist paradigms, it was not equally represented throughout all global modernisms, the Soviet one in particular. What may have been portrayed as a specialized living room in design blueprints became a place of sleep or homework in the $k = n - 1$ Soviet reality and only periodically a space of leisure and socialization within the home.

Perhaps the most famous domestic cultural practice that came to an end with the collapse of the Soviet Union was the political aspect of the "kitchen culture": informal kitchen gatherings that first became widespread among the Soviet intelligentsia in the 1960s and continued until the end of the USSR. The kitchen in this case performed as a salon[24]—"a place for social interaction outside the private sphere."[25] Some of the topics discussed in these kitchen gatherings were too sensitive to discuss in a public space in the context of Soviet censorship. Soviet people talked politics in the kitchen, as in a quote provided by Melissa Caldwell: "We are used to swallowing politics with our meals."[26]

The end of Soviet censorship and the end of kitchen culture went hand in hand, except that kitchen culture did not disappear without a trace. The end of censorship meant that anything could now be discussed anywhere, and the introduction of new establishments outside the home offered different interest groups an alternative space for gathering. Yet, although the political component of the kitchen culture was gone, socialization in the kitchen persisted: twenty four years after the collapse of the Soviet Union, a domestic design portal, *Houzz*, held a poll that asked: "How is the kitchen space being used?" Sixty-three percent of the portal's audience responded that besides cooking (90 percent) and eating (84 percent), it was used for in-home socialization.[27] Instead of dying out, the habit of socializing in the kitchen transformed its meaning from an intellectual, artistic, and political exchange in the 1960s to a normative domesticity and breadth of the soul, like in the post-Soviet television show *Poka vse doma* (While everybody is home).[28]

While kitchen culture is among the most celebrated, unique forms of Soviet socialization in the home, the kitchen was not the only space where socialization happened. Despite each room hosting someone's sleep at night (see chapter 2), a space had to be found to host social functions, such as friend gatherings and celebrations with extended family. Chapter 3 described the character of Soviet domestic celebrations: the mandatory white cloth and the table "groaning under the weight of food" (*stol lomitsia ot iavstsv*, a Russian saying). As shown in the previous chapters, this first part of the celebration could not be performed in the small kitchen and instead had to take place in a room that at night hosted sleep.

From a contemporary perspective, the merging of some cultural practices, like socializing and eating, seems appropriate and even welcome: having a dinner together with friends in the dining room is a stereotype of domestic socialization in many western countries. Other functional overlaps, such as hygiene and socialization or sleep and socialization, at first glance appear problematic, if not bizarre. However, plenty of historical and contemporary examples of such overlaps and merges were not only acceptable but even desirable among urbanites.

For instance, a prominent example of an overlap between socializing and hygiene in the Soviet context can be found in the public bathhouses (*bania*). In the frequent absence of adequate hygiene facilities in apartment homes, particularly prior to the housing construction boom in the second half of the twentieth century, bathhouses fulfilled the needs of urbanites for spaces of hygiene. But besides hygiene, they also provided a space for socialization outside the home. Bania was of special importance to the construction of Soviet post–World War II masculinity[29] and was also a magical and ritualistic place far beyond its formal understanding as a modern hygienic machine.[30]

Of course, bania, where rituals and gender comradery met modernity, was a more exotic example. Socializing in late-Soviet apartments was less exotic: either there was no designated living room at all and every room could take its function or there was a designated living room that had to host someone's sleep at night. This sort of difference depended on the number of people in the household and, most importantly, on the layout of the apartment.

In 1970 Boris Merzhanov, described a living room as follows: "A living room [obshchaia komnata] is usually the biggest room in the apartment that serves for the rest of the entire family, reception of guests, studies, and homework. That is why a living room in a contemporary apartment combines functions of a dining room, parlor, and study. Often in an apartment there is not a possibility to have them as separate spaces. Besides, efficient use of domestic space corresponds with the contemporary lifestyles."[31]

Intentionally or unintentionally, Merzhanov withheld information: the size of a room was not necessarily a definitive factor in designating space in certain apartment types because it mattered more how a room was connected to the rest of the apartment. What mattered was whether an apartment had a walk-through room. In an apartment without a walk-through room, rooms would have been connected with a hallway (figure 5.1). In apartments with a walk-through room, this room became the connective tissue and a circulation space and automatically lost its sleep-related quality—privacy and sound isolation. This meant that most social functions, such as family gatherings next to a television and celebratory dining with guests, became allocated to this room, the least fitting for the privacy of a bedroom.

In an apartment with a hallway (figure 5.1, right), where all the rooms were isolated from each other, the role of a living room could be assigned to any of the rooms. Furthermore, living room functions could have transitioned from room to room rather frequently, depending on the type of socialization happening at the apartment.[32] While small gatherings were held in the kitchen, large gatherings were allocated to the room of the family member(s) that initiated the gathering or based on whether substantial dining and unfolding a gateleg table was involved.

At the same time, there was no major bias against letting guests enter a space that at night served as someone's bedroom. A convertible couch bed would have

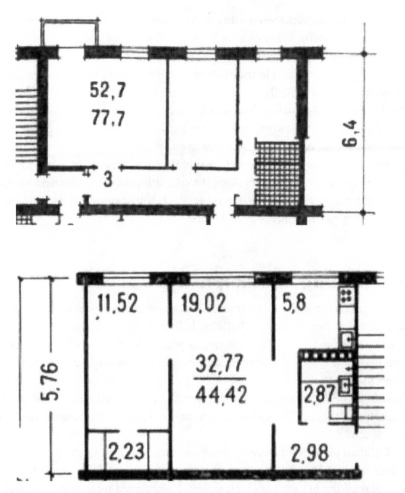

FIGURE 5.1.   *Bottom:* Apartment with a walk-through room from I-464 series; *Top: Stalinka* standardized apartment from II-4 series with a corridor that connects rooms. (Drawings modified by the author.)

been put into a couch position. A single bed would have been modified into a couch form with the help of pillows. From this perspective, the lived rooms of a Soviet apartment were flexible containers where almost any function could be performed on necessity.

Besides celebrations and major gatherings, family time spent at home was increasingly important throughout late-Soviet history. The improvement in housing conditions provided by the mass housing campaign, as well the overall shift from anti-family bias common to the early Soviet history, led to the reintroduction of the home as a cozy place to be.[33] The two spaces that were used most frequently were the kitchen and the room with a television, whether or not it was also some-one's sleeping space. Kitchens were important for the near-religious consump-tion of tea; while the designated living room was a place to watch television (there was rarely a television set in the kitchen; see chapter 3). Television was broadly introduced to the Soviet home as a new form of entertainment in the 1960s.[34] By the 1970s, half of all families had a television set at home, including in rural areas where television ownership was less ubiquitous.[35] Unlike a gateleg table that was unfolded for celebrations, a television and its seating setup was required to be permanently positioned in some part of the apartment for daily use. There-fore, the rise of television stimulated the establishment of a permanent family gathering space, the closest apartment residents would come to having a desig-nated living room in the late-Soviet years.

Socializing in Semiprivate Spaces

A tremendous change also took place in the semipublic spaces contiguous to apartment homes: apartment building hallways, stairwells, and courtyards. Throughout Soviet history, these spaces were extensively used by children, youth, and the elderly. As Alexey Golubev points out, these spaces have been ac-tively used by those marginalized—mostly the working class—whose practices have often been disregarded in the Soviet and post-Soviet intellectual tradi-tions, just as they are invisible in the language of Soviet construction codes and regulations.[36]

Children played in the courtyards,[37] and although the radioactive threat of Chernobyl may have negatively affected the perception of the outdoors for sev-eral years,[38] the presence of children outside continued regardless. Unaccom-panied outdoor play was a rule throughout building types, independent of the character of the courtyards. In the inner cities with historic, Stalin-era, or new urban infill apartment homes, children played in courtyards even in the absence of modern children's infrastructure.[39] In new neighborhoods built according to the modernist principles of extensive outdoor territories with planned play-grounds, children used courtyards as well. Unaccompanied children's social-ization in all kinds of courtyards did not change overnight after the collapse of the USSR.[40] On the contrary, it persisted for several years until the metropoli-tan inner-city courtyards became a highly desirable parking asset with the ex-treme increase in car ownership in large cities in the late 1990s.[41] Although the mikroraion—modernist neighborhood—courtyards experienced an overflow of cars as well, the prescribed infrastructure has somewhat slowed down the car takeover. To this day, many prefabricated building courtyards preserve elements of Soviet infrastructure, including some spaces meant for and occupied by children (now accompanied by adults), but problems with parking are nevertheless a pressing issue. Finally, the growing absence of children in courtyards can also be explained with the change of popular attitude toward childrens' safety in large cities. Children no longer spend as much time outdoors, and this tendency is found in many big Western cities as well.[42]

For the elderly, the situation was somewhat different. Elderly people more than children required an infrastructure to socialize in courtyards, such as benches and other forms of seating.[43] The absolute majority of prefabricated panel buildings had benches by hallway entrances and throughout the adjacent territory. Inner-city courtyards often had seating in front gardens adjacent to pre-1917, Stalin-era, and infill modernist buildings. During the 1990s, some of this infrastructure disappeared to make way for cars; however, when it was preserved, elderly socialization in the courtyards continued.

Youth is another group that has been affected by the new times. Spaces of youth socialization in the territories adjacent to apartment homes were not limited to just courtyards but also included hallways and staircases of apartment buildings. There is a curious disparity in literature between the amount of research produced on courtyards in Soviet and post-Soviet settings and the nearly completely missing mentions of staircases (*pod"ezd*), basements, and even attics and rooftops. The courtyard has been romanticized by Soviet authors, such as Bulat Okudzhava, and international academics, such as Stephen Bittner in his *The Many Lives of Khrushchev's Thaw*.[44] A stairwell, on the contrary, remained barely visible to creative and scholarly literature alike, despite its clear practical importance for youth and working-class social practices. According to Alexey Golubev, the social importance of staircases and hallways is disregarded because their users often did not possess a cultural voice, such as the familiar voice of the Soviet intellectual elites.[45] In addition, they are ignored because despite being utilitarian in design, they show an "incapacity . . . to act in a strictly functional manner, to provide the unobstructed passage for bodies."[46] For different generations of the Soviet working class, the in-between spaces of stairwells, basements, and attics provided an escape from parental or marital control,[47] particularly in the absence of private rooms as described earlier in this book.

Finally, Golubev mentions one more reason for stairwells to be populated with all sorts of activities not planned by the designers: the climate.[48] Most of the former Soviet Union existed in climatic zones with harsh winter conditions. While gatherings in the courtyards, plazas, parks, or natural areas were rather easy in the summer, they became increasingly problematic in winter. At the same time, stairwells were heated, while basements often hosted the heating and water in-frastructure of the entire building.

Perhaps, this imbalance could also be attributed to the semiprivate or private perception of an apartment building stairwell. As if there is a fine line between the semi-public space of the courtyards and the semiprivate of the stairwells, the former are willingly romanticized, while the latter are denied their cultural value. Recognized as significant or not, the practice of gathering in hallways existed during the late-Soviet times and persisted into the 1990s.[49] Furthermore, in the 1990s, stairwells and basements frequently became places for homeless people to hide from the elements in the cold weather.[50] Homelessness was a crime in the Soviet Union, but it was no longer a crime after 1991.[51] Because of the eco-nomic, social, and political turmoil of the 1990s and this partial decriminaliza-tion of their presence, homeless people became increasingly visible in public spaces in Moscow, as described by Stephenson,[52] and other post-Soviet cities. In the absence of social services, they had to find warm places to stay. Inevitably, the presence of homeless individuals in semiprivate spaces of apartment build-ings caused conflict with the residents of the apartments.

Just like children's play spaces, courtyard youth gatherings were affected by parking takeover.[53] But a transformation unique to youth spaces of socialization also happened: the introduction of code or intercom doors to hallways and stair-wells, typically initiated by the residents of the apartments. Although these doors were not always effective at keeping outsiders away, they clearly established hallways as spaces communally belonging to the apartment residents, instead of the Soviet model where apartment dwellers saw hallways as a territory of state and city responsibility.[54] The youth practice of gathering in apartment building hallways, therefore, gained even more traits of trespassing.

Earlier in this chapter I argued that the bulletproof doors of the post-Soviet apartments were not as simple as a desire to fortify a private space against the spirit of communal living in an apartment building block (figure 5.2). In many buildings, the barrier function of the apartment door was quickly followed and doubled by the almost equally fortified entry doors to the communal stairwell. Rather than a means of claiming one's private property, these stairwell entry doors provided another barrier between the community of the apartment build-ing residents and the rest of the world. This world outside was seen as increas-ingly intruding into the semiprivate spaces, as their security was no longer insured by the large-scale state infrastructure. In other words, bulletproof apart-ment doors were not so much a barricade of an individual apartment privacy, but a reaction to the loss of communal control over shared spaces in the entire apartment building.

FIGURE 5.2. A bulletproof metal door and a faux leather-sheathed metal door in a post-Soviet apartment building stairwell. (Photograph by the author.)

Post-Soviet Social Space in the Home

Hanna F., an interviewee for this study, describes a re-planning undertaken by her sister in 1998 and 1999 to modify a two-room apartment for two adults and one child as follows: "They took down the partition wall between the room and the kitchen, the one [room] on the left, that before used to be kind of a bedroom. It was [also] a living room and had a balcony. They enclosed the balcony, and the living room became a leisure zone, parent zone, kind of more private" (figure 3.6).[55]

Hanna continues: "They removed a partition between this, like, bedroom and the kitchen. And they ended up with an open plan, somewhat L-shaped room. The former entrance to this room, on the contrary, got blocked. So, the entrance to this kitchen-dining room turned out to be from the side of the bedroom and the entryway . . ." Furniture relocated too: "At this entrance they put a couch. Closer to the kitchen was the dining zone. Where there used to be an isolated kitchen, they placed kitchen cabinets. And into a niche that used to be the entrance, they put a big fridge. A dining table got placed where the partition used to be."[56]

The former isolated bedroom/living room became a "family and leisure zone," as well as Hanna's nephew's bedroom. "He did not have a bed; he slept on a convertible couch. Later they switched things around [because he got older], and the kid's bedroom and workspace moved to the isolated room. So, when he needed it, he got his own room."

Hanna's definitions speak for themselves: prior to the remodeling, both rooms in her narrative were equally undetermined. After the removal of the partition, one of the rooms permanently became a bedroom, while the other one got assigned living room, kitchen, dining room, and some bedroom functions.

There is a certain irony in the post-Soviet emergence of the designated living room area: while Khrushchev-era apartments, like Hanna's sister's, were built in the best spirit of modernist functionalism, it took residents' initiative to, paraphrasing Judy Attfield's book title, bring the mid-century version of "modernity" home by opening the plans of these apartments.[57] The Soviet modern mass housing project became modern once again, now on post-Soviet terms.

The desire of post-Soviet apartment dwellers to establish functional zoning and provide everyone with a room of their own, outside the shared living room area, had its own side effects. In particular, one interviewee for this study mentioned that when she and her family lived in a small space with no separate rooms for every child, she used to see her children more often and knew what each of the family members was doing. After they moved to a larger apartment with a separate, monofunctional living room and a separate bedroom for each family member, she felt partially alienated from her children inside the home.[58]

Social Findings in Physical Space

Lindsay Asquith lists several common approaches to studying housing: sociological, anthropological, behavioral, and only lastly architectural.[59] In the spirit of vernacular architecture—"an object without a field"—she defines these four components as essential to the integrated study of architecture and architectural history.[60] Although not technically vernacular, mass housing apartments experience the same lack of integrated scholarly attention that Asquith critiqued in the case of a common house. Through what Asquith called an integrated approach, but with a special emphasis on the architectural approach—"the physical spaces themselves"[61]—this project has established that the post-Soviet home improvement boom was not an overnight surprise after the collapse of state socialism. Rather it was a time bomb set in the late-Soviet and perestroika context, ready to explode as soon as the necessary conditions of private labor and access to commodities were met.

What do these shifts in the spatial senses of publicness and privacy, domestic consumption, and the freedom to modify one's dwelling add up to in relation to the post-Soviet society? These shifts in domestic practices and interiors are an inseparable part of assuming a post-Soviet identity. As shown in chapter 2, the late-Soviet trend for home improvement was rooted in decades of Soviet housing policies and practices, became fashionable due to the political and economic shifts of perestroika, and reached its heyday in the first decades after the collapse of the USSR. The resulting domestic architecture became a hybrid between the Soviet and the new—an adaptation to the new reality establishing the post-Soviet "belonging" of interiors and their residents.[62] The hybrid of the Soviet mass housing infrastructure and the individually modified interiors of apartments determined the post-Soviet experience and way of life. In many cities, this hybrid became a structure so stable that it can hardly be addressed as a transitional mode of existence but rather as a way of urban living that is here to stay. Zavisca writes: "Transplanting American housing institutions [mortgage and housing market under neoliberal reforms] to Russia failed, because the resulting housing order did not provide young families with a clear fair path to attain a 'separate apartment.'"[63] Indeed, a separate, owned apartment may not have become an omnipresent reality of every post-Soviet nuclear family; what happened instead was apartment remodeling and associated spatial changes—the actual physical transformation of everyday life that took place along with the collapse of the USSR.

Not unlike how nuclear-family homeownership became a definitive trait of the American middle class in the late 1940s, the desire for remodeling and the spatial transformations that followed became the necessary traits of acclimatized post-Soviet urbanites in the 1990s.[64] If, as Zavisca claims, "desiring a separate apartment for the nuclear family is neither natural nor inevitable,"[65] then it is remodeling and the resulting spatial change within existing homes that should be considered a definition of the post-Soviet condition in the fundamental human category of dwelling.

CONCLUSION

A Note on Time, Style, and the End of the Post-Soviet Era

Eventually, the total remodeling boom ended. Perhaps its end coincided with the time—the first decades of the 2000s—when scholars first started questioning whether the post-Soviet countries were ever going to transition to the Western models of democracy and economy.[1] Or perhaps it ended when Ikea halted its expansion in Russia in 2009, presumably due to corruption concerns.[2] Or when Georgia had its Rose Revolution in 2003, and Ukraine its Orange Revolution in 2004. In any case, at some point, remodeling stopped being among the primary concerns in the post-Soviet societies.

It shifted from the sign of the times, a trend, and the ultimate consumer demand to a more familiar ritual performed by residents when purchasing or otherwise moving into a new home. This is not to say that residents completely exhausted the demand for remodeling their existing apartments; apartments are still being remodeled to this day, often for the second or third time since the collapse of the USSR. Rather the opportunities for apartment purchase grew as new financial tools became available to the general population and the complete distrust of banks, so characteristic of the 1990s, began to ease.[3] There eventually emerged a mortgage market, not quite like the one in the United States. The word "mortgage" firmly entered the post-Soviet languages (*ipoteka* in Russian, Ukrainian, and Belarusian; *hipoteka* in Lithuanian; and so on), while the concept of having a multi-decade housing loan settled into post-Soviet cultures. Mortgage became a substance for folklore and a signifier of class, as in this Russian joke: "Fasting not only is good for your health but also helps you pay off your mortgage."

Ownership of an apartment, not just a fresh remodeling, became a sign of an individual's social success in metropolitan cities. The condition of a home, which used to be of primary importance in the first post-Soviet decades, lost its absolute rule as soon as there emerged some residential mobility, however problematic.

Yet remnants of remont as an overarching societal practice and mode of existence remained. Olga Shevchenko noted that a sense of perpetual crisis developed as a model for dealing with the world in the post-Soviet 1990s, persisted longer than the crisis itself, and "remained a prism" through which post-Soviet subjects navigated the world in the later years.[4] Similarly, remodeling remained as a lens for understanding the world, often in affecting rather unexpected realms of post-Soviet life. One such part of the post-Soviet reality are the ethnic stereotypes. Remodeling and construction fields remain highly ethnically stereotyped in Russia and to lesser degree in other post-Soviet states.

For example, Moldovans were often stereotyped as inherently good at tiling due to the many Moldovan guest laborers working in construction in other post-Soviet republics. These Moldovans were forced to find employment abroad by the war in Transnistria and the depth of the Moldovan economic crisis in the 1990s.[5] Postwar and economically suffering Tajikistan also supplied a large number of laborers to major Russian metropolitan areas, and many of them ended up in small-scale construction with few state regulations, such as apartment remodeling. By the mid-2000s, the television comedy show *Nasha Rasha* (Our Russia) gained extreme popularity on Russian television and in places where Russian television broadcasted. The central recurring characters of this comedy show were guest laborers from Tajikistan named Ravshan and Jamshud, who remodeled expensive apartments in Moscow and were clearly exploited by their local supervisor.[6] Besides the deep roots remodeling took in the post-Soviet cultural lore, these stereotypes also revealed the degree to which the multinational Soviet Union and the equally multi-ethnic Russian Federation failed to positively embrace national differences, without constructing a racist hierarchy of ethnicities and occupations.

Identity, and differences in self-identification, is also essential to another subject of this concluding chapter—the style. This is because "what we think we need is connected to who we think we are."[7] The idea of what constituted a respectable residential interior shifted drastically between the beginning of perestroika in 1985 and the end of the first post-Soviet decade in the 2000s. In the beginning of the 1980s, the desired qualities in a home were primarily determined by the neighborhood, the type of apartment building, the kinds of objects one owned, and the state of repair or disrepair the building and the apartment were in. For instance, central city historic or Stalin-era apartment buildings with tall ceilings were more valued than small, low-ceiling Khrushchev-era apartments in new buildings and new neighborhoods, as long as those historic apartment buildings were in decent shape and were not communal. The limited residential mobility tools that the Soviet citizens did have—to exchange their existing housing for something similar elsewhere, or to receive another apartment from the state or through a cooperative—were mostly used to address one of these variables: communal or individual, building type, and neighborhood. Finally, Soviet urbanites cared about dream domestic possessions: pieces of Czechoslovak furniture, color television sets, Central Asian rugs, and many others. What the majority of the Soviet urbanites did not care about was the style of their interiors. The style was simply not a relevant category in the larger scheme of things since it was determined by housing and consumer goods shortages as well as the square footage and layout of the apartment. What mattered most was owning a television and a cupboard, not the style of these material possessions.

Unlike during the Soviet years, style mattered a lot in the 1990s and the 2000s. Yet before proceeding any further, it is necessary to elaborate what exactly should be understood as style and what should not. The main post-Soviet trope that comes to mind in relation to remodeling style is the term *evroremont*. The very structure of this word starting with "evro" seemingly entails some sort of a stylistic approach. Yet it is hardly possible to find any architectural approach as stylistically inconsistent as the plethora of "evro" remodelings. I deliberately avoided this term as much as possible in this book's narrative until now, but it seems fitting to finally address the elephant in the room in the conclusion. The term evroremont does not just mean "euro" style, whatever such style may entail; it was used to identify the type of remodeling services and the type of construction materials used (such as stretched ceilings and drywall), as well as the look of the interiors resulting from such remodelings. Attempts to identify what exactly evroremont meant stylistically are doomed, as the types of interiors produced under this umbrella term ranged from Neo-Baroque to Minimalism, with Memphis-like fixtures and furniture in between. This is because rather than being a style, evroremont was a framework of thinking and making that for the first time in post-Soviet history allowed for stylistic choices. All of a sudden, post-Soviet apartment dwellers could select finishes, fixtures, and objects they liked (and could afford) out of many different objects of the same type. The quest was no longer about finding a couch but about selecting a couch out of a variety of forms, features, and fabrics available. Of course, this perplexed the post-Soviet consumers, but not for long; they were after all consumers able to embrace choice, just like Westerners, even if their choices may later seem to be unsophisticated to their heirs and even their later selves.[8]

To reiterate my argument from the previous chapters, the incredible effort the post-Soviet populations put into the domestic architecture and interiors undoubtedly had to do with the objective needs for home improvement that gradually grew out of the many late-Soviet circumstances described in chapter 2 ("Remodeling"). However, it also derived from the need to develop a new identity, to become post-Soviet, described in chapter 6 ("Socializing"), a need formulated through social interactions and media access, the zeitgeist of the post-Soviet years, with their hopes and disenchantments alike.

The chapters of this book made an ambitious attempt to describe post-Soviet metropolitan populations at large, emphasizing the similarities in their thinking. Furthermore, I tried to find similarities through the fieldwork conducted outside of Russia, the traditional place to study the Soviet and post-Soviet condition. However, despite my attempt to locate large-scale similarities and connections and make general conclusions about the post-Soviet subjects, it is vital that differences between the post-Soviet subjects and entities are equally acknowledged. Post-Soviet nations have diverged tremendously since 1991. Of course, these national entities were never the same under or prior to the Soviet Union either. But it would be inaccurate to claim that the decades of Soviet rule have not changed its subjects and have not produced similarities across the USSR, near-identical housing infrastructure being a prime example. The similarities were there, even if it now becomes clear that such similarities were temporary. The clash of national identities and linguistic belongings, as well as the conceptions and misconceptions of each other demonstrated by the post-Soviet populations now, grew and matured since 1991 on the foundation of the former USSR, but outside of the late-Soviet circumstances and thinking.

As I am writing these last paragraphs, the post-Soviet cities and apartment blocks in my native Ukraine are being bombed by the Russian army. In Mariupol, Kharkiv, Sumy, Chernihiv, Kyiv, and many other cities, apartment buildings of all kinds—pre-Soviet, Soviet, and post-Soviet—are under attack. Their residents are hiding in basements and subway systems. Civilians are being shot at by the Russian army if they attempt evacuation in places where fighting is especially acute. And for once, the Russian military crimes are not simply swept under the rug like in Chechnya and Syria but are loudly exposed for the entire world to see.

In a moment of dark humor between an architectural friend and me, I suggested that the Russian army shelling Ukrainian cities is an effort to demolish outdated Khrushchev-era housing, like Russians did in Moscow in recent years.[9] My friend countered that Russians should know there are better ways to do urban renewal than shelling. The leading way of thinking about the post-Soviet world in the 1990s and 2000s—the transition paradigm assuming former state-socialisms were on the way to the Western model of democracy—feels particularly irrelevant now in March 2022. Even the finality of the dissolution of the USSR no longer seems to be a concrete fact. The current moment feels like history in the making, and from here the pendulum can still swing either way.

Yet one thing is clear: the post-Soviet era is over. This book, hence, is no longer the history of the present moment, but a proper history of the past.

Notes

INTRODUCTION

1. For instance, V. P. Kolomiets claims that in 1994 furniture and home goods were the third most advertised category of products on Russian television, while in 1995 the second place was occupied by domestic appliances. V. P. Kolomiets, "Televizionnaia reklama kak sredstvo konstruirovaniia smyslov," *Mir Rossii*, no. 1 (1997): 34–35.

2. For example, see *Pole chudes* TV show (1990–present), an analogy of the *Wheel of Fortune* show, where players have to compete to receive prizes such as a car, a television set, a VHS player, or a microwave oven.

3. See Caroline Humphrey, *The Unmaking of Soviet Life: Everyday Economies after Socialism* (Ithaca, NY: Cornell University Press, 2002), 182–185.

4. Since a regular Soviet urbanite could not privately hire an architect or a designer to work on their home design (just like they could not legally hire any private specialist), the profession of a home interior designer simply did not exist until the late 1980s and the beginning of the *remont* era. Prior to that, the term was predominantly used for object and industrial design in publications such as *Dizain v SSSR: 1981–1985* (Vserossiiskii nauchno-issledovatel'skii institut tekhnicheskoi estetiki (VNIITE), 1987).

5. Tatiana Butseva, *Novye slova i znacheniia: Slovar'-spravochnik po materialam pressy i literatury 90-kh godov XX veka v dvukh tomakh* (Saint Petersburg: Institut lingvisticheskikh issledovanii, 2009), 563.

6. Judy Attfield, *Wild Things: The Material Culture of Everyday Life* (Oxford: Berg, 2000), 36.

7. Archie Brown, *Seven Years That Changed the World: Perestroika in Perspective* (Oxford: Oxford University Press, 2007), 5.

8. The argument of Yurchak's *Everything Was Forever, Until It Was No More* is exactly about the system feeling eternal in the late 1980s, even though in retrospect we know that it was no more than a couple of years away from ending. Alexei Yurchak, *Everything Was Forever, Until It Was No More: The Last Soviet Generation* (Princeton, NJ: Princeton University Press, 2013).

9. Philip Hanson, *The Rise and Fall of the Soviet Economy: An Economic History of the USSR 1945–1991* (London: Routledge, 2014).

10. Brown, *Seven Years*, 5.

11. This book specifically looks at remodelings that took place before the financial crisis of 2008. While this is a somewhat arbitrary stopping point historically, this financial crisis slowed down construction and remodeling pace in the post-Soviet states for a while, therefore making it an appropriate date to limit this investigation.

12. Madina Tlostanova, *What Does It Mean to Be Post-Soviet? Decolonial Art from the Ruins of Post-Soviet Empire* (Durham, NC: Duke University Press, 2018), 9.

13. Early Soviet public discourse and art scene was concerned with the upbringing of the New Man: capable of communist selflessness and ruthless to the enemies of the revolution but also possessing certain everyday qualities, such a sense of one's belonging to the state rather than individualist thinking. The old personality type of the pre-Soviet times, such as a kulak or a bourgeois, on the contrary had to be uprooted. See

Mikhail Geller, *Mashyna i vintiki: Istoriia formirovaniia sovetskogo cheloveka* (London: Overseas Publications Interchange, 1985), 7–11.

14. For example, Ron Kerr and Sarah Robinson, "The Hysteresis Effect as Creative Adaptation of the Habitus: Dissent and Transition to the 'Corporate' in Post-Soviet Ukraine," *Organization* 16, no. 6 (November 2009): 829–853; and Aleh Ivanou and Ruben Flores, "Routes into Activism in Post-Soviet Russia: Habitus, Homology, Hysteresis," *Movement Studies* 17, no. 2 (December 2018): 159–174.

15. Erving Goffman, *The Presentation of Self in Everyday Life* (New York: Doubleday, 1959), 22.

16. Goffman, *The Presentation of Self*, 23.

17. The implications of there being relatively few public gathering places in the USSR and in the early post-Soviet years are described in chapter 5: Socializing.

18. There exist multiple theories on the emergence of the term *sovok*. Alexander Genis suggested that "sovok" was used to identify early post-Soviet Russian tourists in the New York City neighborhood Brighton Beach populated by earlier Soviet immigrants. Alexander Genis, "Sovok," *Russian Studies in Literature* 31, no. 11 (1994): 5–11. However, considering the widespread use of this term in the post-Soviet 1990s, it is very likely that the term emerged earlier and inside of the Soviet Union.

19. Nikita Khrushchev, *XXII S'ezd Kommunisticheskoi partii Sovetskogo Soiuza, 17–31 oktiabria 1961 goda: Otchet* (Moscow: Gosudarstevnnoe izdatel'stvo politicheskoi literatury, 1962), 153.

20. See Yurii Levada, ed., *Sovetskii prostoi chelovek: opyt sotsial'nogo portreta na rubezhe 90-kh* (Moskow: Mirovoi Okean, 1993), 8.

21. *Okno v Parizh,* directed by Iurii Mamin (Paris; Moscow: Films du Bouloi, Fontan, La Sept Cinema, Troitskii most, 1993).

22. For example, David Satter, *It Was a Long Time Ago, and It Never Happened Anyway: Russia and the Communist Past* (New Haven, CT: Yale University Press, 2012), 99, 269.

23. Anastasia Miari, "On the Menu in Moscow, Soviet-Era Nostalgia," *New York Times*, December 13, 2019, https://www.nytimes.com/2019/12/11/travel/moscow-restaurants-nostalgia.html.

24. Krisztina Fehérváry, "American Kitchens, Luxury Bathrooms, and the Search for a 'Normal' Life in Postsocialist Hungary," *Ethnos* 67, no. 3 (2002): 370.

25. Fehérváry, "American Kitchens," 370.

26. According to Fukuyama, the resentment of the West expressed by the Russian politicians and public in recent years is the result of the "humiliation" Russia is experiencing for not being treated as the world's great power. Francis Fukuyama, *Identity: Contemporary Identity Politics and the Struggle for Recognition* (London: Profile Books, 2019), 7.

27. Juliane Fürst, *Flowers through Concrete: Explorations in Soviet Hippieland* (Oxford: Oxford University Press, 2021).

28. Olga Shevchenko, *Crisis and the Everyday in Postsocialist Moscow* (Bloomington: Indiana University Press, 2009).

29. "The nostalgia of the late-'90s seems to be posthistorical, a longing for a life of peace and plenty, and an invention of a new tradition of eternal Russian grandeur." Svetlana Boym, "Nostalgia, Moscow Style," *Harvard Design Magazine*, no. 13 (2001), http://www.harvarddesignmagazine.org/issues/13/nostalgia-moscow-style.

30. For scholarship on the global housing crisis, see Ray Forrest and Ngai-Ming Yip, *Housing Markets and the Global Financial Crisis: The Uneven Impact on Households* (Cheltenham, UK: Edward Elgar, 2011). Powerful accounts of housing insecurity in the United States can be found in Matthew Desmond, *Evicted: Poverty and Profit in the American City* (London: Penguin Books, 2017).

31. For example, Graham Tipple, *Extending Themselves: User-Initiated Extensions of Government-Built Housing in Developing Countries* (Liverpool: Liverpool University Press, 2000); Christina Schwenkel, *Building Socialism: The Afterlife of East German Architecture in Urban Vietnam* (Durham, NC: Duke University Press, 2020); Roberto Castillo, "Appropriating Modern Architecture: Designers' Strategies and Dweller's Tactics in the Evolution of the 1950s Venezuelan Superbloques" (PhD diss., University of Chicago, 2015); Sandeep Kumar Agrawal, "Housing Adaptations: A Study of Asian Indian Immigrant Homes in Toronto," *Canadian Ethnic Studies/Etudes Ethniques au Canada* 38, no. 1 (Spring 2006): 117–130; Kirsten Gram-Hanssen and Claus Bech-Danielsen, "Somali, Iraqi and Turkish Immigrants and Their Homes in Danish Social Housing," *Journal of Housing and the Built Environment* 27, no. 1 (April 2012): 89–103.

32. Stefan Bouzarovski, Joseph Salukvadze, and Michael Gentile, "A Socially Resilient Urban Transition? The Contested Landscapes of Apartment Building Extensions in Two Post-Communist Cities," *Urban Studies* 48, no. 13 (October 2011): 2689–2714.

33. Choi Chatterjee, David L. Ransel, Mary Cavender, and Karen Petrone, *Everyday Life in Russia: Past and Present* (Bloomington: Indiana University Press, 2015), 2.

34. Jane Roj Zavisca, *Housing the New Russia* (Ithaca, NY: Cornell University Press, 2012), 90.

35. Elizabeth Cromley, *The Food Axis: Cooking, Eating and the Architecture of the American Houses* (Charlottesville: University of Virginia Press, 2010), 4.

36. Jeffrey Alexander, *The Meanings of Social Life: A Cultural Sociology* (Oxford: Oxford University Press, 2003), 4.

37. For instance, see Celine Rosselin's study of the spatial practices of visiting a home in "Ins and Outs of the Hall: The Parisian Example," in *At Home: An Anthropology of Domestic Space*, ed. Irene Cieraad (Syracuse, NY: Syracuse University Press, 2006), 53–59. For an example of such studies in post-socialist cities, see Krisztina Fehérváry, *Politics in Color and Concrete: Socialist Materialities and the Middle Class in Hungary* (Bloomington: Indiana University Press, 2013).

38. In Michel de Certeau's terms, *The Practice of Everyday Life* (Berkeley: University of California Press, 1984), xix.

39. In Henri Lefebvre's terms, *Rhythmanalysis: Space, Time and Everyday Life* (London: Continuum, 2005).

40. Dell Upton, "Architecture in Everyday Life," *New Literary History* 33, no. 4 (Autumn 2002): 712.

41. Michel de Certeau, "Part III: Spatial Practices," in *The Practice of Everyday Life* (Berkeley: University of California Press, 1984), 91–130.

42. Elizabeth Shove, Mika Pantzar, and Matt Watson, *The Dynamics of Social Practice: Everyday Life and How It Changes* (Los Angeles: SAGE, 2012), 14.

43. For instance, Jordan Sand speaks about the departure from "sleeping, working and playing" all at the same place—a tatami—and into different spatial modes of the table, chairs, and westernized kitchens, along the construction of modern Japan in the end of the 19th century. The description of spatial change is effectively conducted through the constant of common domestic spatial practices. Jordan Sand, *House and Home in Modern Japan: Architecture, Domestic Space and Bourgeois Culture 1880–1930* (Cambridge, MA: Harvard University Asia Center, 2003), 91. While Sand focuses on a historic case of domestic change, another scholar, Sarah Pink, suggests the necessity of understanding the current-day challenge of sustainable living through the everyday life and domestic practices of environmental activists. Sarah Pink, *Situating Everyday Life: Practices and Places* (London: SAGE, 2012), 14–29.

44. Iaroslav D. (architect), interview by the author, May 11, 2017, Kyiv, Ukraine.

45. Olga Shevchenko, "Resisting Resistance: Everyday Life, Practical Competence and Neoliberal Rhetoric in Post-Socialist Russia," in *Everyday Life in Russia Past and Present*, ed. Choi Chatterjee, David L. Ransel, Mary Cavender, and Karen Petrone (Bloomington: Indiana University Press, 2015), 53–54.

46. See Susan Reid, "The Meaning of Home: 'The Only Bit of the World You Can Have to Yourself,'" in *Borders of Socialism: Private Spheres of Soviet Russia*, ed. Lewis Siegelbaum (Basingstoke, UK: Palgrave Macmillan, 2011), 145–170.

47. Florike Egmond and Peter Mason, *The Mammoth and the Mouse: Microhistory and Morphology* (Baltimore, MD: Johns Hopkins University Press, 1997), 1–2.

48. Charles Rice, "Rethinking Histories of Interior," *Journal of Architecture* 9, no. 3 (2004): 282.

49. *Thing-in-itself* or *noumenon*—"(in Kantian philosophy) a thing as it is in itself, as distinct from a thing as it is knowable by the senses through phenomenal attributes." Oxford English Living Dictionaries, s.v. "noumenon," accessed July 5, 2018, https://en .oxforddictionaries.com/definition/noumenon.

50. Alexey Yurchak writes about the dangers of these binaries as reproducing "the master narratives" of the Cold War and the opposition between "the first world" and "the second world." See Alexei Yurchak, *Everything Was Forever, Until It Was No More: The Last Soviet Generation* (Princeton, NJ: Princeton University Press, 2013), 9.

51. Despite the common assumption that the absence of private property was among the most important characteristics of the Soviet Union, forms of private property existed throughout Soviet rule. Even more importantly, certain forms of urban housing property created a sense of ownership strikingly similar to the Western conception of private ownership. See Mark B. Smith, "Individual Forms of Ownership in the Urban Housing Fund of the USSR, 1944–64," *Slavonic and East European Review* 86, no. 2 (2008): 283–305.

52. John Foot, "Micro-History of a House: Memory and Place in a Milanese Neighborhood, 1890–2000," *Urban History* 34, no. 3 (2007): 435.

53. Foot, "Micro-History of a House," 432.

54. Dolores Hayden, "Invisible Angelenos," in *The Power of Place: Urban Landscapes as Public History* (Cambridge, MA: MIT Press, 1997), 82–96.

55. Foot, "Micro-History of a House," 450–452.

56. Nancy Stieber, *Housing Design and Society in Amsterdam: Reconfiguring Urban Order and Identity, 1900–1920* (Chicago: University of Chicago Press, 1998).

57. Stieber, *Housing Design and Society in Amsterdam*, 2.

58. Stieber, *Housing Design and Society in Amsterdam*, 3.

59. Nicole Rudolph, *At Home in Postwar France: Modern Mass Housing and Right to Comfort* (New York: Berghahn, 2015), 1.

60. Gilles Deleuze and Felix Guattari, "May '68 Did Not Take Place," in *Two Regimes of Madness: Texts and Interviews, 1975–1995* (New York: Semiotext(e), 2007), 233.

61. Deleuze and Guattari, "May '68 Did Not Take Place," 234.

62. Deleuze and Guattari, "May '68 Did Not Take Place," 234.

63. Rudolph, *At Home in Postwar France*, 1.

64. Historians Melanie Ilič and Dalia Leinarte claim that the inability of an interviewee to make sense of an event and clearly explain it to others is not necessarily a failed interview but rather an opportunity to observe the missing public discourse that would provide a narrative framework for the interviewee's own story. The omnipresence of the indefinite pronoun "everything" in the post-Soviet discourse in no way means that change did not take place; on the contrary, it indicates the lacking framework to speak about the grandiose change in the life of the late-Soviet and post-Soviet population. Melanie Ilič and Dalia Leinarte, *The Soviet Past in the Post-Socialist Present: Methodology*

and Ethics in Russian, Baltic and Central European Oral History and Memory Studies (New York; London: Routledge, 2016), 13–15.

65. Iaroslav D. (architect), interview.

66. For example, see an interview with the mayor of Moscow and other documents related to the Moscow administrative reform in regards to apartment replanning started in 2011. Sergei Sobianin (mayor of Moscow), interview by *Mestnoe Vremia. Vesti-Moskva. Nedelia v gorode*, September 24, 2011, https://www.mos.ru/mayor/interviews/95214/.

67. Timothy Sosnovy, "The Soviet Housing Situation Today," *Soviet Studies* 11, no. 1 (1959): 21.

68. For instance, Wright mentions a concern with ventilation to show the problems with the early apartments, illustrated with a quote from American Architect praising modern (1879) tenement buildings over the Fifth Avenue apartments. This illustration indicates the shared concern with ventilation transcending building type boundaries and class boundaries. Gwendolyn Wright, *Building the Dream: A Social History of Housing in America* (Cambridge, MA: MIT Press, 1981), 142.

69. Paola Messana, *Soviet Communal Living: An Oral History of the Kommunalka* (Basingstoke, UK: Palgrave Macmillan, 2011); Christine Varga-Harris, *Stories of House and Home: Soviet Apartment Life during the Khrushchev Years* (Ithaca, NY: Cornell University Press, 2015); Steven Harris, *Communism on Tomorrow Street: Mass Housing and Everyday Life after Stalin* (Baltimore, MD: Johns Hopkins University Press, 2013).

70. Victor Buchli, *Materializing Culture: An Archeology of Socialism* (Oxford: Berg, 2000).

71. Varga-Harris, *Stories of House and Home*; Harris, *Communism on Tomorrow Street.*

72. Varga-Harris, *Stories of House and Home*; Harris, *Communism on Tomorrow Street.*

73. Stephen Collier, *Post-Soviet Social: Neoliberalism, Social Modernity, Biopolitics* (Princeton, NJ: Princeton University Press, 2011).

74. Philipp Meuser and Dimitrij Zadorin, *Towards a Typology of Soviet Mass Housing: Prefabrication in the USSR 1955–1991* (Berlin: DOM publishers, 2015), 267.

75. Anna Alekseyeva, "Constructing Soviet Domesticity and Managing Everyday Life from Khrushchev to Collapse," in *Material Culture in Russia and the USSR: Things, Values, Identities*, ed. Graham H. Roberts (London: Bloomsbury Publishing, 2017), 59.

76. *Dacha*—A Soviet summer house. See Stephen Lowell, *Summerfolk: A History of the Dacha, 1710–2000* (Ithaca, NY: Cornell University Press, 2003). For the Soviet "consumer triad," see Vera V. Ageeva, Ilya A. Ageev, Anastasia M. Nikolaeva, and Zoya N. Levashkinac, "Was a Soviet Man a Socialist? The Dichotomy of Consumerist Ideals and Socialist Values in Late Soviet Society (1945–1990)," *European Proceedings of Social & Behavioural Sciences, II International Scientific Symposium on Lifelong Wellbeing in the World*, May 18–22, 2015.

77. Dell Upton, "Vernacular Domestic Architecture in Eighteenth Century Virginia," in *Common Places: Readings in American Vernacular Architecture,* ed. Dell Upton and John Michael Vlach (Athens: University of Georgia Press, 1985), 321.

78. Lizabeth Cohen, "Embellishing a Life of Labor: An Interpretation of the Material Culture of American Working-Class Homes 1885–1915," *Journal of American Culture* 3, no. 4 (January 1980): 763–764.

79. Elizabeth Cromley, "Transforming the Food Axis: Houses, Tools, Modes of Analysis," *Material Culture Review/Revue de la culture matérielle* 44, no. 1 (June 1996): 10.

80. Lindsay Asquith, "Lessons from the Vernacular," in *Vernacular Architecture in the 21st Century: Theory, Education and Practice* (London; New York: Taylor & Francis, 2006), 133.

81. Olga Shevchenko argues that, in the early 1990s, there was a collective shared experience across class lines, despite the different effects the collapse of the USSR had for different social groups. Olga Shevchenko, "Resisting Resistance: Everyday Life, Practical Competence and Neoliberal Rhetoric in Post-Socialist Russia," in *Everyday Life in Russia Past and Present*, ed. Choi Chatterjee, David L. Ransel, Mary Cavender, and Karen Petrone (Bloomington: Indiana University Press, 2015), 55.

82. Varga-Harris, *Stories of House and Home*; Harris, *Communism on Tomorrow Street*, 208.

83. Natalya Chernyshova, *Soviet Consumer Culture in the Brezhnev Era* (London: Routledge, 2013), 83; Steven Harris, "'I Know All the Secrets of My Neighbors': The Quest for Privacy in the Era of the Separate Apartment," in *Borders of Socialism: Private Spheres of Soviet Russia*, ed. Lewis Siegelbaum (New York: Palgrave Macmillan, 2006), 184; Olga Gurova, "Consumer Culture in Socialist Russia," in *The SAGE Handbook of Consumer Culture*, ed. Olga Kravets, Pauline Maclaran, Steven Miles, and Alladi Venkatesh (London: SAGE Publications, 2018), 116–117.

84. Judy Attfield, *Wild Things*, 36.

85. Svetlana Boym, *Common Places: Mythologies of Everyday Life in Russia* (Cambridge, MA: Harvard University Press, 1994), 147–148.

86. See Anya Von Bremzen, *Mastering the Art of Soviet Cooking: A Memoir of Food and Longing* (New York: Crown Publishers, 2013).

87. Although this study concentrates on individual rather than communal apartments, the pre-1917 buildings that predominantly hosted communal apartments need to be mentioned for two reasons. First, many patterns of everyday life in the Soviet Union were found in both individual and communal apartments. Second, these same pre-1917 buildings were frequently converted into individual apartments, starting as early as the 1970s along the state capital reconstruction program, as well as both privately and under a state initiative after the collapse of the USSR in 1991.

88. For instance, some former Soviet republics had higher numbers of large families, resulting in more four- to six-room apartments and sometimes more than one sanitary block (bathroom) per apartment. Meuser and Zadorin, *Towards a Typology of Soviet Mass Housing*, 419.

89. Daniel Baldwin Hess and Tiit Tammaru, eds., *Housing Estates in the Baltic Countries: The Legacy of Central Planning in Estonia, Latvia and Lithuania* (Cham, UK: Springer Open, 2019), 46, 82–84.

90. Joanna Szostek, "The Mass Media and Russia's 'Sphere of Interests': Mechanisms of Regional Hegemony in Belarus and Ukraine," *Geopolitics* 23, no. 2 (2018): 307–329.

91. Natalya Ryabinska, "The Media Market and Media Ownership in Post-Communist Ukraine: Impact on Media Independence and Pluralism," *Problems of Post-Communism* 58, no. 6 (2011): 12.

92. For information on Russian-published media in Ukraine, see Stephen Velychenko, "Introduction," in *The EU and Russia: History, Culture and International Relations* (Basingstoke, UK: Palgrave Macmillan, 2007), 1–26.

93. It should be noted that there are several exclusions. Some of the post-Soviet urban populations, particularly those in Tajikistan and Chechnya, experienced extreme hardship that may have prevented them from concentrating their resources and efforts on individual home improvement in the first decade after the collapse of the USSR.

94. For example, Stefan Bouzarovski, Joseph Salukvadze, and Michael Gentile, "A Socially Resilient Urban Transition? The Contested Landscapes of Apartment Building Extensions in Two Post-communist Cities," *Urban Studies* 48, no. 13 (October 2011): 2689–2714.

95. For a photographic library of Kyiv balconies, see Oleksandr Burlaka, *Balcony Chic* (Kyiv: Osnovy, 2019).

96. "Proshchai khrushchevka: kak v Moskve snosiat vetkhoe nasledie sovetskoi epokhi," *BBC News|Russkaia sluzhba*, April 6, 2017, https://www.bbc.com/russian /features-39505267.

97. "Renovatsiia p'iatypoverkhivok: De u Kyievi znosytymut' Khrushchovky," *UA.NEWS*, January 23, 2018, https://ua.news/ua/renovatsiya-p-yatipoverhivok-de-u -kiyevi-znositimut-hrushhovki.

98. See, for example, Volodymyr Ishchenko, "Fighting Fences vs Fighting Monuments: Politics of Memory and Protest Mobilization in Ukraine," *Debatte: Journal of Contemporary Central and Eastern Europe* 19, nos. 1–2 (2011): 375–380.

99. "Proshchai khrushchevka," ibid.

100. "Piat' let spustia: Zashitniki Khimkinskogo lesa—o skorostnoi trasse Moskva-Sankt Peterburg," *The Village*, August 21, 2015, https://www.the-village.ru/city/city /220205-khimki.

101. Joseph Giovanni, "A Funny Thing Happened to Soviet Architecture," *New York Times*, May 28, 1989, https://www.nytimes.com/1989/05/28/arts/architecture-design -funny-thing-happened-soviet-architecture-photo-ascencion.html.

102. For example, in Alekseyeva, "Constructing Soviet Domesticity," 59; Buchli, *An Archeology of Socialism*, 142, 144–145.

103. See chapter 3.

104. For instance, this popular Russian idiom is used as a title of Anton Chekhov's short story "Woman's Kingdom."

105. Natasha Tolstikova, "Rabotnitsa: The Paradoxical Success of a Soviet Women's Magazine," *Journalism History* 30, no. 3 (2004): 131.

106. Vera Zvereva, "Lifestyle Programs on Russian Television," *Russian Journal of Communication* 3, nos. 3–4 (2010): 267.

107. For a detailed explanation of SNiP development see Philipp Meuser and Dmitrij Zadorin, *Towards a Typology of Soviet Mass Housing: Prefabrication in the USSR 1955–1991* (Berlin: Dom Publishers, 2015), 21–25.

108. For instance, this chapter on the Soviet home is written without a single blueprint: Alekseyeva, "Constructing Soviet Domesticity," 55–70.

109. Such as Sanitary Norms and Regulations (*Sanitarnye normy i pravila*) and apartment series booklets.

110. These competitions were organized by Gosstroi (State Construction Committee) or other institutions and typically did not lead to actual construction. For more information on the Soviet "paper architecture" tradition, see Inez Weizman, "Interior Exile and Paper Architecture," in *Agency: Working with Uncertain Architectures*, eds. Florian Kossak, Doina Petrescu, Tatjana Schneider, Renata Tyszczuk, and Stephen Walker (London: Routledge, 2010).

111. Josephine Mylan and Dale Southerton, "The Social Ordering of an Everyday Practice: The Case of Laundry," *Sociology* 52, no. 6 (December 2018): 1136.

112. Jennifer Patico, *Consumption and Social Change in a Post-Soviet Middle Class* (Stanford, CA: Stanford University Press, 2008), 68.

113. Boym, *Common Places*, 132, 150–157.

114. Anastasiia Dubrovina, "Kak soedenit' sovetskoe retro i sovremennyi inter'er," *Idei vashego doma*, January 30, 2019, https://www.ivd.ru/dizajn-i-dekor/kvartira/kak -soedinit-sovetskoe-retro-i-sovremennyj-interer-36821.

115. Jeffrey M. Hornstein, *A Nation of Realtors: A Cultural History of the Twentieth-Century American Middle Class* (Durham, NC: Duke University Press, 2005), 202.

1. REMODELING

1. Vladimir Dal, "Remont," in *Tolkovyi slovar' zhyvogo velikorusskogo iazyka* (Moscow: Olma Press, 2001), t.3.

2. Svetlana Boym, *The Future of Nostalgia* (New York: Basic Books, 2001), 96.

3. Walter Benjamin, *Moscow Diaries* (Cambridge, MA: Harvard University Press, 1986), 36.

4. For example, see Susan E. Reid, "Cold War in the Kitchen: Gender and the De-Stalinization of Consumer Taste in the Soviet Union under Khrushchev," *Slavic Review* 61, no. 2 (2002): 211–252.

5. V. Poluboiarinov, "Zona remonta," *Rabotnitsa* 4 (April 1985): 28. This article specifically cites an eight-month wait and says that the state agencies offering remodeling services could only supply customers with one or two types of wallpaper.

6. Ekaterina Gerasimova and Sofia Chuikina, "The Repair Society," *Russian Studies in History* 48, no. 1 (2009): 58–74; Catherine Alexander, "Remont: Works in Progress," in *Economies of Recycling: The Global Transformation of Materials, Values and Social Relations*, ed. Catherine Alexander and Joshua Reno (London: ZED Books, 2012), 255–275.

7. For example, see Krisztina Fehérváry, "American Kitchens, Luxury Bathrooms, and the Search for a 'Normal' Life in Postsocialist Hungary," *Ethnos* 67, no. 3 (2002): 369–400.

8. Michael Gentile, "The Post-Soviet Urban Poor and where They Live: Khrushchev-Era Blocks, 'Bad' Areas, and the Vertical Dimension in Luhansk, Ukraine," *Annals of the Association of American Geographers* 105, no. 3 (2015): 583–603.

9. Lynne Attwood, "Privatization of Housing in Post-Soviet Russia: A New Understanding of Home?" *Europe-Asia Studies* 64, no. 5 (2012): 903–928.

10. Jane Roj Zavisca, *Housing the New Russia* (Ithaca, NY: Cornell University Press, 2012).

11. Stephen Collier, *Post-Soviet Social: Neoliberalism, Social Modernity, Biopolitics* (Princeton, NJ: Princeton University Press, 2011). See also Sasha Tsenkova, *Housing Policy Reforms in Post-Socialist Europe: Lost in Transition* (Heidelberg: Physica-Verlag, 2011); Stuart Lowe and Sasha Tsenkova, *Housing Change in East and Central Europe: Integration or Fragmentation* (Aldershot, UK: Ashgate, 2003); and many others.

12. Olga Shevchenko, *Crisis and the Everyday in Postsocialist Moscow* (Bloomington: Indiana University Press, 2009).

13. Obsession with apartment remont, the ineffective approaches to remont, and the social and gender patterns in relation to remont became a usual subject for satire. For instance, in 1996, the Ukrainian *Shou dovgonosykiv* premiered an episode (15) about *evroremont*; in 2001, the Russian comedy show *Gorodok* dedicated an entire episode (89) to remont; and in 2007, Russian ska-punk band Leningrad released a song titled "Remont." *Shou dovgonosykiv*, episode 15, "Evroremont"; *Gorodok*, episode 89, "Gorodok na remonte"; and Leningrad (Russian ska-punk band), "Remont," released November 20, 2007, track 10 on *Avrora* album.

14. In the last several decades of the Soviet Union, Stroibank (Construction Bank of the USSR) conducted quality surveys for new residential construction. The results of such surveys showed multiple quality and technology issues that Stroibank tried to regulate through a system of fines and changes in the payment mechanism. Fond R-337, Opis' 26, Delo 667, Tsentral'nyi derzhavnyi arkhiv vyshchykh organiv vlady ta upravlinnia Ukrainy, Kyiv, Ukraine, 129–133.

15. Natasha Tolstikova, "Rabotnitsa: The Paradoxical Success of a Soviet Women's Magazine," *Journalism History* 30, no. 3 (2004): 131.

16. "Pod kryshey doma svoego," *Rabotnitsa* 10 (October 1984): 28.

17. V. Poluboiarinov, "Zona remonta," *Rabotnitsa* 4 (April 1985): 28.

18. "Tsena remonta," *Rabotnitsa* 6 (June 1986): 21–22.

19. V. Stepanishev, "10 metrov na 100 chelovek," *Rabotnitsa* 3 (March 1989): 8. Many individual apartment kitchens in the Soviet apartment block buildings were rather small and typically ranged from fifty-three to seventy-five square feet.

20. *Burda Moden* in Russian, Spring 1987.

21. "Interesnye idei oformleniia okon" and "Komnatnye rastenia," *Burda Moden*, 1988, 60–63.

22. M. V. Bakiev, *Domashaniaia academiia*, vol. 1 (Ufa: Bashkirskoe oblastnoe prav-lenie Soyza nauchnyh i inzhenernyh obshchestv SSSR, 1990), introduction.

23. Radmila Milosavlevich, *Inter'er zhilogo doma* (Moscow: Stroizdat, 1988), 4.

24. "Pereplanirovka dvukhkomnatnoi kvartiry v dome serii P-44," *Idei vashego doma*, January 1999, https://www.ivd.ru/custom_category/custom_subcategory/pereplanirovka -dvuhkomnatnoj-kvartiry-v-dome-serii-p-44-4094.

25. Kitchens starting at eight square meters (86 square feet) and rooms starting at eleven square meters (118 square feet).

26. For the history and meaning of open plan, see Judy Attfield, "Bringing Modernity Home: Open Plan in the British Domestic Interior," in *At Home: An Anthropology of Do-mestic Space*, ed. Irene Cieraad (Syracuse, NY: Syracuse University Press, 2006), 72–83.

27. Gregory D. Andrusz, "A Note on the Financing of Housing in the Soviet Union," *Soviet Studies* 42, no. 3 (July 1990): 555–570.

28. For instance, see Attwood, "Privatization of Housing in Post-Soviet Russia," 903–928.

29. Alina E. (apartment dweller), interview by the author, June 24, 2017, Kyiv, Ukraine.

30. Lewis H. Siegelbaum and Leslie Page Moch, *Broad Is My Native Land: Repertoires and Regimes of Migration in Russia's Twentieth Century* (Ithaca, NY: Cornell University Press, 2014). The name of this book on the Russian and Soviet migration refers to the Soviet song "Broad is My Native Land," which celebrates the vastness of the Soviet ter-ritory and the supposed freedom of the Soviet citizens.

31. Siegelbaum and Moch, *Broad Is My Native Land*, Russian Terms and Abbreviations.

32. Baikal–Amur Mainline (BAM) is a railroad traversing through most of the terri-tory of the Russian Federation, from eastern Siberia to the Russian Far East. Active con-struction lasted from the 1930s to the 1980s. Prior to Stalin's death in 1952, BAM and other Great Constructions were conducted by prisoners. See Christopher J. Ward, *Brezhnev's Folly: The Building of BAM and Late Soviet Socialism* (Pittsburgh, PA: Uni-versity of Pittsburgh Press, 2009).

33. Petty trade practices at the Soviet-socialist camp borders increased significantly in 1989. See Krystyna Iglicka, "The Economics of Petty Trade on the Eastern Polish Bor-der," in *The Challenge of East-West Migration for Poland*, ed. Keith Sword and Krystyna Iglicka (New York: St. Martin's Press, 1999), 120–144.

34. The Decree of the Cabinet of Ministers of the USSR, No. 261, "Ob uporiadochenii peresecheniia grazhdanami gosudarstvennoi granitsy SSSR i o dopolnitel'nykh merakh po regulirovaniiu vyvoza za granitsu tovarov narodnogo potrebleniia" [About the or-dering of the state border crossing by the citizens of the USSR and the additional mea-sures on export of the consumer goods], March 12, 1990.

35. William Moskoff, *Hard Times: Impoverishment and Protest in the Perestroika Years: The Soviet Union 1985–1991* (Armonk, NY: M. E. Sharpe, 1993).

36. Moskoff, *Hard Times*.

37. Alexei Yurchak, *Everything Was Forever, Until It Was No More: The Last Soviet Generation* (Princeton, NJ: Princeton University Press, 2005), 1.

38. Werner Rödiger, Herbert Schumacher, and Wilfried Demel, *Rost i stanovlenie: Bi-ographia sem'i predprinematelei Knauf* (Iphofen: Knauf Gips KG, 2003), 372.

39. Oleksandr Startschenko, interview by the author, May 21, 2021, Kyiv, Ukraine.

40. Moskoff, *Hard Times*, 169–171, 183–186.

41. Moskoff, *Hard Times*, 169–171.

42. Coal miners played a crucial role in the dissolution of the USSR through their economic and political strikes in the late 1980s. The early economic reasoning for strikes came from the slowdown in the distribution of benefits and raise in salaries that coal miners (unlike other workers) regularly enjoyed earlier in late-Soviet history. More information on the subject can be found in Donald Filtzer, *Soviet Workers and the Collapse of Perestroika: The Soviet Labour Process and Gorbachev's Reforms, 1985–1991* (Cambridge: Cambridge University Press, 2008), or Lewis Siegelbaum and Daniel Walkowitz, *Workers of the Donbass Speak: Survival and Identity in the New Ukraine, 1989–1992* (Albany: State University of New York Press, 1995).

43. Mykola N. (construction business owner), interview by the author, April 28, 2017, Kyiv, Ukraine.

44. Ivan G. (construction brigade head), interview by the author, June 26, 2017, Kyiv, Ukraine.

45. Mykola N. (construction business owner), interview.

46. Oleksii R. (architect), interview by the author, May 4, 2017, Kyiv, Ukraine.

47. Vitalii F. (construction worker), interview by the author, May 28, 2017, Kyiv, Ukraine.

48. Soviet troops were relocated back to the USSR after the fall of the Berlin Wall.

49. Moskoff, *Hard Times*, 65.

50. A curious example can be found in the widespread 1990s and early 2000s fashion for creating arched openings between apartment spaces. The readily available, high-quality drywall was easy to bend; as a result, an arched doorway, earlier an element perceived as Western and luxurious, became readily available for post-Soviet citizens.

51. Svetlana Boym, *Common Places: Mythologies of Everyday Life in Russia* (Cambridge, MA: Harvard University Press, 1994), 29–40.

52. Boym, *Common Places*; David Crowley and Susan Emily Reid, *Socialist Spaces: Sites of Everyday Life in the Eastern Bloc* (Oxford: Berg, 2002).

53. Joseph Brodsky, "Room and a Half," in *Less Than One: Selected Essays* (London: Penguin, 2011); *Pokrovskie vorota*, directed by Mikhail Kazakov (Moscow: Mosfilm, 1982).

54. "Kurs No.15: Antropologiia kommunalki," Arzamas Academy, accessed October 10, 2017, http://arzamas.academy/courses/6.

55. State Committee of Construction of the USSR Decree, "Ob utverzhdenii polozheniia o provedenii planovo-predupreditel'nogo remonta zhilykh i obshchestvennykh zdanii" [Provision on the carrying of the planned prevention remodeling of the residential and public buildings], September 8, 1964.

56. Provision of the Soviet of Ministers of the USSR, No. 740, "O merakh po dal'neishemu uluchsheniiu ekspluatatsii i remonta zhilishchnogo fonda" [On the measures for further improvement of exploitation and repair (remont) of the housing resources], September 4, 1978.

57. "O merakh po dal'neishemu," ibid.

58. Provision of the State Committee of Construction of the USSR, No. 113, "On the Recognition of the Decree of the State Committee of Construction from September 8th, 1964, No.147 'About the regulations on the carrying of the planned prevention remodeling of the residential and public buildings' as No Longer Valid," June 30, 1989.

59. Moskoff, *Hard Times*, 64–65.

60. Housing Code of the Russian Federation, Section 106, "Provision of the Residential Spaces of the Maneuver Fund," December 19, 2004.

61. Additionally, capital reconstructions offered a shift from the shared communal apartment occupancy, where many family members had to all share one room and multiple unrelated families had to share utilities with no functional separation or privacy possible whatsoever. Analysis of the Soviet communal apartments may be found in Ekaterina Gerasimova, "Public Privacy in the Soviet Communal Apartment," in *Socialist Spaces: Sites of Everyday Life in the Eastern Bloc*, ed. David Crowley and Susan E. Reid (Oxford: Berg, 2002), 207–230; or Steven Harris, "'I Know All the Secrets of My Neighbors': The Quest for Privacy in the Era of the Separate Apartment," in *Borders of Socialism: Private Spheres of Soviet Russia*, ed. Lewis Siegelbaum (New York: Palgrave Macmillan, 2006), 171–189.

62. *Homes of Moderate Cost* (Chicago: National Plan Service, 1952).

63. Steven Harris, *Communism on Tomorrow Street: Mass Housing and Everyday Life after Stalin* (Washington, DC: Woodrow Wilson Center Press with John Hopkins University Press, 2013).

64. Christine Varga-Harris, *Stories of House and Home: Soviet Apartment Life during the Khrushchev Years* (Ithaca, NY: Cornell University Press, 2015).

65. Harris, *Communism on Tomorrow Street*, 41.

66. *Homes of Moderate Cost*.

67. "Zasedanie . . . na kukhne, kotoraia mogla by byt v kazhdom dome," *Rabotnitsa* 1 (January 1988): 8.

68. Mervyn Matthews, *Privilege in the Soviet Union: A Study of Elite Life-Styles under Communism* (London: Allen and Unwin, 1979), 45.

69. *Moskva slezam ne verit*, directed by Vladimir Menshov (Moscow: Mosfilm, 1979).

70. *Ironiia sud'by, ili s legkim parom!*, directed by El'dar Riazanov (Moscow: Mosfilm, 1976).

71. A reflection on the role of soap operas in the late-Soviet and early post-Soviet everyday life can be found in Boym, *Common Places*, 247–249.

72. See Sheila Fitzpatrick, "Things under Socialism: The Soviet Experience," in *The Oxford Handbook of the History of Consumption*, ed. Frank Trentmann (Oxford: Oxford University Press, 2012), 464–467.

73. In the late 1970s and 1980s, the State Committee of Construction (Gosstroi) of the USSR held multiple architectural competitions for Khrushchev-era housing modernization and reconstruction projects. For instance, *Illiustrirovannyi catalog proektov otkrytogo konkursa na razrabotku proektnykh predlozhenii po novym tipam maloetazhnykh zhilykh domov i prinzipov plotno-nizkoi gorodskoi zastroiki* (Moscow: Gosstroi SSSR, 1981) and *Illiustrirovannyi catalog proektov otkrytogo konkursa "Modernizatsiia i rekonstruktsiia zhilykh domov pervykh massovykh serii"* (Moscow: Gosstroi SSSR, 1987).

74. Oleksii R. (architect), interview. Additionally, see Mariia Boyarova, "Istoriia dizaina inter'era postsovetskoi Moskvy v 1990e gody," *Houzz*, November 23, 2016, https://www.houzz.ru/ideabooks/76622145/list/istoriya-dizayna-interyery-postsovetskoy-moskvy-v-1990-e-gody.

75. Anastasiia Romashkevich, "Skanflot" gotov sozdat' rai v otdel'no vziatykh pomeshcheniakh," *Kommersant*, December 12, 1991, https://www.kommersant.ru/doc/1815.

76. *Katalog tipovykh reshenii pereplanirovok kvartir v zhilykh domakh massovykh serii* (Moscow: MNIITEP, 2011).

77. Epitsentr is a construction material and furniture store that first opened in Kyiv in 1996 as a small business and by 2003 opened the first superstore. Roman Mal'chevskiy, "Aleksandr Gerega—o pervykh den'gakh i o tom kak sozdavalsia Epitsentr," *Politrada. ua*, September 25, 2013, https://politrada.com/news/aleksandr-gerega-o-pervykh-dengakh-i-tom-kak-sozdavalsya-epitsentr/. IKEA opened its first store in Russia in 2000. "IKEA v Rossii," IKEA in Russia (official website), https://www.ikea.com/ms/ru_RU/about_ikea/ikea_in_russia/ikea_in_russia.html.

78. "Dom v kotorom my zhivem," *Rabotnitsa*, monthly heading.

79. Edward Casey, "Body, Self, and Landscape: A Geophilosophical Inquiry into the Place-World," in *Textures of Place: Exploring Humanist Geographies*, ed. Paul Adams (Minneapolis: University of Minnesota Press, 2004), 409.

80. A comparison can be drawn between permanent remont and Olga Shevchenko's permanent crisis in *Crisis and the Everyday in Postsocialist Moscow*, where she addresses the sense of crisis as a "the postsoviet hysteresis of habitus."

81. Natalia S. (apartment dweller), interview by the author, May 2, 2017, Kyiv, Ukraine.

82. Oksana H. (apartment dweller), interview by the author, May 14, 2017, Kyiv, Ukraine.

83. Maryna D. (apartment dweller), interview by the author, May 6, 2017, Kyiv, Ukraine.

84. Mykola I. (apartment dweller), interview by the author, June 26, 2019, Lviv, Ukraine.

85. Mykola I. (apartment dweller), interview.

86. See Ekaterina Gerasimova and Sofia Chuikina, "The Repair Society," *Russian Studies in History* 48, no. 1 (2009): 58–74; Alexander, "Remont: Work in Progress," 255–275; Wladimir Sgibnev, "Remont: Do-It-Yourself-Urbanism in Post-Soviet Tajikistan" (presentation paper, RC21 Conference, Berlin, Germany, August 29–31, 2013).

87. Tatiana Bulakh, "The Enchantment of Imaginary Europe: Consumer Practices in Post-Soviet Ukraine," in *The Socialist Good Life: Desire, Development and Standards of Living in Eastern Europe*, ed. Christopher Scarboro, Diana Mincyte, and Zsuzsa Gille (Bloomington: Indiana University Press, 2020), 162.

88. The Law of the USSR, Section 24, "Prevention and Elimination of Noise," in "About the Fundaments of the USSR and Republican Healthcare," December 19, 1969.

89. The Law of Ukraine, Section 24, "Protection of the Population from the Harmful Influence of Noise, Non-Ionizing Emissions and Other Physical Factors," in "About the Provision of Sanitary and Epidemical Wellbeing of the Population," April 8, 1994.

90. Anton C. (top-floor apartment dweller), interview by the author, May 10, 2017, Kyiv, Ukraine.

91. Leningrad, "Remont," released November 20, 2007, track 10 on *Avrora* album.

92. Krisztina Fehérváry, *Politics in Color and Concrete: Socialist Materialities and the Middle Class in Hungary* (Bloomington: Indiana University Press, 2013), 1.

2. SLEEPING

1. For information on apartments without bedrooms in the United States, see John Hancock, "The Apartment House in Urban America," in *Buildings and Society: Essays on the Social Development of the Built Environment*, ed. Anthony King (London: Routledge, 2003), 92, 96.

2. For example, Steven Harris, *Communism on Tomorrow Street: Mass Housing and Everyday Life after Stalin* (Baltimore, MD: Johns Hopkins University Press, 2013); Christine Varga-Harris, *Stories of House and Home: Soviet Apartment Life during the Khrushchev Years* (Ithaca, NY: Cornell University Press, 2015).

3. Fedor Dostoevsky, *Crime and Punishment* (Oxford: Benediction Classics, 2016), 28.

4. In addition to communal apartments, many urbanites, particularly in smaller cities and prior to mass housing construction, lived in barracks. Barracks—temporary wooden or masonry housing split into rooms or even apartments—were typically built to house workers in new industrial locations around the Soviet Union. Since they were considered temporary, they often lacked amenities and were not properly maintained over time. However, like most temporary solutions, they turned out to be very persistent. For example, in 1980, two and a half decades after the beginning of the mass housing

campaign, there were still 54 thousand people living in barracks and basements in the Ukrainian SSR alone. Fond R-582, Opys' 12, Sprava 2938, 1, Tsentral'nyi derzhavnyi arkhiv vyshchykh organiv vlady ta upravlinnia Ukrainy, Kyiv, Ukraine.

5. Varga-Harris, *Stories of House and Home*, 2.

6. Most importantly this includes fluid space use rather than identifiable room functions.

7. Yuri Trifonov, "Obmen,"in *Moskovskie povesti* (Moscow: Litres, 2017) (first published in 1969; author's translation).

8. The Soviet and post-Soviet conventional meaning for a room is a separate domestic space other than the kitchen, bathroom, or entryway. The quality of a home is not defined by the number of bedrooms like in the United States but rather by the number of rooms. In this chapter the term is used accordingly.

9. Early modular (composed of panel) apartment series, nicknamed after Khrushchev, the general secretary of the Communist Party of the USSR between 1953 and 1964.

10. According to Soviet housing regulations, a family of three could not have received more than a two-room apartment.

11. Iu. S. Kukushkin and O. I. Chistiakov, *Ocherk istorii sovetskoi konstitutsii* (Moscow: Politizdat, 1987), 331.

12. Deirdre Harshman, "A Space Called Home: Housing and the Management of Everyday in Russia, 1890–1935" (PhD Diss., University of Urbana-Champaign, 2018), 40.

13. Vladimir Lenin, *Polnoe sobranie sochinenii*, vol. 54 (Moscow: Izdatel'stvo Politicheskoi Literatury, 1975), 350.

14. A. N. Fedorov, "Zhilishche v poslerevoliutsionnoi Moskve kak ob'iekt politiki i povsednevnoi zhizni," *Vestnik RUDN: Istoriia Rossii* 1 (2008): 56–57.

15. This number varied at different times in different republics but has never gone above nine square meters per person. See Katherine Zubovich, "Housing and Meaning in Soviet and Post-Soviet Russia," *Kritika: Explorations in Russian and Eurasian History* 16, no. 4 (Fall 2015): 1007.

16. k stands for *komnata* (a room). In the 1950s and 1960s, this formula called *formula rasseleniia* (formula of settlement) sometimes reached $k=n-2$ or even $k=n-3$ values. Boris Rubanenko (ed.), *Tipizatsiia zhilykh zdanii, ikh elementov i detalei* (Moscow: Stroiizdat, 1974), 91.

17. Vladimir Papernyi, *Kul'tura dva* (Moscow: Novoe literaturnoe obozrenie, 2011), 103.

18. Isadora Duncan (1877–1927)—a famous American dancer who resided in Moscow 1921–1924.

19. Mikhail Bulgakov, *Heart of a Dog* (New York: Grove Press, 1987), 26–27.

20. "In the next three five-year plans every family will have a separate apartment!" Nikita Khrushchev claimed at the 20th Congress of the Communist Party of the Soviet Union in 1956.

21. The format of the Sanitary Norms and Regulations was first introduced in 1954 to replace the previous scattered rules. See *SNiP II-V.10–58 Zhilye zdaniia* (Moscow: Stroiizdat, 1954).

22. Jane Roj Zavisca, *Housing the New Russia* (Ithaca, NY: Cornell University Press, 2012), 30.

23. V. D. Elizarov, *Massovoe zhilishchnoe stroitel'stvo v USSR* (Kyiv: Budivel'nyk, 1966), 39–44.

24. A rare exclusion, when kitchens became big enough to occasionally accommodate sleep, is described in chapter 4.

25. *Illustrirovannyi katalog proektov otkrytogo konkursa na razrabotku proektnykh predlozhenii po novym tipam maloetazhnykh zhilykh domov i prinzipov plotno-nizkoi gorodskoi zastroiki* (Moscow: Gosstroi SSSR, 1981), 24.

26. Svetlana Boym, *Common Places: Mythologies of Everyday Life in Russia* (Cambridge, MA: Harvard University Press, 1994), 150–159.

27. Compact housing (*malogabaritnoe zhil'e*) is a term typically used to define Khrushchev-era and post-Khrushchev-era Soviet apartments due to their small dimensions.

28. Trifonov, "Obmen."

29. *Pora bol'shogo novoselia*, directed by Nebylitskii B. (Moscow: Tsentral'naia studiia dokumental'nykh filmov, 1959).

30. Merzhanov describes an intensively used common room as having "a dining and a living room zone" and at night "transforming into a bedroom, say, for a young couple." Boris Merzhanov, *Inter'er zhilishcha* (Moscow: Znanie, 1970), 21.

31. For an in-depth exploration into the Soviet *byt*, see Boym, *Common Places*, 29–40.

32. "Russian Property Law, Privatization, and the Right of 'Full Economic Control,'" *Harvard Law Review* 107, no. 5 (March 1994): 1044.

33. "Russian Property Law, Privatization, and the Right of 'Full Economic Control,'" 1044.

34. "Russian Property Law, Privatization, and the Right of 'Full Economic Control,'" 1044.

35. Verkhovna Rada URSR, *Zakon URSR "Pro vlasnist'" (697-12) z 15 kvitnia 1991 roku* (Kyiv: Vidomosti Verkhovnoi Rady URSR, 1991), http://zakon.rada.gov.ua/laws/show /885-12.

36. See Filip Novokmet, Thomas Piketty, and Gabriel Zucman, "From Soviets to Oligarchs: Inequality and Property in Russia, 1905–2016" (NBER Working Paper No. 23712, August 2017).

37. *Sanitarnye normy i pravila I-B.II Stroitel'nye materialy, detali i konstruktsii* (Moscow: Gosudarstvennoe izdatel'stvo literatury po stroitel'stvu, arkhitekture i stroitel'nym materialam, 1955), 48.

38. *Gosudarstvennyi standard Soiuza SSR 6428-52 Plity gipsovye dlia peregorodok* (Moscow: Gosudarstvennyi komitet SSR po delam stroitel'stva, 1952).

39. *Gosudarstvennyi standard Soiuza SSR 6428-74 Plity gipsovye dlia peregorodok* (Moscow: Gosudarstvennyi komitet SSR po delam stroitel'stva, 1974); *Gosudarstvennyi standard Soiuza SSR 6428-83 Plity gipsovye dlia peregorodok* (Moscow: Gosudarstvennyi komitet SSR po delam stroitel'stva, 1983).

40. Werner Rödiger, Herbert Schumacher, and Wilfried Demel, *Rost i stanovlenie: Biografia sem'i predprinematelei Knauf* (Iphofen: Knauf Gips KG, 2003), 362–370.

41. "V khrushchevke," *Idei vashego doma* 61, no. 4 (April 2003), https://www.ivd.ru /custom_category/custom_subcategory/v-hrusevke-4463.

42. "Prevrashchenia khrushchevki," *Idei vashego doma*, no. 2 (2005), https://www.ivd .ru/custom_category/custom_subcategory/prevrasenia-hrusevki-5411; "Nemnogo sveta i tepla," *Idei vashego doma*, no. 2 (2005), https://www.ivd.ru/custom_category/custom _subcategory/nemnogo-sveta-i-tepla-5413.

43. T. A. Korostleva, *Pereplanirovka kvartiry* (Moscow: Gammapress, 2000), 23.

44. Hanna F. (architect), interview by the author, May 15, 2017, Kyiv, Ukraine.

45. Hanna F. (architect), interview.

46. Hanna F. (architect), interview.

47. Valerii M. (apartment dweller), interview by the author, April 27, 2017, Kyiv, Ukraine.

48. Recorder of Deeds engineers, personal conversation with the author; anonymized Recorder of Deeds plans reproduced by the author, Kyiv, Ukraine, April 2017.

49. See chapter 5.

50. Since state-supplied housing for the most part no longer functioned after 1991, families who were unable to afford bigger homes continued living and growing in small

apartments. To this day, several generations of the same family (more than one core family) commonly live together, with occupants outnumbering rooms. For more information on economic disparity, see Branko Milanović and Lire Ersado, "Reform and Inequality during the Transition: An Analysis Using Panel Household Survey Data, 1990–2005" (No. wp-2010-062, WIDER Working Paper Series, World Institute for Development Economic Research [UNU-WIDER]) and Zavisca, *Housing the New Russia*. According to Tsenkova and Turner, in 2002, 33.5 percent (Latvia) and 44.1 percent (Ukraine) of three-member families lived in two or fewer rooms. Another 25.5 percent (Latvia) and 23.7 percent (Ukraine) of three-member families lived in three-room apartments. Sasha Tsenkova and Bengt Turner, "The Future of Social Housing in Eastern Europe: Reforms in Latvia and Ukraine," *European Journal of Housing Policy* 4, no. 2 (2004): 141.

51. Valerii M. (apartment dweller), interview.

52. Ekaterina Gerasimova and Sof'ia Chuikina, "Obshchestvo remonta," *Neprikos-novennyi zapas* 34, no. 2 (2004).

53. See Natalya Chernyshova, "Philistines on the Big Screen: Consumerism in Soviet Cinema of the Brezhnev Era," *Studies in Russian and Soviet Cinema* 5, no. 2 (2014): 227–254; and Natalya Chernyshova, "Consuming Technology in a Closed Society: Household Appliances in Soviet Urban Homes of the Brezhnev Era," *Ab Imperio* 2011, no. 2 (2011): 188–220.

54. Because of the consumer goods deficit, many goods could not be bought freely but had to be obtained through contrivances. For information about the consumer goods deficit, see Steven Sampson, "The Second Economy of the Soviet Union and Eastern Europe," *The Annals of the American Academy of Political and Social Science* 493, no. 1 (2016): 120–136.

55. Gerasimova and Chuikina, "Obshchestvo remonta."

56. IKEA first opened in the Russian Federation in 2000.

57. JYSK first opened in the Russian Federation in 1996 and in Ukraine in 2004.

58. Boym, *Common Places*, 150–159.

59. David Stea, "House and Home: Identity, Dichotomy or Dialectic?" in *Domestic Space Reader*, ed. Chiara Briganti and Kathy Mezei (Toronto: University of Toronto Press, 2012), 48.

60. Boym, *Common Places*, 155–157.

61. A detailed account of the growing housing inequality after the collapse of the Soviet Union can be found in Zavisca, *Housing the New Russia*, 89.

62. Oksana H. (apartment dweller), interview by the author, May 14, 2017, Kyiv, Ukraine.

63. Oleksandra H. (apartment dweller), interview by the author, May 14, 2017, Kyiv, Ukraine.

64. Aleksander Kuliapin and Olga Skubach, *Mifologiia sovetskoi povsednevnosti* (Moscow: Iazyki slavianskoi kul'tury [IaSK], 2013), 128.

65. Norbert Elias, *The Civilizing Process* (London: Blackwell, 1982), 132–138, quoted in Chiara Briganti and Kathy Mezei, eds., *Domestic Space Reader* (Toronto, Ontario: University of Toronto Press, 2012), 227–229.

66. It seems that out of all bourgeois habits, shame of the naked body was not one the Soviet society was ready to abandon: radical nudists were physically interrogated, taken off public transport, and finally condemned by the communist state itself. The Soviet People's Commissar of Healthcare, Nickolay Semashko, stated in an interview to the major Soviet newspaper *Izvestiia* that "when such capitalist ugliness as prostitution and hooliganism, are not yet outlived in the Soviet society, nudity only promotes immorality, and not good morals." *Izvestiia*, "Kul'tura ili bezobrazie?" September 12, 1924, cover.

67. See Papernyi, *Kul'tura dva*, 148 on Konstantin Melnikov's house.

68. "Socialism in One Country"—A theory broadly accepted in the Soviet Union after the defeat of socialist revolutions in European countries. Formally introduced by Nickolay

Bukharin in 1925. "Communism in One Apartment" was a running Soviet joke, meaning the promised communist paradise was created in a single apartment, often obtaining commodities through the informal economy and bribery.

69. "Vasha mechta—sobstvennaia spal'nia," *Rabotnitsa* 3/4 (1992): 8/11.

70. Valerii M. (apartment dweller), interview.

71. Henri Lefebvre, *Rhythmanalysis* (London: Bloomsbury, 2014), 83.

72. While rhythmanalysis did appear in the field of post-Soviet studies, it was only used in a couple studies and applied predominantly to public space. Wladimir Sgibnev, "Rhythms of Being Together: Public Space in Urban Tajikistan through the Lens of Rhythmanalysis," *International Journal of Sociology and Social Policy* 35, no. 7/8 (2015): 533–549.

3. EATING

Parts of chapter 3 have been previously published in Kateryna Malaia, "Transforming the Architecture of Food: From the Soviet to the Post-Soviet Apartment," *Journal of the Society of Architectural Historians* 80, no. 4 (2021): 460–476.

1. Oksana H. (apartment dweller), interview by the author, May 14, 2017, Kyiv, Ukraine.

2. Elizabeth Cromley, *The Food Axis: Cooking, Eating and the Architecture of the American Houses* (Charlottesville: University of Virginia Press, 2010), 3.

3. Late-Soviet housing stock, a product of seven decades of Communist rule, predominantly consisted of pre-Revolutionary communal, Stalin-era, prefabricated Khrushchev-era (first-generation), and Brezhnev-era (second- and third-generation) apartments. The intervention of the state into the apartment life of the Khrushchev-era is described in Victor Buchli, "Khrushchev, Modernism, and the Fight against 'Petit-Bourgeois' Consciousness in the Soviet Home," *Journal of Design History* 10, no. 2 (1997): 161–176. The relationship between the home and the state in the Brezhnev era is addressed in Natalya Chernyshova, "Closing the Door on Socialism: Furniture and the Domestic Interior," in *Soviet Consumer Culture in the Brezhnev Era* (London: Routledge, 2013).

4. In Victor Buchli, *Materializing Culture: An Archeology of Socialism* (Oxford: Berg, 2000), Buchli writes that the elimination of a dining room took place during the de-Stalinization effort and with the introduction of the utilitarian prefabricated housing in the late 1950s. According to Buchli, it was not until the 1950s that Soviet apartments shifted toward multifunctional rather than monofunctional spaces. However, it is possible to argue that Soviet apartments shifted toward multifunctional spaces with the introduction of $k = n - 1$ rule in the 1918 decree: *O vselenii semei krasnoarmeitsev i bezrabotnykh rabochikh v zhil'e burzhuazii i normirovke zhilykh pomeshchenii* (About moving red army soldiers and unemployed workers into the housing of bourgeoisie, and the norms for housing spaces). Rooms remained multifunctional in most Soviet urban households until 1991, excluding only the elites of the Soviet society. The decree meant that the number of people always exceeded the number of rooms in the apartment. Having a dining room was impossible for most urbanites throughout Soviet history. What Buchli identifies as a dining room was rather a multifunctional area in one of the available rooms, used for different purposes throughout the day. Despite Buchli's examples drawn from a Soviet domestic interior advice book, the actual apartments constructed in the 1960s were too modestly sized for an open plan or for Buchli's illustration to be realized. Except for a small number of first-generation apartments designed with kitchenettes, the rooms remained as segregated as they were before. A transformation shown by Buchli could only have taken place in a large communal apartment room, which made this scenario practically impossible due to the necessity to replace all furniture at once for no real reason in the society of an omnipresent commodity shortage. *An Archeology*

of Socialism refers to the formal modernist discourse in Soviet domestic architecture rather than real domestic interior in practice.

5. In some experimental Constructivist housing, Narkomfin apartment buildings in particular, architects abolished apartment kitchens in favor of a communal canteen that was supposed to feed the entire population of the building. The experiment largely failed: apartment dwellers established and expanded individual kitchenettes inside their apartments.

6. Soviet bureaucracy divided domestic space into the so-called lived and auxiliary spaces, with auxiliary spaces being kitchens, bathrooms, lavatories, hallways, balconies, and storage, and lived space being everything else. In other words, everything other than auxiliary spaces was considered to be a lived room (*zhilaia komnata*).

7. See Paola Messana, *Soviet Communal Living: An Oral History of the Kommunalka* (Basingstoke, UK: Palgrave Macmillan, 2011), 117; or Ilya Utekhin, Alice Nakhimovsky, Slava Paperno, and Nancy Ries, *Communal Living in Russia: A Virtual Museum of Soviet Everyday Life*, http://kommunalka.colgate.edu/cfm/essays.cfm?ClipID=250&TourID=910.

8. Svetlana Boym, *Common Places: Mythologies of Everyday Life in Russia* (Cambridge, MA: Harvard University Press, 1994), 147.

9. Lynne Attwood, *Gender and Housing in Soviet Russia: Private Life in a Public Space* (Manchester, UK: Manchester University Press, 2010), 224–226.

10. Attwood, *Gender and Housing in Soviet Russia*, 223.

11. Prigov poetically suggests that all the most important events took place in the communal kitchens. These events later "flooded the rooms, as the secondary signs of offenses, spiteful looks, greetings, and sweet pies . . ." Dmitrii Prigov, *Zhivite v Moskve: Rukopis' na pravakh romana* (Moscow: Novoe literaturnoe obozrenie, 2000), 96.

12. For instance, in the movie *Dobrovol'tsy*, directed by Yurii Egorov (Moscow: Kinostudiia im. Gor'kogo, 1958), and the painting *Utro* (1954) by Tatiana Iablonskaia.

13. Sarah Bonnemaison, "Performing the Modernist Dwelling: The Unite d'Habitation of Marseille," in *Architecture as Performing Art*, ed. Marcia Feuerstein and Gray Read (Burlington, VT: Ashgate, 2013), 64.

14. Susan E. Reid, "The Khrushchev Kitchen: Domesticating the Scientific-Technological Revolution" *Journal of Contemporary History* 40, no. 2 (2005): 289. The effects of the disappearance of servant labor from the kitchen are relevant far beyond just Soviet geographies. However, the effects of this labor disappearance vary and have taken different spans of time to unwrap. For instance, Elizabeth Cromley associates the merging between the cooking, dining and living room spaces in the American homes with the "change towards the servantless household evident since 1910." Cromley, *The Food Axis*, 204.

15. Christine Varga-Harris, *Stories of House and Home: Soviet Apartment Life during the Khrushchev Years* (Ithaca, NY: Cornell University Press, 2015), 64.

16. Frankfurt kitchen is a commonly used name for the modernist fitted kitchen designed by Margarete Schutte-Lihotsky for the Frankfurt housing projects in 1926–1927. Christopher Wilk, ed., *Modernism: 1914–1939; Designing a New World* (London: Victoria & Albert Publications, 2006), 180.

17. Varga-Harris, *Stories of House and Home*, 27.

18. Plans from Philipp Meuser and Dimitrij Zadorin, *Towards a Typology of Soviet Mass Housing: Prefabrication in the USSR 1955–1991* (Berlin: DOM publishers, 2015), 267.

19. *Sanitarnye Normy i Pravila II-B.10-58 Zhilye zdaniia* (Moskva: Gosudarstvennoe izdatel'stvo literatury po stroitel'stvu, arkhitekture i stroitel'nym materialam, 1958), 20.

20. Varga-Harris, *Stories of House and Home*, 26–28.

21. Varga-Harris, *Stories of House and Home*, 150; and "Norma zhiloi ploshchadi," in *Zhilishchnyi kodeks RSFSR* (Moskva: Iuridicheskaia literatura, 1986).

22. *Sanitarnye Normy i Pravila II-B.10-58 Zhilye zdaniia*, 20.

23. *Sanitarnye Normy i Pravila II-B.10-58 Zhilye zdaniia*, 20.

24. Buchli, "Khrushchev, Modernism," 166.

25. "Programma otkrytogo konkursa na luchshie tipovye proekty domov 3-4-5 etazhei," Gosstroi SSR, 1956, Fond R-1657, Opys' 1, Sprava 97, 16, Desrzhavnyi oblastnyi arkhiv L'vivs'koi Oblasti, Lviv, Ukraine.

26. Susan E. Reid, "Cold War in the Kitchen: Gender and the De-Stalinization of Consumer Taste in the Soviet Union under Khrushchev," *Slavic Review* 61, no. 2 (2002): 223–228.

27. Varga-Harris, *Stories of House and Home*, 65.

28. Buchli, "Khrushchev, Modernism," 167–168.

29. "Down with the Kitchen Slavery! Let There Be New Everyday Life [*Byt*]!" is a Soviet political poster promoting female liberation widely used in the 1920s and 1930s. Also see Reid, "The Khrushchev Kitchen," 291–292.

30. "Programma otkrytogo konkursa na luchshie tipovye proekty domov 3-4-5 etazhei," Gosstroi SSR, Fond R-1657, Opys' 1, Sprava 97, 16, Desrzhavnyi oblastnyi arkhiv L'vivs'koi Oblasti, Lviv, Ukraine.

31. Meuser and Zadorin, *Towards a Typology of Soviet Mass Housing*, 171.

32. O. Ia. Smirnova, "Vliianie bytovykh processov na formirovanie zhiloi iacheiki," *Stroitel'stvo i arkhitektura*, no. 22 (1986): 13.

33. *Dom v kotorom ia zhivu*, directed by Lev Kulidzhanov, (Moscow: Kinostudiia im. Gor'kogo, 1957); *Iiul'skii dozhd'*, directed by Marlen Khutsiev, (Moscow: Mosfilm, 1966).

34. *Operatsiia Y i drugie prikliucheniia Shurika*, directed by Leonid Gaidai, (Moscow, Mosfilm, 1965).

35. *Ivan Vasil'evich meniaet professiiu*, directed by Leonid Gaidai, (Moscow, Mosfilm, 1973).

36. Yurii Poliakov, "Podruzhka: Moi milyi chto tebe ia sdelala," *Rabotnitsa* 6 (June 1984): 28.

37. V. Stepanishev, "10 metrov na 100 chelovek," *Rabotnitsa* 3 (March 1989): 8. Although this example is a consumer ideal of a late-Soviet urbanite—two television sets in an apartment, one of them in the kitchen—this does not mean that every single family had two television sets in their home. Nevertheless, this description would appear familiar and relevant to the general public.

38. Boym, *Common Places*, 142.

39. Stepanishev, "10 metrov na 100 chelovek," 8.

40. Anna Alekseyeva, "Constructing Soviet Domesticity and Managing Everyday Life from Khrushchev to Collapse," in *Material Culture in Russia and the USSR: Things, Values, Identities*, ed. Graham H. Roberts (London: Bloomsbury Publishing, 2017), 61–63.

41. Alekseyeva, "Constructing Soviet Domesticity," 63.

42. See Buchli on transformable furniture: Buchli, *Materializing Culture*, 143.

43. Owning a television was an important element of the late-Soviet idea of prosperity (Andrey Trofimov and Marina Klinova, "'Sovetskii potrebitel' v otechestvennom gumanitarnom diskurse 1950–1980kh godov," *Izvestiia UrGEU* 4, no. 54 (2014): 110), while owning a second television set in the kitchen was a sign of particular comfortable living [for instance, a late-Soviet movie *The Most Charming and Attractive* (*Samaia obaiatel'naia i privlekatel'naia*) uses a second kitchen television set to illustrate the well-being of a secondary character, Susanna]. The growing late-Soviet consumerism is described and explained in Chernyshova, *Soviet Consumer Culture in the Brezhnev Era*. Gerald Bezhanov, *Samaia obaiatel'naia i privlekatel'naia* (Moscow: Mosfilm, 1985).

44. On celebratory food and its meaning, see Albert Baiburin and Alexandra Piir, "When We Were Happy: Remembering Soviet Holidays," in *Petrified Utopia: Happiness Soviet Style*, ed. Marina Balina and Evgeny Dobrenko (London: Anthem Press, 2011), 247.

45. William Moskoff, *Hard Times: Impoverishment and Protest in the Perestroika Years: The Soviet Union 1985–1991* (Armonk, NY: M. E. Sharpe, 1993), 28–43.

46. Adrianne Jacobs, "The Many Flavors of Socialism: Modernity and Tradition in Late Soviet Food Culture, 1965–1985" (PhD diss., University of North Carolina at Chapel Hill, 2015), 240, https://cdr.lib.unc.edu/indexablecontent/uuid:123695e5-654d-4112-8efb-38980ad8e51a.

47. Anna Kushkova, "V tsentre stola: Zenit i zakat salata Olivye," *Novoe literaturnoe obozrenie* 76 (2005): 278–313.

48. Nika Zh. (apartment dweller), personal conversation and photoshoot with the author, June 30, 2019, Kyiv, Ukraine.

49. Natalia S. (apartment dweller), interview by the author, May 2, 2017, Kyiv, Ukraine; as well as Boym, *Common Places*, 150–157.

50. Jennifer A. Jordan, *Edible Memory: The Lure of Heirloom Tomatoes and Other Forgotten Foods* (Chicago: University of Chicago Press, 2015), 36.

51. Jennifer Patico, *Consumption and Social Change in a Post-Soviet Middle Class* (Stanford, CA: Stanford University Press, 2008), 177.

52. Meuser and Zadorin, *Towards a Typology of Soviet Mass Housing*, 267.

53. *Sanitarnye normy i pravila* 2.08.01-89* *Zhilye zdaniia* (Moscow: TsITP Gosstroiia SSSR, 1989).

54. Out of the nine apartment dwellers interviewed for this project, four indicated kitchens as the primary spaces they remodeled and attempted to improve, either with efficient organization or by physically enlarging or connecting them with other spaces of their apartment.

55. Stepanishev, "10 metrov na 100 chelovek," 8. This passage has an additional implication other than pointing out a perception of kitchens as insufficiently small. In this quote, the fridge is no longer treated as a technical breakthrough or a sign of social and economic well-being of its owners. On the contrary, it is shown as a bulky, inconvenient object that needs to be partially hidden inside the wall. This is in tune with Sandy Isenstadt's argument that by the 1950s, in the United States, refrigerators became so commonplace they were no longer treated as a technological miracle, and their physical presence was downplayed in the interiors by their "spectacularization" as a vision of food abundance. While the quote by Stepanishev clearly shows an attempt to downplay the refrigerator in the kitchen interior, the social context of this quote from *Rabotnitsa* is quite different from the American case. It similarly suggests that refrigerators and accessible food also became commonplace in the late Soviet Union. However, the quality of this food supply was quite different from the "vision of plenty" described in Isenstadt's article. Sandy Isenstadt, "Visions of Plenty: Refrigerators in America around 1950," *Journal of Design History* 11, no. 4 (1998): 311.

56. Although there was no written rule to not use monolith concrete for floor slab construction, it is clearly evident in the recommendations for residential construction. The reason to limit the use of monolith concrete was the omnipresence of House Building Factories [*domostroitel'nyi kombinat* (DSK)]—factories that produced prefabricated panels. For instance, Yurii Dykhovichii suggests only using concrete panels in residential construction. Yurii Dykhovichii, *Zhilye i obshchestvennye zdaniia: Kratkii spravochnik inzhenera-konstruktora* (Moscow: Stroiizdat, 1991), 9; Kateryna Malaia, "A Unit of Homemaking: The Prefabricated Panel and Domestic Architecture in the Late Soviet Union," *Architectural Histories* 8, no. 1 (2020): 11.

57. For the discussion of the limited possibilities of prefabricated panel construction and the necessity to shift to monolith construction in housing, see N. K. Buts, "Puti i metody razvitiia monolitnogo domostroeniia," *Stroitel'stvo i arkhitektura* 8 (1989): 14–15.

58. Some standardized housing construction did not stop immediately after the collapse of the Soviet Union but rather continued for a couple more years, if money and materials were allocated for the construction before 1991. Typically, these projects took longer than predicted and were frequently finished by a funder different than the state.

59. Arsenii R. (engineer), interview by the author, May 18, 2017, Kyiv, Ukraine.

60. Iaroslav D. (architect), interview by the author, May 11, 2017, Kyiv, Ukraine.

61. Iaroslav D. (architect), interview.

62. Andrii K. (architect), interview by the author, May 24, 2017, Kyiv, Ukraine. During an interview, Andrii K. recalled that in 1992–1993, imported cabinet elements replaced locally produced cabinet parts.

63. Taras S. (architect), interview by the author, April 22, 2017, Kyiv, Ukraine.

64. Boym, *Common Places*, 155.

65. Stepanishev, "10 metrov na 100 chelovek," 8.

66. "Of all spaces of an apartment the most universally used is the kitchen" from Smirnova, "Vliianie bytovykh processov na formirovanie zhiloi iacheiki," 13.

67. For more information on anti-Soviet (dissident) gatherings in the kitchen, see Nancy Ries, *Russian Talk Culture and Conversation during Perestroika* (Ithaca, NY: Cornell University, 1997), 92.

68. The damage from a potential gas explosion would be minimized as the window structures would be the first to burst.

69. *Sanitarnye normy i pravila II-B.10-58 Zhilye zdaniia*, 20; *Sanitarnye normy i pravila II-L.1-71* Zhilye zdaniia* (Moscow: Stroiizadat, 1978), 16, 23.

70. "Ob izmenenii i dopolnenii glavy SNiP II-L.1-71," in *Sanitarnye normy i pravila II-L.1-71* Zhilye zdaniia*, 11 (dopolnenie).

71. Arsenii R. (engineer), interview. This interviewee worked on an apartment building reconstruction in the 1980s. Since this apartment building was located in the very center of a republican capital, the apartments were supposed to house Soviet elites after the reconstruction was over. Unlike in regular cases, future dwellers were able to put in personal requests. One of the future residents requested that engineers and architects develop his apartment with two kitchens, since the apartment was to be populated by both his and his child's family and the two families wanted to cook separately.

72. A comprehensive account of the American National Exhibition that demonstrated American commodities to the Soviet public in Moscow in 1959 can be found in Reid, "Cold War in the Kitchen," 211–252.

73. Krisztina Fehérváry, "American Kitchens, Luxury Bathrooms, and the Search for a 'Normal' Life in Postsocialist Hungary," *Ethnos* 67, 3 (2002): 369.

74. Fehérváry, "American Kitchens," 380.

75. For studies on Socialist Bloc suburbanization (i.e., urban decentralization), see Sonia Hirt, *Iron Curtains: Gates, Suburbs, and Privatization of Space in the Post-Socialist City* (Hoboken, NJ: Wiley & Sons, 2012), 106–110, 127–128; K. Leetmaa, T. Tammaru, and K. Anniste, "From Priority-Led to Market-Led Suburbanization in a Post-Communist Metropolis," *Tijdschrigt Voor Economische En Sociale Geografie* 100, 4 (2009): 436–453, and many others.

76. Matas Cirtautas, "Urban Sprawl of Major Cities in the Baltic States," *Arhitektura un pilsetplanosana* 7, no. 10 (2013): 72.

77. Robert J. Mason and Liliya Nigmatullina, "Suburbanization and Sustainability in Metropolitan Moscow," *Geographical Review* 101, no. 3 (July 2011): 316–333.

78. Irene Cieraad, "'Out of My Kitchen!' Architecture, Gender and Domestic Efficiency," *The Journal of Architecture* 7, no. 3 (2002): 263–279.

79. Cieraad, "'Out of My Kitchen!' Architecture, Gender and Domestic Efficiency," 263–279.

80. Stepanishev, "10 metrov na 100 chelovek," 8.

81. Iurii Ivanov, *Pereplanirovka, remont i dizain kvartiry: Sovremennye otdelochnye materialy i technologii raboty s nimi* (Moscow: Ast. Astrel', 2006), 18.

82. Hanna F. (architect), interview by the author, May 15, 2017, Kyiv, Ukraine.

83. For instance, II-57 series and PP-44 series apartments had a load-bearing wall between the kitchen and the adjacent room.

84. "Fabrika komforta," *Idei vashego doma*, accessed April 25, 2018, https://www.ivd .ru/custom_category/custom_subcategory/fabrika-komforta-5002.

85. *Buro tekhnichnoi inventaryzatsii* engineers, personal conversations with the author.

86. *GOST 13025.2-85 Mebel' bytovaia: Funktsional'nye razmery mebeli dlia sideniia i lezhaniia* (Moscow: Izdatel'stvo standartov, 1987).

87. *Bol'shaia sovetskaia entsyklopediia* (Moscow: Sovetskaia entsyklopediia, 1972), s.vv. "mebel'" and "mebel'naia promyshlennost'." Since furniture production in the Soviet Union was centralized, if a piece did not appear in the catalogues of the Soviet furniture industry and did not make it into *Bol'shaia sovetskaia entsyklopediia* (*Great Soviet encyclopedia*), it means that it was not produced and virtually did not exist in Soviet homes.

88. Stepanishev, "10 metrov na 100 chelovek," 8.

89. The comfort of fixed kitchen sitting may appear to be questionable when it comes to daily eating.

90. Stepanishev, "10 metrov na 100 chelovek," 8.

91. Maryna D. (apartment dweller), interview by the author, May 6, 2017, Kyiv, Ukraine.

92. Mykola H. (apartment dweller), interview by the author, June 26, 2019, Lviv, Ukraine.

93. Iryna M. (apartment dweller), interview by the author, July 11, 2019, Lviv, Ukraine.

94. Iryna M. (apartment dweller), interview.

95. Mariia K. (apartment dweller), interview by the author, August 22, 2019, Kyiv, Ukraine.

96. Mariia K. (apartment dweller), interview.

97. Cromley, *The Food Axis*, 207.

98. Cromley, *The Food Axis*, 207.

99. Stepanishev, "10 metrov na 100 chelovek," 8.

100. See for example, "Sobianin: Kvartaly v Moskve budut pereseliat' i snosit' tol'ko po zhelaniiu zhitelei," *TASS: Informatsionnoe agenstvo Rossii*, updated March 9, 2017, http://tass.ru/obschestvo/4081517.

4. CLEANING

Programma KPSS (Moscow: Gospolitizdat, 1961), 94.

1. Svetlana Boym speaks of the "communal duties" in "Archeology of Banality: The Soviet Home," *Public Culture* 6, no. 2 (1994): 266.

2. Between 1987 and 1991, *Rabotnitsa* magazine published a number of articles on remodeling kitchens, living rooms, and other rooms but not a single article on remodeling bathrooms.

3. Valentyna B., personal conversation with the author, Summer 2017, Kyiv, Ukraine.

4. Krisztina Fehérváry, "American Kitchens, Luxury Bathrooms, and the Search for a 'Normal' Life in Postsocialist Hungary," *Ethnos* 67, no. 3 (2002): 383.

5. *Ironiia sud'by, ili s legkim parom!*, directed by Il'dar Riazanov (Moscow: Mosfilm, 1975); *Afonia*, directed by Georgii Danelia (Moscow: Mosfilm, 1975).

6. Lilya Kaganovsky, "The Cultural Logic of Late Socialism," *Studies in Russian and Soviet Cinema* 3, no. 2 (2009): 192.

7. *Moskva slezam ne verit*, directed by Vladimir Menshov (Moscow: Mosfilm, 1979).

8. Christine Varga-Harris, "Foundation: Revolution Realized," in *Stories of House and Home: Soviet Apartment Life during the Khrushchev Years* (Ithaca, NY: Cornell University Press, 2015), 53–80.

9. For example, see Boris Merzhanov, *Inter'er zhilishcha* (Moscow: Znanie, 1970), 34.

10. Although not an image, another major introduction of the toilet to the discourse happened with Victor Pelevin's "Vera Pavlovna's Ninth Dream," a short story first published in 1991.

11. Many communal apartments were established in pre-1917 apartment buildings. In these buildings, story heights sometimes reached 4.5 meters or almost fifteen feet.

12. Svetlana Boym, "Ilya Kabakov: The Soviet Toilet and the Palace of Utopias," *ARTMargins*, December 31, 1999, https://artmargins.com/ilya-kabakov-the-soviet-toilet-and-the-palace-of-utopias.

13. "Respectable inter'er v panel'nom dome," *Salon inter'er*, no. 1 (1994), https://salon.ru/article/respectable-interer-v-panelnom-dome-1744.

14. Boym, "Ilya Kabakov."

15. For an example of a reference to "golden toilets," see Mikhail Kolomenskii, "K voprosu o formirovanii vneshnepoliticheskogo imidzha sovremennoi Rossii," *Vlast'* (March 2008): 83. For further reading on Russian nouveau riche homes, see Caroline Humphrey, *The Unmaking of Soviet Life: Everyday Economies after Socialism* (Ithaca, NY: Cornell University Press, 2002), 175–201.

16. "Respectable inter'er v panel'nom dome."

17. For example, see Merzhanov, *Inter'er zhilishcha*, 33, where the author claims combined and separate sanitary blocks to be the two main sanitary types available. Out of nine (K-7, G (Gi), I-464, I-335, I-467, I-447/I-447C, I-507, II-18, and II-38) prefabricated apartment building series of the first generation that Meuser and Zadorin list in their book on Soviet prefabricated construction, only one (II-38) had a separate bathroom and toilet room for one- and two-room apartments. At the same time, all of them had a separate bathroom and toilet room in three-or-more-room apartments. Philipp Meuser and Dimitrij Zadorin, *Towards a Typology of Soviet Mass Housing: Prefabrication in the USSR 1955–1991* (Berlin: DOM publishers, 2015), 167–256.

18. Christine Varga-Harris, *Stories of House and Home: Apartment Life during the Khrushchev Years* (Ithaca, NY: Cornell University Press, 2015), 152–153; Ekaterina Gerasimova, "The Soviet Communal Apartment," in *Beyond the Limits: The Concept of Space in Russian History and Culture*, ed. Jeremy Smith (Helsinki: SHS, 1999); Steven Harris, "In Search of 'Ordinary' Russia: Everyday Life in the NEP, the Thaw, and the Communal Apartment," *Kritika: Explorations in Russian and Eurasian History* 6, no. 3 (2005): 583–614; Svetlana Boym, *Common Places: Mythologies of Everyday Life in Russia* (Cambridge, MA: Harvard University Press, 1994), 121–167.

19. Christine Varga-Harris, "Homemaking and the Aesthetic and Moral Perimeters of the Soviet Home during the Khrushchev Era," *Journal of Social History* 41, no. 3 (Spring 2008): 567.

20. *Sanitarnye normy i pravila II-B.10–58 Zhilye zdaniia* (Moscow: Gosudarstvennoe izdatel'stvo literatury po stroitel'stvu, arkhitekture i stroitel'nym materialam, 1958), 19.

21. *Sanitarnye normy i pravila II-B.10–58 Zhiliye zdaniia*, 19.

22. Varga-Harris, *Stories of House and Home*, 2.

23. For example, the KOPE series developed in 1981. Meuser and Zadorin, *Towards a Typology of Soviet Mass Housing*, 399–405.

24. Natalia S. (apartment dweller), interview by the author, May 2, 2017, Kyiv, Ukraine.

25. Soviet literature provides numerous examples of limited access to hygiene facilities in a communal apartment. One such example can be seen in Aleksei Nikolaevich Tolstoy's novel *The Viper*. The female protagonist carries out daily hygienic procedures in the communal kitchen, and the spectrum of these procedures varies depending on the presence of men. Aleksei Nikolaevich Tolstoy, "The Viper" in *The Marie Antoinette Tapestry* (Moscow: Raduga Pub., 1991).

26. For example, the KOPE series was designed to have only separate sanitary blocks, even in the small two-room apartments.

27. Henry W. Morton, "Who Gets What, When and How? Housing in the Soviet Union," *Soviet Studies* 32, no. 2 (April 1980): 245.

28. Cooperatives and institutions had a little more freedom in deciding on the number of square meters per apartment than they would with state-owned housing. This often resulted in larger kitchens and separate bathrooms and lavatories. See Mervyn Matthews, *Poverty in the Soviet Union: The Life-Styles of the Underprivileged in Recent Years* (Cambridge: Cambridge University Press, 1986), 67.

29. For example, see an interview with the head of Moscow State Housing Inspection Aleksandr Matveevich Strazhnikov, "Vse o pereplanirovke kvartiry," interview by Svetlana Olifirova, *Komsomol'skaia pravda*, May 5, 2005, https://www.kp.ru/daily/23519/40426/. Another example can be found in an article on the resettlement of the first-generation prefabricated housing in Moscow, where the vice director of the Department of Housing Policy and Housing Funds in Moscow states: "As for the new apartments, they are offered not on a square-meter-for-square-meter basis, but on a room-for-room. Take a two-room khrushchevka. It has 42–44 square meters, a small kitchen, typically a combined sanitary block, and walk-through rooms. Resettling from this housing, people will receive a two-room apartment of no less than 50 square meters, with isolated rooms, a large kitchen, loggia, and separate bathroom and toilet room. Is this person going to improve their housing situation? Of course, they will!" From "Zhiteliam moskovskikh khrushchevok predlozhat kvartity za MKAD," *Komsomol'skaia pravda*, March 27, 2012, https://www.msk.kp.ru/daily/25858/2825855/.

30. The discrepancies between the Soviet texts and reality are a subject for Mikhail Epstein's "The Origins and Meaning of Russian Postmodernism," in *After the Future: The Paradoxes of Postmodernism and Contemporary Russian Culture* (Amherst: University of Massachusetts Press, 1995), 188–210. Epstein sees Soviet texts as inventing models of reality that "replace reality itself" (189).

31. Except for the homes of extreme elites, who could request individually designed layouts or were offered an outstanding apartment composition in the so-called institutional (*vedomstvennye*) buildings.

32. Boris Merzhanov, *Sovremennaia kvartira* (Moscow: Stroiizdat, 1974), title page.

33. Merzhanov, *Sovremennaia kvartira*, 27.

34. Ol'khova A. P., *Novye serii tipovykh proektov zhilykh domov dlia massovogo stroitel'stva: Arkhitekturno-planirovochnye resheniia (obzor)* (Moscow: Tsentr nauchno-tekhnicheskoi informatsii po grazhdanskomu stroitel'stvu i arkhitekture, 1972), 46.

35. Merzhanov, *Sovremennaia kvartira*, 35–37.

36. Merzhanov, *Sovremennaia kvartira*, 35–37.

37. Anna Bronivitskaia and Nikolai Malinin, *Moskva: Arkhitektura sovetskogo modernizma 1955–1991: Spravochnik-putevoditel'* (Moscow: Garazh, 2016), 123.

38. Meuser and Zadorin list two third-generation series of apartment buildings equipped with two bathrooms: 112 and 148. The 112 series was originally developed for Vorkuta and soon became widespread in Norilsk, making it a general regional series for climatic zone 1. The 112 series built in Tashkent "over-compensated for the shortage of four- and five-room apartments with the additional conveniences such as large entrance

halls and two sanitary blocks." The abundance of four- and five-room apartments was regionally specific to Central Asian republics, as they were considered to have large families. Meuser and Zadorin, *Towards a Typology of Soviet Mass Housing*, 407, 419.

39. Iaroslav D. (architect), interview by the author, May 11, 2017, Kyiv, Ukraine.

40. Iaroslav D. (architect), interview.

41. *Illiustrirovannyi katalog proektov otkrytogo konkursa "Modernizatsiia i rekonstruktsiia zhilykh domov pervykh massovikh serii"* (Moscow: Gosstroi SSSR, 1987), 11.

42. *Illiustrirovannyi katalog proektov otkrytogo konkursa*, 16.

43. *Illiustrirovannyi katalog proektov otkrytogo konkursa*, 19.

44. *Illiustrirovannyi katalog proektov otkrytogo konkursa na razrabotku proektnykh predlozhenii po novym tipam maloetazhnykh zhilykh domov I prinzipov plotno-nizkoi gorodskoi zastrojki* (Moscow: Gosstroi SSSR, 1981), 6, 26–27, 67.

45. *Sanitarnye normy i pravila II-B.10–58 Zhilye zdaniia*.

46. *Sanitarnye normy i pravila II-L.1–62 Zhilye zdaniia* (Moscow: Izdatel'stvo literatury po stroitel'stvu, 1964).

47. *Sanitarnye normy i pravila II-L.1–71* Zhilye zdaniia* (Moscow: Stroiizadat, 1978).

48. *Sanitarnye normy i pravila 2.08.01–89 Zhilye zdaniia* (Moscow: TsITP Gosstroiia SSSR, 1989).

49. See Jane Roj Zavisca, *Housing the New Russia* (Ithaca, NY: Cornell University Press, 2012), 52.

50. This is despite the preservation of many elements of Soviet norms in the early post-Soviet building codes. The first construction regulations developed in the post-Soviet states often resembled the late-Soviet ones, but some received a new nomenclature; for instance, construction regulations became known as Derzhavni Budivel'ni Normy in Ukraine and Noteikumi par Latvijas būvnormatīvu in Latvia.

51. P-44 is described in detail in Meuser and Zadorin, *Towards a Typology of Soviet Mass Housing*, 375–385.

52. I. N. Shkaruba, "Razvitie panel'nogo domostroeniia v Moskve," *Zhilishchnoe stroitel'stvo*, no. 8 (2003): 11

53. Shkaruba, "Razvitie panel'nogo domostroeniia v Moskve," 11–12.

54. Kateryna Malaia, "A Unit of Homemaking: The Prefabricated Panel and Domestic Architecture in the Late Soviet Union," *Architectural Histories* 8, no. 1 (2020): 12, 13.

55. Iaroslav D. (architect), interview.

56. The scale of influence projected by Western expatriates in the large post-Soviet cities can be seen in Yuri Medvedkov and Olga Medvedkov, "Upscale Housing in Post-Soviet Moscow and its Environs," in *The Post-Socialist City: Urban Form and Space Transformations in Central and Eastern Europe after Socialism*, ed. Kiril Stanilov (Dordrecht, the Netherlands: Springer Verlag, 2007), 252. For more information on expats in post-Soviet states, see Natasza Camiah and Graham Hollinshead, "Assessing the Potential for Effective Cross-Cultural Working between 'New' Russian Managers and Western Expatriates," *Journal of World Business* 38, no. 3 (August 2003): 245–326.

57. Oleksii R. (architect), interview by the author, May 4, 2017, Kyiv, Ukraine; Mykola N. (construction firm owner), interview by the author, April 24, 2017, Kyiv, Ukraine.

58. Selection of typical plans granted by Biuro Tekhnichnoi Dokumentatsii in Kyiv, Ukraine.

59. See apartment plans in Meuser and Zadorin, *Towards a Typology of Soviet Mass Housing*.

60. Oleksii R. (architect), interview; Mykola N. (construction firm owner), interview.

61. Olga Gurova, *Sovetskoe nizhnee bel'e: Mezhdu ideologiei i povsednevnost'iu* (Moscow: Novoe literaturnoe obozrenie, 2008), 46.

62. Oksana Fomina, "Grozu domokhoziaek toshnit ot slov: 'Vy vse eshche kipiatite?' kak Bordovskikh ot gazirovki," *Komsomol'skaia pravda*, November 20, 2003, https://www .kp.ru/daily/23161/24803.

63. Melanie Ilič, Susan Emily Reid, and Lynne Attwood, *Women in the Khrushchev Era* (Houndmills, UK: Palgrave Macmillan, 2004), 11; Natalya Chernyshova, *Soviet Consumer Culture in the Brezhnev Era* (London: Routledge, 2013), 82, 186.

64. Susan Reid, "Cold War at the Kitchen: Gender and the De-Stalinization of Consumer Taste in the Soviet Union under Khrushchev," *Slavic Review* 61, no. 2 (Summer 2002): 227–228.

65. Ilič, Reid, Attwood, *Women in the Khrushchev Era*, 193.

66. For instance, one of the Soviet washing machines, Maliutka (first manufactured in 1973), had a height dimension of fifty-seven centimeters and could be stored under a standard sink (fifty-nine centimeters at the lowest point). The instructions for the machine suggest using a special structure if installing the machine on top of the bathtub. *Mashina stiral'naia bytovaia SM-1 Maliutka-2: Rukovodstvo po ekspluatatsii* (Sverdlovsk: Proizvodstvennoe ob"edinenie "Uralmash," 1988), 8.

67. Chernyshova, *Soviet Consumer Culture in the Brezhnev Era*, 186.

68. See Natalya Chershova, "Household Technology in the Brezhnev Era Home," in *Soviet Consumer Culture in the Brezhnev Era*, 184–201.

69. *Sanitarnye normy i pravila II-V.10 Zhilye zdaniia* (Moscow: Gosudarstvennoe izdatel'stvo literatury po stroitel'stvu, arkhitekture i stroitel'nym materialam 1954), 227.

70. *Sanitarnye normy i pravila II-B.10–58 Zhilye zdaniia* (Moscow: Gosudarstvennoe izdatel'stvo literatury po stroitel'stvu, arkhitekture i stroitel'nym materialam, 1958), 11.

71. Biuro Tekhnichnoi Dokumentatsii engineers, personal conversation with the author, 2017, Kyiv, Ukraine.

72. Jennifer Patico, *Consumption and Social Change in a Post-Soviet Middle Class* (Stanford, CA: Stanford University Press, 2008), 209.

73. Fehérváry, "American Kitchens," 372.

74. Beverly Skeggs, *Formations of Class & Gender: Becoming Respectable* (London: SAGE Publications, 1997), 65.

5. SOCIALIZING

1. William J. Tompson, *Khrushchev: A Political Life* (New York: St. Martin's Press, 1997), 238.

2. See Christine Varga-Harris, *Stories of House and Home: Soviet Apartment Life during the Khrushchev Years* (Ithaca, NY: Cornell University Press, 2015).

3. Jean Baudrillard, *The System of Objects* (London: Verso, 2005), 15–29.

4. William Moskoff, *Hard Times: Impoverishment and Protest in the Perestroika Years: The Soviet Union 1985–1991* (Armonk, NY: M. E. Sharpe, 1993), 64–44.

5. A detailed discussion of this issue can be found in chapter 2.

6. Jane Zavisca writes that although there was a 1992 agreement between the United States and the new Russian government to implement a housing reform and introduce a housing market, such initiatives did not take off until later in the first decade of the 2000s. Jane Roj Zavisca, *Housing the New Russia* (Ithaca, NY: Cornell University Press, 2016), 1.

7. Birgit Glock and Hartmut Häußermann, "New Trends in Urban Development and Public Policy in Eastern Germany: Dealing with the Vacant Housing Problem at the Local Level," *International Journal of Urban and Regional Research* 28, no. 4 (December 2004): 920–923.

8. Glock and Häußermann, "New Trends in Urban Development," 920–923.

9. For instance, in both the Russian Federation and Belarus, the Soviet norms for apartment housing construction were only replaced in 2003. (SNiP 2.08.01-89* was replaced by SNiP 31-01-2003 in Russia and by SNB 3.02.04-03 in Belarus.)

10. For example, the earlier versions of Ukrainian building codes—Desrzhavni budivel'ni normy (DBN)—have repeated the language and the standards of the Soviet norms. A 2005 DBN for residential buildings contains lower and upper limits of apartment area, just like its Ukrainian (1992) and Soviet (1989) counterparts.

11. "Prichinoi obvala doma v tsentre Kieva stala rekonstruktsiia i pereplanirovka kvartir pod gostinitsu," *Korrespondent.net*, July 25, 2003, https://korrespondent.net /ukraine/events/75805-prichinoj-obvala-doma-v-centre-kieva-stala-rekonstrukciya-i -pereplanirovka-kvartir-pod-gostinicu.

12. Derzhavnyi komitet budivnytstva, arkhitektury ta zhytlovoi polityky Ukrainy, "Pro zatverdzhennia instruktsii pro poriadok derzhavnoi reiestratsii prava vlasnosti na ob'iekty nerukhomogo maina, shcho perebuvaiut' u vlasnosti iurydychnykh ta fizychnykh osib," June 26, 1998, no. 399/2839, http://zakon.rada.gov.ua/laws/show/z0399-98 /ed19980609.

13. Oleksii R. (architect), interview by the author, May 4, 2017, Kyiv, Ukraine.

14. Michael Gentile and Tiit Tammaru, "Housing and Ethnicity in the Post-Soviet City: Ust'-Kamenogorsk, Kazakhstan," *Urban Studies* 43, no. 10 (September 2006): 1764.

15. For instance, in Moscow a simplified procedure for legal apartment replanning was introduced in 2011. See Moscow Government Decree No. 508-PP, "Ob organizatsii pereustroistva i (ili) pereplanirovki zhilykh i nezhilykh pomeshchenii v mnogokvartirnykh domakh," Ofitsial'nyi sait Mera Moskvy, October 25, 2011, https://www.mos.ru /authority/documents/doc/9600220/.

16. Florian Urban noted that in the late 1990s, state authorities and other institutions still owned 40 percent of all housing stock (not just apartments). Florian Urban, *Tower and Slab: Histories of Global Mass Housing* (London: Routledge, 2012), 141.

17. Oleh P. (former handy worker), interview by the author, May 8, 2017, Kyiv, Ukraine.

18. Maryna D. (apartment dweller), interview by the author, May 6, 2017, Kyiv, Ukraine.

19. Hanna F. (apartment dweller/architect), interview by the author, May 5, 2017, Kyiv, Ukraine.

20. "Obrushenie zhilykh domov v RF v rezul'tate nezakonnykh pereplanirovok s 2006 goda. Dos'e," TASS-Dos'e, May 31, 2016, https://tass.ru/info/3328058.

21. Elizabeth Cromley, "Domestic Space Transformed, 1850–2000," in *Architectures: Modernism and After*, ed. Andrew Ballantyne (Malden, MA: Blackwell Publishing, 2004), 173.

22. James A. Jacobs, "Social and Spatial Change in the Postwar Family Room," *Perspectives in Vernacular Architecture* 13, no. 1 (2006): 70–85.

23. Judy Attfield, "Bringing Modernity Home: Open Plan in the British Domestic Interior," in *At Home: An Anthropology of Domestic Space*, ed. Irene Cieraad (Syracuse, NY: Syracuse University Press, 2006), 73–74.

24. Svetlana Boym, *Common Places: Mythologies of Everyday Life in Russia* (Cambridge, MA: Harvard University Press, 1994), 148.

25. Bonnie Calhoun, "Shaping the Public Sphere: English Coffeehouses and French Salons and the Age of the Enlightenment," *Colgate Academic Review* 3 (Spring 2008): 75.

26. Melissa Caldwell, *Food & Everyday Life in the Postsocialist World* (Bloomington: Indiana University Press, 2009), 11.

27. Evgenii Ivanov, "Houzz issledovanie: Chto rossiiane deistvitel'no delaiut pri remonte kukhni," *Houzz*, February 2, 2016, https://www.houzz.ru/ideabooks/60830940/list /houzz-issledovanie-chto-rossiyane-deystvitelyno-delayut-pri-remonte-kuhni.

28. *Poka vse doma* (Moscow: RGTRK Ostankino, 1992–1994); and *Poka vse doma* (Moscow: Telekompaniia Klass, 1994–2005).

29. Ethan Pollock, "'Real Men Go to the Bania': Postwar Soviet Masculinities and the Bathhouse," *Kritika: Explorations in Russian and Eurasian History* 11, no. 1 (Winter 2010): 47–76.

30. Tijana Vujosevic, "The Soviet Banya and the Mass Production of Hygiene," *Hygiene. Architectural Histories* 1, no. 1 (2013).

31. Boris Merzhanov, *Inter'er zhilishcha* (Moscow: Znanie, 1970), 21.

32. Mila D. (apartment dweller), interview by the author, May 7, 2017, Kyiv, Ukraine.

33. Vladimir Shlapentokh, "The Soviet Family in the Period of the Decay of Socialism," *Journal of Comparative Family Studies* 22, no. 2 (Summer 1991): 269.

34. Lynne Attwood, *Gender and Housing in Soviet Russia: Private Life in a Public Space* (Manchester: Manchester University Press, 2010), 195.

35. Christine Evans, *Between Truth and Time: A History of Soviet Central Television* (New Haven, CT: Yale University Press, 2016), 4.

36. Alexey Golubev, "When Spaces of Transit Fail Their Designers: Social Antagonisms of Soviet Stairwells and Streets," in *The Things of Life: Materiality in Late Soviet Russia* (Ithaca, NY: Cornell University Press, 2020), 91.

37. For an in-depth analysis of the culture of children's play in urban courtyards, see Iulia Cherniavskaia, "Sovetskoe kak detskoe: Opyt dvora," *Logos* 27, no. 5 (2017): 224–226.

38. M. Rahu, "Health Effects of the Chernobyl Accident: Fears, Rumors and the Truth," *European Journal of Cancer* 39, no. 3 (February 2003): 295–299.

39. Cherniavskaia, "Sovetskoe kak detskoe," 224.

40. For a recent account of a persisting social meaning of a post-Soviet courtyard, see Mateusz Laszczkowski, "Scraps, Neighbors, and Committees: Material Things, Place-Making, and the State in an Astana Apartment Block," *City & Society* 27, no. 2 (August 2015): 136–159.

41. For data on parking assets at the apartment building territory, see Tamara Uskova and Sergei Kozhevnikov, "Monitoring uslovii prozhyvaniia naseleniia oblasnogo tsentra," *Problemy razvitiia territorii* 62, no. 2 (2012): 35–36.

42. For example, see Lia Karsten, "It All Used to Be Better? Different Generations on Continuity and Change in Urban Children's Daily Use of Space," *Children's Geographies* 3, no. 3 (2005): 275–290.

43. Cherniavskaia formulates this as follows: "The enclave of benches by the hallways was assigned to the elderly ladies, the rest of the space [of the courtyard] belonged to the children." Cherniavskaia, "Sovetskoe kak detskoe," 226.

44. See Stephen Bittner, "History and Myth of Arbat," in *The Many Lives of Khrushchev's Thaw: Experience and Memory in Moscow's Arbat* (Ithaca, NY: Cornell University Press, 2008), 19–39.

45. Golubev, *The Things of Life*, 91.

46. Golubev, *The Things of Life*, 91.

47. Golubev, *The Things of Life*, 96–97.

48. Golubev, *The Things of Life*, 97.

49. For an analysis of the post-Soviet stairwell youth gatherings, see Irina Kosterina, "Konstrukty i praktiki maskulinnosti v provintsial'nom gorode: Gabitus 'normal'nykh patsanov," *Zhurnal sotsiologii i sotsial'noi antropologii* XI, no. 4 (2008): 122–140.

50. Living in basements or cellars of apartment buildings is described throughout Svetlana Stephenson, *Crossing the Line: Vagrancy, Homelessness and Social Displacement in Russia* (Aldershot, UK: Ashgate, 2006).

51. Being homeless in certain cities could have been an administrative misdemeanor due to the rules of local registration. Stephenson, *Crossing the Line*, 19.

52. Stephenson, *Crossing the Line*, 19.

53. Emil Nasritdinov and Philipp Schröder, "From Frunze to Bishkek: Soviet Territorial Youth Formations and Their Decline in the 1990s and 2000s," *Central Asian Affairs* 3, no. 1 (2016): 24–25.

54. For example, see the descriptions of dilapidated common areas—hallways and staircases—in contrast to well-maintained apartments in George J. Neimanis, *The Collapse of the Soviet Empire: A View from Riga* (Westport, CT: Praeger, 1997), 13. For another example of hallway and staircase door study, see Rosa Vihavainen, "Common and Dividing Things in Homeowners Associations," in *Political Theory and Community Building in Post-Soviet Russia*, eds. Oleg Kharkhordin and Risto Alapuro (London: Routledge, 2011), 155–158.

55. Hanna F. (apartment dweller/architect), interview.

56. Hanna F. (apartment dweller/architect), interview.

57. Judy Attfield, "Bringing Modernity Home."

58. Oksana H. (apartment dweller), interview by the author, May 14, 2017, Kyiv, Ukraine. In addition to a different apartment composition, such decrease in family contacts could be explained with the shift of importance from television to personal computers that coincided with the first decade after the collapse of the USSR.

59. Lindsay Asquith and Marcel Vellinga, *Vernacular Architecture in the 21st Century: Theory, Education and Practice* (London: Taylor & Francis, 2006), 130.

60. Asquith and Vellinga, *Vernacular Architecture in the 21st Century*, 131.

61. Asquith and Vellinga, *Vernacular Architecture in the 21st Century*, 131.

62. For the analysis of hybrid building identities and spatial practices, see Arijit Sen, "Staged Disappointment: Interpreting the Architectural Facade of the Vedanta Temple, San Francisco," *Winterthur Portfolio* 47, no. 4 (Winter 2013): 207–244.

63. Zavisca, *Housing the New Russia*, 194.

64. Jeffrey M. Hornstein, *A Nation of Realtors: A Cultural History of the Twentieth-Century American Middle Class* (Durham, NC: Duke University Press, 2005), 202.

65. Zavisca, *Housing the New Russia*, 194.

CONCLUSION

1. See, for example, Thomas Carothers, "The End of the Transition Paradigm," *Journal of Democracy* 13, no. 1 (January 2002): 5–21.

2. Andrew E. Kramer, "Ikea Plans to Halt Its Investment in Russia," *New York Times*, June 23, 2009, https://www.nytimes.com/2009/06/24/business/global/24ruble.html.

3. For distrust of the post-Soviet institutions, see Roger Sapsford et al., "Trust in Post-Soviet Countries, Ten Years On," *European Politics and Society* 16, no. 4 (2015): 523–539. http://dx.doi.org/10.1080/23745118.2015.1039286.

4. Olga Shevchenko, *Crisis and the Everyday in the Post-Socialist Moscow* (Bloomington: Indiana University Press, 2009), 173.

5. Dorzhi Dondokov, "Verbalizatsiia etnicheskikh stereotipov i reprezentatsiia povsednevnosti v russkoiazychnykh sotsial'nykh setiakh (kraudsorsingovoe issledovaniie)" (conference paper, Russkii iazyk i kul'tura v zerkale perevoda, Proceedings of the 10th International Conference, Moscow, 2020), 526. Stuart Hensel and Anatol Gudim, "Moldova's Economic Transition: Slow and Contradictory," in *The EU & Moldova: On a Fault-line of Europe*, ed. Ann Lewis (London: Federal Trust for Education and Research, 2004), 89.

6. *Nasha Rasha*, TNT, 2006–2011. For information on abuse of migrant laborers in the construction field, see Jane Buchanan, "Abuse and Exploitation of Migrant Construction Workers in Russia," part 3 in *"Are You Happy to Cheat Us?": Exploitation of Migrant Construction Workers in Russia* (New York: Human Rights Watch, 2009), 28–76.

7. Ronald Grigor Suny, "Provisional Stabilities: The Politics of Identities in Post-Soviet Eurasia," *International Security* 24, no. 3 (Winter 1999/2000), 139.

8. Natalia Chernyshova, *Soviet Consumer Culture in the Brezhnev Era* (London: Routledge, 2013), 17.

9. "Sobianin: Kvartaly v Moskve budut pereseliat' i snosit' tol'ko po zhelaniiu zhitelei," *TASS: Informatsionnoe agenstvo Rossii*, March 9, 2017, http://tass.ru/obschestvo/4081517.

BIBLIOGRAPHY

Ageeva, Vera V., Ilya A. Ageev, Anastasia M. Nikolaeva, and Zoya N. Levashkinac. "Was a Soviet Man a Socialist? The Dichotomy of Consumerist Ideals and Socialist Values in Late Soviet Society (1945–1990)." *European Proceedings of Social & Behavioural Sciences EpSBS, II International Scientific Symposium on Lifelong Wellbeing in the World*, May 18–22, 2015.

Agrawal, Sandeep Kumar. "Housing Adaptations: A Study of Asian Indian Immigrant Homes in Toronto." *Canadian Ethnic Studies/Etudes Ethniques au Canada* 38, no. 1 (Spring 2006): 117–130.

Alekseyeva, Anna. "Constructing Soviet Domesticity and Managing Everyday Life from Khrushchev to Collapse." In *Material Culture in Russia and the USSR: Things, Values, Identities*, edited by Graham H. Roberts, 55–70. London: Bloomsbury Publishing, 2017.

Alexander, Catherine. "Remont: Works in Progress." In *Economies of Recycling: The Global Transformation of Materials, Values and Social Relations*, edited by Catherine Alexander and Joshua Reno, 255–275. London: ZED Books, 2012.

Alexander, Jeffrey. *The Meanings of Social Life: A Cultural Sociology*. Oxford: Oxford University Press, 2003.

Andrusz, Gregory D. "A Note on the Financing of Housing in the Soviet Union." *Soviet Studies* 42, no. 3 (July 1990): 555–570.

Arzamas Academy. "Kurs No.15: Antropologiia kommunalki." http://arzamas.academy/courses/6.

Asquith, Lindsay, and Marcel Vellinga. *Vernacular Architecture in the 21st Century: Theory, Education and Practice*. London: Taylor & Francis, 2006.

Attfield, Judy. "Bringing Modernity Home: Open Plan in the British Domestic Interior." In *At Home: An Anthropology of Domestic Space*, edited by Irene Cieraad, 72–83. Syracuse, NY: Syracuse University Press, 2006.

Attfield, Judy. *Wild Things: The Material Culture of Everyday Life*. Oxford: Berg, 2000.

Attwood, Lynne. *Gender and Housing in Soviet Russia: Private Life in a Public Space*. Manchester, UK: Manchester University Press, 2010.

Attwood, Lynne. "Privatization of Housing in Post-Soviet Russia: A New Understanding of Home?" *Europe-Asia Studies* 64, no. 5 (2012): 903–928.

Baiburin, Albert, and Alexandra Piir. "When We Were Happy: Remembering Soviet Holidays." In *Petrified Utopia: Happiness Soviet Style*, edited by Marina Balina and Evgeny Dobrenko, 161–186. London: Anthem Press, 2011.

Bakiev, M. V. *Domashniaia academiia*. Vol. 1. Ufa: Bashkirskoe oblastnoe pravlenie Soiuza nauchnykh i inzhenernykh obshchestv SSSR, 1990.

Baudrillard, Jean. *The System of Objects*. London: Verso, 2005.

Benjamin, Walter. *Moscow Diaries*. Cambridge, MA: Harvard University Press, 1986.

Bezhanov, Gerald, dir. *Samaia obaiatel'naia i privlekatel'naia*. Moscow: Mosfilm, 1985.

Bittner, Stephen. *The Many Lives of Khrushchev's Thaw: Experience and Memory in Moscow's Arbat*. Ithaca, NY: Cornell University Press, 2008.

Blashkevich, R. N. *Inter'er sovremennoi kvartiry*. Moscow: Stroiizdat, 1988.

Bonnemaison, Sarah. "Performing the Modernist Dwelling: The Unite d'Habitation of Marseille." In *Architecture as Performing Art*, edited by Marcia Feuerstein and Gray Read, 61–72. Burlington, VT: Ashgate, 2013.

Bouzarovski, Stefan, Joseph Salukvadze, and Michael Gentile. "A Socially Resilient Urban Transition? The Contested Landscapes of Apartment Building Extensions in Two Post-Communist Cities." *Urban Studies* 48, no. 13 (October 2011): 2689–2714.

Boyarova, Mariia. "Istoriia dizaina inter'era postsovetskoi Moskvy v 1990e gody." *Houzz*, November 23, 2016. https://www.houzz.ru/ideabooks/76622145/list/istoriya-dizayna-interyery-postsovetskoy-moskvy-v-1990-e-gody.

Boym, Svetlana. "Archeology of Banality: The Soviet Home." *Public Culture* 6, no. 2 (1994): 263–292.

Boym, Svetlana. *Common Places: Mythologies of Everyday Life in Russia*. Cambridge, MA: Harvard University Press, 1994.

Boym, Svetlana. *The Future of Nostalgia*. New York: Basic Books, 2001.

Boym, Svetlana. "Ilya Kabakov: The Soviet Toilet and the Palace of Utopias." *ARTMargins*, December 31, 1999.

Boym, Svetlana. "Nostalgia, Moscow Style." *Harvard Design Magazine*, no. 13. http://www.harvarddesignmagazine.org/issues/13/nostalgia-moscow-style.

Brodsky, Joseph. "Room and a Half." In *Less Than One: Selected Essays*. London: Penguin, 2011.

Bronivitskaia, Anna, and Nikolai Malinin. *Moskva: Arkhitektura sovetskogo modernizma 1955–1991: Spravochnik-putevoditel'*. Moscow: Garazh, 2016.

Buchanan, Jane. "Abuse and Exploitation of Migrant Construction Workers in Russia" in *Are You Happy to Cheat Us?": Exploitation of Migrant Construction Workers in Russia*. New York: Human Rights Watch, 2009.

Buchli, Victor. "Khrushchev, Modernism, and the Fight against 'Petit-bourgeois' Consciousness in the Soviet Home." *Journal of Design History* 10, no. 2 (1997): 161–176.

Buchli. Victor. *Materializing Culture: An Archeology of Socialism*. Oxford: Berg, 2000.

Bulakh, Tatiana. "The Enchantment of Imaginary Europe: Consumer Practices in Post-Soviet Ukraine." In *The Socialist Good Life: Desire, Development and Standards of Living in Eastern Europe*, edited by Christopher Scarboro, Diana Mincyte, and Zsuzsa Gille. Bloomington: Indiana University Press, 2020.

Bulgakov, Mikhail. *Heart of a Dog*. New York: Grove Press, 1987.

Buts, N. K. "Puti i metody razvitiia monolitnogo domostroeniia." *Stroitel'stvo i arkhitektura* 8 (1989).

Butseva, Tatiana. *Novye slova i znacheniia: Slovar'-spravochnik po materialam pressy i literatury 90-kh godov XX veka v dvukh tomakh*. Saint Petersburg: Institut lingvisticheskikh issledovanii, 2009.

Caldwell, Melissa. *Food & Everyday Life in the Postsocialist World*. Bloomington: Indiana University Press, 2009.

Calhoun, Bonnie. "Shaping the Public Sphere: English Coffeehouses and French Salons and the Age of the Enlightenment." *Colgate Academic Review* 3 (Spring 2008): 75–99.

Camiah, Natasza, and Graham Hollinshead. "Assessing the Potential for Effective Cross-Cultural Working between 'New' Russian Managers and Western Expatriates." *Journal of World Business* 38, no. 3 (August 2003): 245–326.

Carothers, Thomas. "The End of the Transition Paradigm." *Journal of Democracy* 13, no. 1 (January 2002): 5–21.

Casey, Edward. "Body, Self, and Landscape: A Geophilosophical Inquiry into the Place-World." In *Textures of Place: Exploring Humanist Geographies*, edited by Paul Adams, 403–419. Minneapolis: University of Minnesota Press, 2004.

Castillo, Roberto. "Appropriating Modern Architecture: Designers' Strategies and Dweller's Tactics in the Evolution of the 1950s Venezuelan Superbloques." PhD diss., University of Chicago, 2015.

Cherniavskaia, Iulia. "Sovetskoe kak detskoe: Opyt dvora." *Logos* 27, no. 5 (2017): 219–240.

Chernyshova, Natalya. "Consuming Technology in a Closed Society: Household Appliances in Soviet Urban Homes of the Brezhnev Era." *Ab Imperio*, no. 2 (2011): 188–220.

Chernyshova, Natalya. *Soviet Consumer Culture in the Brezhnev Era*. London: Routledge, 2013.

Chernyshova, Natalya. "Philistines on the Big Screen: Consumerism in Soviet Cinema of the Brezhnev Era." *Studies in Russian and Soviet Cinema* 5, no. 2 (2014): 227–254.

Cieraad, Irene. "'Out of My Kitchen!' Architecture, Gender and Domestic Efficiency." *The Journal of Architecture* 7, no. 3 (2002): 263–279.

Cirtautas, Matas. "Urban Sprawl of Major Cities in the Baltic States." *Arhitektura un Pilsetplanosana* 7, no. 10 (2013): 72–79.

Cohen, Lizabeth. "Embellishing a Life of Labor: An Interpretation of the Material Culture of American Working-Class Homes 1885–1915." *Journal of American Culture* 3, no. 4 (January 1980): 752–775.

Collier, Stephen. *Post-Soviet Social: Neoliberalism, Social Modernity, Biopolitics*. Princeton, NJ: Princeton University Press, 2011.

Cromley, Elizabeth. "Domestic Space Transformed, 1850–2000." In *Architectures: Modernism and After*, edited by Andrew Ballantyne, 163–201. Malden, MA: Blackwell Publishing, 2004.

Cromley, Elizabeth. *The Food Axis: Cooking, Eating and the Architecture of the American Houses*. Charlottesville: University of Virginia Press, 2010.

Crowley, David, and Susan Emily Reid. *Socialist Spaces: Sites of Everyday Life in the Eastern Bloc*. Oxford: Berg, 2002.

Dal', Vladimir. *Tolkovyi slovar' zhyvogo velikorusskogo iazyka*. Moscow: Olma Press, 2001.

Danelia, Georgii, dir. *Afonia*. Moscow: Mosfilm, 1975.

de Certeau, Michel. *The Practice of Everyday Life*. Berkeley: University of California Press, 1984.

Deleuze, Gilles, and Felix Guattari. "May '68 Did Not Take Place." In *Two Regimes of Madness: Texts and Interviews, 1975–1995*, 233–236. New York: Semiotext(e), 2007.

Derzhavnyi komitet budivnytstva, arkhitektury ta zhytlovoi polityky Ukrainy. "Pro zatverdzhennia instruktsii pro poriadok derzhavnoi reiestratsii prava vlasnosti na ob'iekty nerukhomogo maina, shcho perebuvaiut' u vlasnosti iurydychnykh ta fizychnykh osib." June 26, 1998, no. 399/2839. http://zakon.rada.gov.ua/laws/show/z0399-98/ed19980609.

Design v SSSR: 1981–1985. Vserossiiskii nauchno-issledovatel'skii institut tekhnicheskoi estetiki (Moscow: VNIITE), 1987.

Desmond, Matthew. *Evicted: Poverty and Profit in the American City*. London: Penguin Books, 2017.

Dondokov, Dorzhi. "Verbalizatsiia etnicheskikh stereotipov i reprezentatsiia povsednevnosti v russkoiazychnykh sotsial'nykh setiakh (kraudsorsingovoe issledovaniie." Conference paper, Russkii iazyk i kul'tura v zerkale perevoda: Proceedings of the 10th International Conference, Moscow, 2020.

Dostoevsky, Fedor. *Crime and Punishment*. Oxford: Benediction Classics, 2016.

Dubrovina, Anastasiia. "Kak soedenit' sovetskoe retro i sovremennyi inter'er." *Idei vashego doma*, January 30, 2019. https://www.ivd.ru/dizajn-i-dekor/kvartira/kak-soedinit-sovetskoe-retro-i-sovremennyj-interer-36821.

Dykhovichii, Iurii. *Zhilye i obshchestvennye zdaniia: Kratkii spravochnik inzhenera-konstruktora.* Moscow: Stroiizdat, 1991.

Egmond, Florike, and Peter Mason. *The Mammoth and the Mouse: Microhistory and Morphology.* Baltimore, MD: Johns Hopkins University Press, 1997.

Egorov, Iurii, dir. *Dobrovol'tsy.* Moscow: Kinostudiia im. Gor'kogo, 1958.

Elias, Norbert. *The Civilizing Process.* London: Blackwell, 1982. Quoted in Chiara Briganti and Kathy Mezei, eds., *Domestic Space Reader*, 227–229. Toronto, Ontario: University of Toronto Press, 2012.

Elizarov, V. D. *Massovoe zhilishchnoe stroitel'stvo v USSR.* Kyiv: Budivel'nyk, 1966.

Epstein, Mikhail. "The Origins and Meaning of Russian Postmodernism." In *After the Future: The Paradoxes of Postmodernism and Contemporary Russian Culture.* Amherst: University of Massachusetts Press, 1995.

Evans, Christine. *Between Truth and Time: A History of Soviet Central Television.* New Haven, CT: Yale University Press, 2016.

"Fabrika komforta." *Idei vashego doma*, accessed April 25, 2018. https://www.ivd.ru/custom_category/custom_subcategory/fabrika-komforta-5002.

Fedorov, A. N. "Zhilishche v poslerevoliutsionnoi Moskve kak ob'iekt politiki i povsednevnoi zhizni." *Vestnik RUDN: Istoriia Rossii* 1 (2008).

Fehérváry, Krisztina. "American Kitchens, Luxury Bathrooms, and the Search for a 'Normal' Life in Postsocialist Hungary." *Ethnos* 67, no. 3 (2002): 369–400.

Fehérváry, Krisztina. *Politics in Color and Concrete: Socialist Materialities and the Middle Class in Hungary.* Bloomington: Indiana University Press, 2013.

Filtzer, Donald. *Soviet Workers and the Collapse of Perestroika: The Soviet Labour Process and Gorbachev's Reforms, 1985–1991.* Cambridge: Cambridge University Press, 2008.

Fitzpatrick, Sheila. "Things under Socialism: The Soviet Experience." In *The Oxford Handbook of the History of Consumption*, edited by Frank Trentmann, 451–466. Oxford: Oxford University Press, 2012.

Fomina, Oksana. "Grozu domokhoziaek toshnit ot slov: 'Vy vse eshche kipiatite?' kak Bordovskikh ot gazirovki." *Komsomol'skaia Pravda*, November 20, 2003. https://www.kp.ru/daily/23161/24803.

Fond R-337, Opis' 26, Delo 667. Tsentral'nyi derzhavnyi arkhiv vyshchykh organiv vlady ta upravlinnia Ukrainy, Kyiv, Ukraine.

Fond R-582, Opys 12, Sprava 2938. Tsentral'nyi derzhavnyi arkhiv vyshchykh organiv vlady ta upravlinnia Ukrainy, Kyiv, Ukraine.

Fond R-1657, Opys 1, Sprava 97, 16. Desrzhavnyi oblastnyi arkhiv L'vivs'koi Oblasti, Lviv, Ukraine.

Foot, John. "Micro-History of a House: Memory and Place in a Milanese Neighborhood, 1890–2000." *Urban History* 34, no. 3 (2007): 431–452.

Forrest, Ray, and Ngai-Ming Yip. *Housing Markets and the Global Financial Crisis: The Uneven Impact on Households.* Cheltenham, UK: Edward Elgar, 2011.

Fukuyama, Francis. *Identity: Contemporary Identity Politics and the Struggle for Recognition.* London: Profile Books, 2019.

Fürst, Juliane. *Flowers Through Concrete: Explorations in Soviet Hippieland.* Oxford: Oxford University Press, 2021.

Gaidai, Leonid, dir. *Operatsiia Y i drugie prikliucheniia Shurika.* Moscow: Mosfilm, 1965.

Gaidai, Leonid. dir. *Ivan Vasil'evich meniaet professiiu.* Moscow: Mosfilm, 1973.

Geller, Mikhail. *Mashyna i vintiki: Istoriia formirovaniia sovetskogo cheloveka.* London: Overseas Publications Interchange, 1985.

Gentile, Michael. "The Post-Soviet Urban Poor and where They Live: Khrushchev-Era Blocks, 'Bad' Areas, and the Vertical Dimension in Luhansk, Ukraine." *Annals of the Association of American Geographers* 105, no. 3 (2015): 583–603.

Gerasimova, Ekaterina. "Public Privacy in the Soviet Communal Apartment." In *Socialist Spaces. Sites of Everyday Life in the Eastern Bloc*, edited by David Crowley and Susan E. Reid, 207–230. Oxford: Berg, 2002.

Gerasimova, Ekaterina. "The Soviet Communal Apartment." In *Beyond the Limits: The Concept of Space in Russian History and Culture*, edited by Jeremy Smith. Helsinki: SHS, 1999.

Gerasimova, Ekaterina, and Sof'ia Chuikina. "Obshchestvo remonta," *Neprikosnovennyi zapas* 34, no. 2 (2004).

Gerasimova, Ekaterina, and Sof'ia Chuikina. "The Repair Society." *Russian Studies in History* 48, no. 1 (2009): 58–74.

Giovanni, Joseph. "A Funny Thing Happened to Soviet Architecture." *New York Times*, May 28, 1989. https://www.nytimes.com/1989/05/28/arts/architecture-design -funny-thing-happened-soviet-architecture-photo-ascencion.html.

Glock, Birgit, and Hartmut Häußermann. "New Trends in Urban Development and Public Policy in Eastern Germany: Dealing with the Vacant Housing Problem at the Local Level." *International Journal of Urban and Regional Research* 28, no. 4 (December 2004): 920–923.

Goffman, Erving. *The Presentation of Self in Everyday Life*. New York: Doubleday, 1959.

Golubev, Alexey. *The Things of Life: Materiality in Late Soviet Russia*. Ithaca, NY: Cornell University Press, 2020.

Gosudarstvennyi standard Soiuza SSR 6428-52 Plity gipsovye dlia peregorodok. Moscow: Gosudarstvennyi komitet SSR po delam stroitel'stva, 1952.

Gosudarstvennyi standard Soiuza SSR 6428-74 Plity gipsovye dlia peregorodok. Moscow: Gosudarstvennyi komitet SSR po delam stroitel'stva, 1974.

Gosudarstvennyi standard Soiuza SSR 6428-83 Plity gipsovye dlia peregorodok. Moscow: Gosudarstvennyi komitet SSR po delam stroitel'stva, 1983.

GOST 13025.2-85, Mebel' bytovaia: Funktsional'nye razmery mebeli dlia sideniia i lezhaniia. Moscow: Izdatel'stvo standartov, 1987.

Gram-Hanssen, Kirsten, and Claus Bech-Danielsen. "Somali, Iraqi and Turkish Immigrants and Their Homes in Danish Social Housing." *Journal of Housing and the Built Environment* 27, no. 1 (April 2012): 89–103.

Gurova, Olga. "Consumer Culture in Socialist Russia." In *The SAGE Handbook of Consumer Culture*, edited by Olga Kravets, Pauline Maclaran, Steven Miles, and Alladi Venkatesh, 102–123. London: SAGE Publications, 2018.

Gurova, Olga. *Sovetskoe nizhnee bel'e: Mezhdu ideologiei i povsednevnost'iu*. Moscow: Novoe literaturnoe obozrenie, 2008.

Hancock, John. "The Apartment House in Urban America." In *Buildings and Society; Essays on the Social Development of the Built Environment*, edited by Anthony King, 83–105. London: Routledge, 2003.

Harris, Steven. *Communism on Tomorrow Street: Mass Housing and Everyday Life after Stalin*. Baltimore, MD: Johns Hopkins University Press and Washington DC: Woodrow Wilson Center Press, 2013.

Harris, Steven. "'I Know All the Secrets of My Neighbors': The Quest for Privacy in the Era of the Separate Apartment." In *Borders of Socialism: Private Spheres of Soviet Russia*, edited by Lewis Siegelbaum, 171–190. New York: Palgrave Macmillan, 2006.

Harris, Steven. "In Search of 'Ordinary' Russia: Everyday Life in the NEP, the Thaw, and the Communal Apartment." *Kritika: Explorations in Russian and Eurasian History* 6, no. 3 (2005): 583–614.

Harshman, Deirdre. "A Space Called Home: Housing and the Management of Everyday in Russia, 1890–1935." PhD Diss., University of Urbana-Champaign, 2018.

Hayden, Dolores. *The Power of Place: Urban Landscapes as Public History*. Cambridge, MA: MIT Press, 1997.

Hensel, Stuart and Anatol Gudim, "Moldova's Economic Transition: Slow and Contradictory." In *The EU & Moldova: On a Fault-line of Europe*, edited by Ann Lewis. London: Federal Trust for Education and Research, 2004.

Hess, Daniel Baldwin, and Tiit Tammaru, eds. *Housing Estates in the Baltic Countries: The Legacy of Central Planning in Estonia, Latvia and Lithuania*. Cham, UK: Springer Open, 2019.

Hirt, Sonia. *Iron Curtains: Gates, Suburbs, and Privatization of Space in the Post-Socialist City*. Hoboken, NJ: Wiley & Sons, 2012.

Homes of Moderate Cost. Chicago: National Plan Service, 1952.

Humphrey, Caroline. *The Unmaking of Soviet Life: Everyday Economies after Socialism*. Ithaca, NY: Cornell University Press, 2002.

Iablonskaia, Tatiana. *Utro*. 1954.

Iglicka, Krystyna. "The Economics of Petty Trade on the Eastern Polish Border." In *The Challenge of East-West Migration for Poland*, edited by Keith Sword and Krystyna Iglicka, 120–144. New York: St. Martin's Press, 1999.

"IKEA v Rossii." IKEA in Russia (official website). https://www.ikea.com/ms/ru_RU/about_ikea/ikea_in_russia/ikea_in_russia.html.

Ilič, Melanie, and Dalia Leinarte. *The Soviet Past in the Post-Socialist Present: Methodology and Ethics in Russian, Baltic and Central European Oral History and Memory Studies*. New York: Routledge, 2016.

Ilič, Melanie, Susan Emily Reid, and Lynne Attwood. *Women in the Khrushchev Era*. Houndmills, UK: Palgrave Macmillan, 2004.

Illiustrirovannyi katalog proektov otkrytogo konkursa na razrabotku proektnykh predlozhenii po novym tipam maloetazhnykh zhilykh domov i printsipov plotno-nizkoi gorodskoi zastroiki. Moscow: Gosstroi SSSR, 1981.

Illiustrirovannyi katalog proektov otkrytogo konkursa. "*Modernizatsiia i rekonstruktsiia zhilykh domov pervykh massovykh serii*." Moscow: Gosstroi SSSR, 1987.

"Interesnye idei oformleniia okon." *Burda Moden*, 1988, 60–63.

Isenstadt, Sandy. "Visions of Plenty: Refrigerators in America around 1950." *Journal of Design History* 11, no. 4 (1998): 311–332.

Ivanou, Aleh, and Ruben Flores. "Routes into Activism in Post-Soviet Russia: Habitus, Homology, Hysteresis." *Movement Studies* 17, no. 2 (December 2018): 159–174.

Ivanov, Evgenii. "Houzz issledovanie: Chto rossiane deistvitel'no delaiut pri remonte kukhni." *Houzz*, February 2, 2016. https://www.houzz.ru/ideabooks/60830940/list/houzz-issledovanie-chto-rossiyane-deystvitelyno-delayut-pri-remonte-kuhni.

Ivanov, Iurii. *Pereplanirovka, remont i dizain kvartiry: Sovremennye otdelochnye materialy i technologii raboty s nimi*. Moscow: Ast. Astrel', 2006.

Jacobs, Adrianne. "The Many Flavors of Socialism: Modernity and Tradition in Late Soviet Food Culture, 1965–1985." PhD diss., University of North Carolina at Chapel Hill, 2015. https://cdr.lib.unc.edu/indexablecontent/uuid:123695e5-654d-4112-8efb-38980ad8e51a.

Jacobs, James A. "Social and Spatial Change in the Postwar Family Room." *Perspectives in Vernacular Architecture* 13, no. 1 (2006): 70–85.

Jordan, Jennifer A. *Edible Memory: The Lure of Heirloom Tomatoes and Other Forgotten Foods*. Chicago: University of Chicago Press, 2015.

Kaganovsky, Lilya. "The Cultural Logic of Late Socialism." *Studies in Russian and Soviet Cinema* 3, no. 2 (2009): 185–199.

Karsten, Lia. "It All Used to Be Better? Different Generations on Continuity and Change in Urban Children's Daily Use of Space." *Children's Geographies* 3, no. 3 (2005): 275–290.

Katalog tipovykh reshenii pereplanirovok kvartir v zhilykh domakh massovykh serii. Moscow: MNIITEP, 2011.

Kerr, Ron, and Sarah Robinson. "The Hysteresis Effect as Creative Adaptation of the Habitus: Dissent and Transition to the 'Corporate' in Post-Soviet Ukraine." *Organization* 16, no. 6 (November 2009): 829–853.

Khutsiev, Marlen, dir. *Iiul'skii dozhd'*. Moscow: Mosfilm, 1966.

Khrushchev, Nikita. *XXII S"ezd Kommunisticheskoi partii Sovetskogo Soiuza, 17–31 oktiabria 1961 goda: Otchet*. Moscow: Gosudarstevnnoe izdatel'stvo politicheskoi literatury, 1962.

Kirnichanskiy, Ruslan. "Pereplanirovka: Modernizatsiia dvukhkomnatnoi kvartiry v khrushchevke I-515/5." *Houzz*, September 3, 2015. https://www.houzz.ru/ideabooks /52262255/list/pereplanirovka-modernizatsiya-dvuhkomnatnoy-kvartiry-v -hrushchevke-1-515-5.

Kolomenskii, Mikhail. "K voprosu o formirovanii vneshnepoliticheskogo imidzha sovremennoi Rossii." *Vlast'* (March 2008).

Kolomiets, V. P. "Televizionnaia reklama kak sredstvo konstruirovaniia smyslov." *Mir Rossii*, no. 1 (1997).

"Komnatnye rastenia," *Burda Moden*, 1988, 60–63.

Korostleva, T.A. *Pereplanirovka kvartiry*. Moscow: Gammapress, 2000.

Kosterina, Irina. "Konstrukty i praktiki maskulinnotsi v provintsial'nom gorode: Gabitus 'normal'nykh patsanov'." *Sotsiologiia molodezhi* 11, no. 4 (2008): 122–140.

Kuliapin, Aleksander, and Olga Skubach. *Mifologiia sovetskoi povsednevnosti*. Moscow: Iazyki slavianskoi kul'tury (IaSK), 2013.

Kulidzhanov, Lev, and Jakov Segel', dirs. *Dom v kotorom ia zhivu*. Moscow: Gorky Film Studio, 1957.

Kushkova, Anna. "V tsentre stola: Zenit i zakat salata Oliv'e." *Novoe literaturnoe obozrenie* 76 (2005): 278–313.

Laszczkowski, Mateusz. "Scraps, Neighbors, and Committees: Material Things, Place-Making, and the State in an Astana Apartment Block." *City & Society* 27, no. 2 (August 2015): 136–159.

Leetmaa, K., T. Tammaru, and K. Anniste. "From Priority-Led to Market-Led Suburbanization in a Post-Communist Metropolis." *Tijdschrigt Voor Economische En Sociale Geografie* 100, no. 4 (2009): 436–453.

Lefebvre, Henri. *Rhythmanalysis: Space, Time and Everyday Life*. London: Continuum, 2005.

Lenin, Vladimir. *Polnoe sobranie sochinenii*. Vol. 54. Moscow: Izdatel'stvo Politicheskoi Literatury, 1975.

Levada, Yuri, ed. *Sovetskii prostoi chelovek: opyt sotsialnogo potreta na rubezhe 90-kh*. Moscow: Mirovoi Okean, 1993.

Lowe, Stuart, and Sasha Tsenkova. *Housing Change in East and Central Europe: Integration or Fragmentation*. Aldershot, UK: Ashgate, 2003.

Lowell, Stephen. *Summerfolk: A History of the Dacha, 1710–2000*. Ithaca, NY: Cornell University Press, 2003.

Madden, David, and Peter Marcuse. *In Defense of Housing: The Politics of Crisis*. London: Verso, 2016.

Malaia, Kateryna. "A Unit of Homemaking: The Prefabricated Panel and Domestic Architecture in the Late Soviet Union." *Architectural Histories* 8, no. 1 (2020): 1–16.

Malaia, Kateryna. "Transforming the Architecture of Food: From the Soviet to the Post-Soviet Apartment." *Journal of the Society of Architectural Historians* 80, no. 4 (2021): 460–476.

Mal'chevskii, Roman. "Aleksandr Gerega—o pervykh den'gakh i o tom kak sozdavalsia Epitsentr." *Politrada.ua*, September 25, 2013. https://politrada.com/news/aleksandr -gerega-o-pervykh-dengakh-i-tom-kak-sozdavalsya-epitsentr/.

Mamin, Iurii, dir. *Okno v Parizh*. Paris: Films du Bouloi, Fontan, La Sept Cinema, Troitskii most, 1993.

Mashina stiral'naia bytovaia SM-1 Maliutka-2: Rukovodstvo po ekspluatatsii. Sverdlovsk: Proizvodstvennoe Ob"edinenie "Uralmash," 1988.

Mason, Robert J., and Liliya Nigmatullina. "Suburbanization and Sustainability in Metropolitan Moscow." *Geographical Review* 101, no. 3 (July 2011): 316–333.

Matthews, Mervyn. *Poverty in the Soviet Union: The Life-Styles of the Underprivileged in Recent Years*. Cambridge: Cambridge University Press, 1986.

Matthews, Mervyn. *Privilege in the Soviet Union: A Study of Elite Life-Styles under Communism*. London: Allen and Unwin, 1979.

"Mebel'" and "mebel'naia promyshlennost.'" In *Bol'shaia sovetskaia entsyklopediia*. Moscow: Sovetskaia entsyklopediia, 1972.

Medvedkov, Yuri, and Olga Medvedkov. "Upscale Housing in Post-Soviet Moscow and its Environs." In *The Post-Socialist City: Urban Form and Space Transformations in Central and Eastern Europe after Socialism*, edited by Kiril Stanilov, 245–268. Dordrecht, the Netherlands: Springer Verlag, 2007.

Menshov, Vladimir, dir. *Moskva slezam ne verit*. Moscow: Mosfilm, 1979.

Messana, Paola. *Soviet Communal Living: An Oral History of the Kommunalka*. Basingstoke, UK: Palgrave Macmillan, 2011.

Merzhanov, Boris. *Inter'er zhilishcha*. Moscow: Znanie, 1970.

Merzhanov, Boris. *Sovremennaia kvartira*. Moscow: Stroiizdat, 1974.

Meuser, Philipp, and Dimitrij Zadorin. *Towards a Typology of Soviet Mass Housing: Prefabrication in the USSR 1955–1991*. Berlin: DOM Publishers, 2015.

Miari, Anastasia. "On the Menu in Moscow, Soviet-Era Nostalgia." *New York Times*, December 13, 2019. https://www.nytimes.com/2019/12/11/travel/moscow-restaurants -nostalgia.html.

Milosavlevich, Radmila. *Inter'er zhilogo doma*. Moscow: Stroiizdat, 1988.

Morton, Henry W. "Who Gets What, When and How? Housing in the Soviet Union." *Soviet Studies* 32, no. 2 (April 1980): 235–259.

Moskoff, William. *Hard Times: Impoverishment and Protest in the Perestroika Years: The Soviet Union 1985–1991*. Armonk, NY: M. E. Sharpe, 1993.

Mylan, Josephine, and Dale Southerton. "The Social Ordering of an Everyday Practice: The Case of Laundry." *Sociology* 52, no. 6 (December 2018): 1134–1151.

Nasritdinov, Emil, and Philipp Schröder. "From Frunze to Bishkek: Soviet Territorial Youth Formations and Their Decline in the 1990s and 2000s." *Central Asian Affairs* 3, no. 1 (2016): 1–28.

Nebylitskii, B., dir. *Pora bol'shogo novosel'ia*. Moscow: Tsentral'naia studiia dokumental'nykh filmov, 1959.

Neimanis, George J. *The Collapse of the Soviet Empire: A View from Riga*. Westport, CT: Praeger, 1997.

"Nemnogo sveta i tepla." *Idei vashego doma*, no. 2 (2005). https://www.ivd.ru/custom _category/custom_subcategory/nemnogo-sveta-i-tepla-5413.

Novokmet, Filip, Thomas Piketty, and Gabriel Zucman. "From Soviets to Oligarchs: Inequality and Property in Russia, 1905–2016." NBER Working Paper No. 23712, August 2017.

"Ob izmenenii i dopolnenii glavy *SNiP* II-L.1–71." In *Sanitarnye Normy i Pravila* II-L.1 –71* *Zhilye zdaniia*. Moscow: Stroiizadat, 1978.

"Ob utverzhdenii polozheniia o provedenii planovo-predupreditel'nogo remonta zhilykh i obshchestvennykh zdanii." State Committee of Construction of the USSR Decree, September 8, 1964.

"Obrushenie zhilykh domov v RF v rezul'tate nezakonnykh pereplanirovok s 2006 goda. Dos'e." *TASS-Dos'e*, May 31, 2016. https://tass.ru/info/3328058.

Ol'khova, A. P. *Novye serii tipovykh proektov zhilykh domov dlia massovogo stroitel'stva: Arkhitekturno-planirovochnye resheniia (obzor)*. Moscow: Tsentr nauchno-tekhnicheskoi informatsii po grazhdanskomu stroitel'stvu i arkhitekture, 1972.

Papernyi, Vladimir. *Kul'tura dva*. Moscow: Novoe literaturnoe obozrenie, 2011.

Patico, Jennifer. *Consumption and Social Change in a Post-Soviet Middle Class*. Stanford, CA: Stanford University Press, 2008.

"Pereplanirovka dvukhkomnatnoi kvartiry v dome serii P-44." *Idei vashego doma*, January 1999. https://www.ivd.ru/custom_category/custom_subcategory/pereplanirovka -dvuhkomnatnoj-kvartiry-v-dome-serii-p-44-4094.

Pink, Sarah. *Situating Everyday Life: Practices and Places*. London: SAGE, 2012.

Plan of an individually designed apartment building. Folder #098833.AR-2, 2 Avgustyn Voloshyn Street, Kyiv, Ukraine. Kyivproekt archives.

"Pod kryshei doma svoego." *Rabotnitsa* 10 (October 1984): 28.

Pokrovskie vorota. Mikhail Kazakov, dir. Moscow: Mosfilm, 1982.

Poliakov, Iurii. "Podruzhka: Moi milyi chto tebe ia sdelala." *Rabotnitsa* 6 (June 1984): 28.

Pollock, Ethan. "'Real Men Go to the Bania': Postwar Soviet Masculinities and the Bathhouse." *Kritika: Explorations in Russian and Eurasian History* 11, no. 1 (Winter 2010): 47–76.

Poluboiarinov, V. "Zona remonta." *Rabotnitsa* 4 (April 1985): 28.

"Prevrashchenia khrushchevki," *Idei vashego doma*, no. 2 (2005). https://www.ivd.ru /custom_category/custom_subcategory/prevrasenia-hrusevki-5411.

"Prichinoi obvala doma v tsentre Kieva stala rekonstruktsiia i pereplanirovka kvartir pod gostinitsu." *Korrespondent.net*, July 25, 2003. https://korrespondent.net/ukraine /events/75805-prichinoj-obvala-doma-v-centre-kieva-stala-rekonstrukciya-i -pereplanirovka-kvartir-pod-gostinicu.

Prigov, Dmitriy. *Zhivite v Moskve: Rukopis' na pravakh romana*. Moscow: Novoe literaturnoe obozrenie, 2000.

Programma KPSS. Moscow: Gospolitizdat, 1961.

Rahu, M. "Health Effects of the Chernobyl Accident: Fears, Rumors and the Truth." *European Journal of Cancer* 39, no. 3 (February 2003): 295–299.

Reid, Susan E. "Cold War in the Kitchen: Gender and the De-Stalinization of Consumer Taste in the Soviet Union under Khrushchev." *Slavic Review* 61, no. 2 (2002): 211–252.

Reid, Susan E. "The Khrushchev Kitchen: Domesticating the Scientific-Technological Revolution." *Journal of Contemporary History* 40, no. 2 (2005): 289–316.

Reid, Susan E. "The Meaning of Home: 'The Only Bit of the World You Can Have to Yourself.'" In *Borders of Socialism: Private Spheres of Soviet Russia*, edited by Lewis Siegelbaum, 145–170. Basingstoke, UK: Palgrave Macmillan, 2011.

"Respectable inter'er v panel'nom dome." *Salon inter'er*, no. 1 (1994). https://salon.ru /article/respectable-interer-v-panelnom-dome-1744.

Riazanov, El'dar, dir. *Ironiia Sud'by ili s legkim parom!* Moscow: Mosfilm, 1975.

Rice, Charles. "Rethinking Histories of Interior." *Journal of Architecture* 9, no. 3 (2004): 275–287.

Ries, Nancy. *Russian Talk Culture and Conversation during Perestroika*. Ithaca, NY: Cornell University, 1997.

Romashkevich, Anastasiia. "Scanflot" gotov sozdat' rai v otdel'no vziatykh pomeshche-niakh." *Kommersant*, December 12, 1991. https://www.kommersant.ru/doc/1815.

Rosselin, Celine. "Ins and Outs of the Hall: The Parisian Example." In *At Home: An Anthropology of Domestic Space*, edited by Irene Cieraad, 53–59. Syracuse, NY: Syracuse University Press, 2006.

Rudolph, Nicole. *At Home in Postwar France: Modern Mass Housing and Right to Comfort*. New York: Berghahn, 2015.

Ryabinska, Natalya. "The Media Market and Media Ownership in Post-Communist Ukraine: Impact on Media Independence and Pluralism." *Problems of Post-Communism* 58, no. 6 (2011): 3–20.

Sampson, Steven. "The Second Economy of the Soviet Union and Eastern Europe." *The Annals of the American Academy of Political and Social Science* 493, no. 1 (2016): 120–136.

Sand, Jordan. *House and Home in Modern Japan: Architecture, Domestic Space and Bourgeois Culture 1880–1930*. Cambridge, MA: Harvard University Asia Center, 2003.

Sanitarnye normy i pravila II-V.10–58 Zhilye zdaniia. Moscow: Stroiizdat, 1954.

Sanitarnye normy i pravila II-B.10–58 Zhilye zdaniia. Moscow: Gosudarstvennoe izdatel'stvo literatury po stroitel'stvu, arkhitekture i stroitel'nym materialam, 1958.

Sanitarnye normy i pravila II-L.1–62 Zhilye zdaniia. Moscow: Izdatel'stvo literatury po stroitel'stvu, 1964.

Sanitarnye normy i pravila II-L.1–71* Zhilye zdaniia. Moscow: Stroiizadat, 1978.

Sanitarnye normy i pravila 2.08.01-89* Zhilye zdaniia. Moscow: TsITP Gosstroiia SSSR, 1989.

Sapsford, Roger, Pamela Abbot, Christian Haerpfer, and Claire Wallace. "Trust in Post-Soviet Countries, Ten Years On." *European Politics and Society* 16, no. 4 (2015): 523–539. http://dx.doi.org/10.1080/23745118.2015.1039286.

Satter, David. *It Was a Long Time Ago, and It Never Happened Anyway: Russia and the Communist Past*. New Haven, CT: Yale University Press, 2012.

Schwenkel, Christina. *Building Socialism: The Afterlife of East German Architecture in Urban Vietnam*. Durham, NC: Duke University Press, 2020.

Sen, Arijit. "Staged Disappointment: Interpreting the Architectural Facade of the Vedanta Temple, San Francisco." *Winterthur Portfolio* 47, no. 4 (Winter 2013): 207–244.

Seriia 84: Krupnopanel'nye doma i blok-sektsii. Moscow: TsNIIEP zhilishcha, 1979.

Sgibnev, Wladimir. "Remont: Do-It-Yourself-Urbanism in Post-Soviet Tajikistan." Paper presented at the RC21 Conference, Berlin, Germany, August 29–31, 2013.

Sgibnev, Wladimir. "Rhythms of Being Together: Public Space in Urban Tajikistan through the Lens of Rhythmanalysis." *International Journal of Sociology and Social Policy* 35, no. 7/8 (2015): 533–549.

Shevchenko, Olga. *Crisis and the Everyday in Postsocialist Moscow*. Bloomington: Indiana University Press, 2009.

Shevchenko, Olga. "Resisting Resistance: Everyday Life, Practical Competence and Neo-liberal Rhetoric in Post-Socialist Russia." In *Everyday Life in Russia Past and Present*, edited by Choi Chatterjee, David L. Ransel, Mary Cavender, and Karen Petrone, 52–71. Bloomington: Indiana University Press, 2015.

Shkaruba, I. N. "Razvitie panel'nogo domostroeniia v Moskve." *Zhilishnoe stroitel'stvo*, no. 8 (2003).

Shlapentokh, Vladimir. "The Soviet Family in the Period of the Decay of Socialism." *Journal of Comparative Family Studies* 22, no. 2 (Summer 1991).

Siegelbaum, Lewis, and Daniel Walkowitz. *Workers of the Donbass Speak: Survival and Identity in the new Ukraine, 1989–1992*. Albany, NY: State University of New York Press, 1995.

Skeggs, Beverly. *Formations of Class & Gender: Becoming Respectable*. London: SAGE Publications, 1997.

Smirnova, O. Ia. "Vliianie bytovykh processov na formirovanie zhiloi iacheiki." *Stroitel'stvo i arkhitektura*, no. 22 (1986).

Smith, Mark B. "Individual Forms of Ownership in the Urban Housing Fund of the USSR, 1944–64." *Slavonic and East European Review* 86, no. 2 (2008): 283–305.

Sobianin, Sergei. Interview by *Mestnoe vremia. Vesti-Moskva. Nedelia v gorode*, September 24, 2011. https://www.mos.ru/mayor/interviews/95214/.

"Sobianin: kvartaly v Moskve budut pereseliat' i snosit' tol'ko po zhelaniiu zhitelei." *TASS: Informatsionnoe agenstvo Rossii*, March 9, 2017. http://tass.ru/obschestvo/4081517.

Sosnovy, Timothy. "The Soviet Housing Situation Today." *Soviet Studies* 11, no. 1 (1959).

Stea, David. "House and Home: Identity, Dichotomy or Dialectic?" In *Domestic Space Reader*, edited by Chiara Briganti and Kathy Mezei, 45–49. Toronto: University of Toronto Press, 2012.

Stepanishev, V. "10 metrov na 100 chelovek." *Rabotnitsa* 3 (March 1989): 8.

Stephenson, Svetlana. *Crossing the Line: Vagrancy, Homelessness and Social Displacement in Russia*. Aldershot, UK: Ashgate, 2006.

Stieber, Nancy. *Housing Design and Society in Amsterdam: Reconfiguring Urban Order and Identity, 1900–1920*. Chicago: University of Chicago Press, 1998.

Strazhnikov, Aleksandr Matveevich. "Vse o pereplanirovke kvartiry." Interview by Svetlana Olifirova. *Komsomol'skaia pravda*, May 5, 2005. https://www.kp.ru/daily/23519/40426/.

Suny, Ronald Grigor. "Provisional Stabilities: The Politics of Identities in Post-Soviet Eurasia." *International Security* 24, no. 3 (Winter 1999/2000).

Szostek, Joanna. "The Mass Media and Russia's 'Sphere of Interests': Mechanisms of Regional Hegemony in Belarus and Ukraine." *Geopolitics* 23, no. 2 (2018).

Tipple, Graham. *Extending Themselves: User-Initiated Extensions of Government-Built Housing in Developing Countries*. Liverpool, UK: Liverpool University Press, 2000.

Tolstikova, Natasha. "Rabotnitsa: The Paradoxical Success of a Soviet Women's Magazine." *Journalism History* 30, no. 3 (2004).

Tolstoy, Aleksei Nikolaevich. *The Viper*. In *The Marie Antoinette Tapestry*. Moscow: Raduga, 1991.

Tompson, William J. *Khrushchev: A Political Life*. New York: St. Martin's Press, 1997.

Trifonov, Yuri. "Obmen." In *Moskovskie povesti*. Moscow: Litres, 2017.

Trofimov, Andrey, and Marina Klinova. "'Sovetskii potrebitel'' v otechestvennom gumanitarnom diskurse 1950–1980kh godov." *Izvestiia UrGEU* 4, no. 54 (2014).

Tsenkova, Sasha. *Housing Policy Reforms in Post-Socialist Europe: Lost in Transition*. Heidelberg, Germany: Physica-Verlag, 2011.

Tsenkova, Sasha, and Bengt Turner. "The Future of Social Housing in Eastern Europe: Reforms in Latvia and Ukraine." *European Journal of Housing Policy* 4, no. 2 (2004): 133–149.

Upton, Dell. "Architecture in Everyday Life." *New Literary History* 33, no. 4 (Autumn 2002): 707–723.

Upton, Dell, and John Michael Vlach, eds. *Common Places: Readings in American Vernacular Architecture*. Athens: University of Georgia Press, 1985.

Urban, Florian. *Tower and Slab: Histories of Global Mass Housing*. London: Routledge, 2012.

Uskova, Tamara, and Sergei Kozhevnikov. "Monitoring uslovii prozhyvaniia naseleniia obalsnogo tsentra." *Problemi razvitiia teritorii* 62, no. 2 (2012): 31–44.

Utekhin, Ilya, Alice Nakhimovsky, Slava Paperno, and Nancy Ries. *Communal Living in Russia: A Virtual Museum of Soviet Everyday Life*. https://kommunalka.colgate.edu/index.cfm.

"V khrushchevke." *Idei vashego doma* 61, no. 4 (April 2003). https://www.ivd.ru/custom_category/custom_subcategory/v-hrusevke-4463.

Varga-Harris, Christine. "Homemaking and the Aesthetic and Moral Perimeters of the Soviet Home during the Khrushchev Era." *Journal of Social History* 41, no. 3 (Spring 2008): 561–589.

Varga-Harris, Christine. *Stories of House and Home: Soviet Apartment Life during the Khrushchev Years*. Ithaca, NY: Cornell University Press, 2015.

"Vasha mechta—sobstvennaia spal'nia." *Rabotnitsa* 3/4 (1992): 8/11.

Velychenko, Stephen. *The EU and Russia: History, Culture and International Relations*. Basingstoke, UK: Palgrave Macmillan, 2007.

Vihavainen, Rosa. "Common and Dividing Things in Homeowners Associations." In *Political Theory and Community Building in Post-Soviet Russia*, edited by Oleg Kharkhordin and Risto Alapuro, 139–163. London: Routledge, 2011.

Von Bremzen, Anya. *Mastering the Art of Soviet Cooking: A Memoir of Food and Longing*. New York: Crown Publishers, 2013.

Vujosevic, Tijana. "The Soviet Banya and the Mass Production of Hygiene." *Hygiene. Architectural Histories* 1, no. 1 (2013).

Ward, Christopher J. *Brezhnev's Folly: The Building of BAM and Late Soviet Socialism*. Pittsburgh, PA: University of Pittsburgh Press, 2009.

Weizman, Inez. "Interior Exile and Paper Architecture." In *Agency: Working with Uncertain Architectures*, edited by Florian Kossak, Doina Petrescu, Tatjana Schneider, Renata Tyszczuk, and Stephen Walker, 154–164. London: Routledge, 2010.

Wilk, Christopher, ed. *Modernism: 1914–1939; Designing a New World*. London: Victoria & Albert Publications, 2006.

Wright, Gwendolyn. *Building the Dream: A Social History of Housing in America*. Cambridge, MA: MIT Press, 1981.

Yurchak, Alexei. *Everything Was Forever, Until It Was No More: The Last Soviet Generation*. Princeton, NJ: Princeton University Press, 2013.

Zavisca, Jane Roj. *Housing the New Russia*. Ithaca, NY: Cornell University Press, 2012.

"Zhiteliam moskovskikh khrushchevok predlozhat kvartity za MKAD." *Komsomol'skaia pravda*, March 27, 2012. https://www.msk.kp.ru/daily/25858/2825855/.

Zubovich, Katherine. "Housing and Meaning in Soviet and Post-Soviet Russia." *Kritika: Explorations in Russian and Eurasian History* 16, no. 4 (Fall 2015): 1003–1011.

Index

Page numbers in *italics* indicate figures.

Kabakov, Ilia and Emilia: *The Toilet*, 97
Khrushchev, Nikita, 3, 4, 55, 113
khrushchevka apartments: demand for remont
    of, 41–43; eating-related spaces in, 41–42,
    76–77; replanning of, 62–66, 126; Russian
    invasion of Ukraine in destruction of,
    131–32; size of, 41–42, 55–56, 82–83;
    sleeping spaces in, 50–51, 55–57, 62–66;
    social spaces in, 126
Kitchen Debate, 1959, 78–79
kitchens: in late-Soviet homes, 79–83; in politics,
    17, 79, 81, 94, 119; post-Soviet, 83–94; size
    of, 41–42, 79, 91–92, 94; as social spaces, 82,
    119; space from, for sanitary blocks, 102; as
    utilitarian workspace, 76; washing machines
    in, 108–9. *See also* eating spaces; food
$k = n - 1$ formula, 51–53, 55–56, 60–61, 75–76,
    148–49n4
Knauf Gips, 36, 62
Krasivye kvartiry (Beautiful apartments)
    magazine, 33
Kvartirnyi vopros (Apartment question), 19, 24
Kyiv, Ukraine, 18, 20, 22, 37

labor: domestic, and kitchens, 76–77, 149n14;
    ethnic stereotyping of, 129; gendered, 23–24;
    in the rise of the bedroom, 62; supply and
    demand in availability of, 28–29, 30, 34–38,
    105–7
layout, spatial: of eating spaces, 74–75, 76–77,
    78, 84–85, 86–89; of hygienic spaces,
    100–101; in media on remodeling, 33–34;
    remont in, 47; of sleeping space, 48–49,
    55–57, 59, 62, 67–73; of social space, 115,
    120–21; standardization of, 12–15. *See also*
    evroremont (Euro-remodeling); replanning
    (*pereplanirovka*)
Lefebvre, Henri: *Rhythmanalysis*, 72
Leinarte, Dalia, 136–37n64
Lenin, Vladimir, 51–53
liberalization, economic, 2–3, 85
living conditions. *See* conditions of housing
    and living
living rooms/spaces: and eating spaces, 74,
    80–81, *87*, 88–92, 93–94; floor
    space for, in demand for remont, 41–42;
    post-Soviet emergence of, 125–26; and
    sleeping space, 55–56, 64–65, 66, 69, *70–71*;
    as social space, 118, 120, 121–22
Lviv, Ukraine, 12, 18, 20, *21*

magazines, 19, 31–32, 33. *See also under*
    magazine title
maintenance, 29, 30, 33–34, 40, 95, 98–99

Mason, Peter, 9–10
mass housing: in the Baltic Soviet republics,
    19; eating-related spaces in, 76–77; as
    modern, 16; remont as habitus in, 29;
    sleeping spaces in, 50–51, 55, 57; social
    findings in, 126–27; social spaces in,
    121–23; standardization in, 13–14.
    See also khrushchevka apartments
materiality, 8–9, 66–67
materials, construction: in popular sources,
    31–32; in post-Soviet style and evroremont,
    130; in the rise of the bedroom, 61–62; supply
    and demand in remont, 35–36, 38, 43–44
media: food-related spaces in, 93; hygiene-
    related spaces in, 96–98; remont in, 31–34;
    replanning in, 64; as sources, 23–24
memorabilia, 81
Merzhanov, Boris, 57, 100–102, 120
mobility: of labor, 30, 35–37; residential, 63,
    129–30; social, 42
Moch, Leslie Page: *Broad Is My Native Land*, 35
models, spatial, 25–26, 83–84
Modernism, 12, 76–78, 79–80, 89, 113, 118,
    122–23
modernization: architectural competitions
    in, 56, *58–59*; in post-Soviet discourses
    of normalcy, 5–6; in post-Soviet kitchen
    remodeling, 89; and remont, 31, 41;
    replanning for social space as, 126; and
    social spaces, 113, 114
Moldovans, 129
mortgage markets, 128
Moscow, 20, 22, 27–28, 94, 124
Moscow Does Not Believe in Tears (*Moskva
    slezam ne verit*, 1981) film, 42–43, 96
Moscow Scientific-Research and Project
    Institute of Typology and Experimental
    Design (MNIITEP), 43–44
Moskoff, William, 40
multi/mono-functionality: of eating spaces,
    78, 82–83, 84–85, 90–91, 92–94; of furniture
    in Soviet architecture, 13–15; $k = n - 1$
    formula in, 148–49n4; of sleeping spaces
    and furniture, 8, 48–49, 50–51, 52–53,
    55–57, 58–60, 65, 66, 67–68; of social
    spaces, 56, 58, *60*, 118, 119–21. *See also*
    functionality

Narkomfin apartment building, 149n5
Nasha Rasha (Our Russia) television show, 129
neoliberalism, 29–30
New *byt* apartment buildings, 102
noise of remodeling, 46–47
normalcy, post-Soviet, 5–6, 26

popular sources, 33–34, 95; remodeling as, 1; in sanitary blocks, 95, 105–7

Trifonov, Yuri: "Exchange," 50–51, 57

"Tsena remonta" (*Rabonitsa* magazine), 31

Ukraine: diversity of housing in, 18; replanning documentation in, 115; Russian war and military crimes in, 131–32; size of family housing in, 55; traits of urban homes in, 20

Ukrainian Soviet Socialist Republic, 60–61

United States, 88, 118

Upton, Dell, 8, 15–16

urban lore, 129

Varga-Harris, Christine, 96

ventilation, 137n68

vernacular architecture, 15–16, 126–27

walk-through rooms: in daily personal rhythms, 68, 69, 72–73; in domestic practices, 16; multifunctionality of, 56, 57, 67–68; in post-Soviet kitchen remodeling,

90–91; and the rise of the bedroom, 62, 63, 65–66; as social space, 120, *121*

walls. *See* partitions/partition walls

washing machines, 107–11

water heaters, 99

Westernness/the West, 4–5, 29, 35–36, 37, 97–98, 105–7, 111–12

Window to Paris (Okno v Parizh), 4

women: and the domestic sphere, 23–24, 28–29, 31; kitchen technology and liberation of, 79; Soviet, in *Rabonitsa* magazine, 31; Soviet rhetoric on liberation of, 107–8

workspace: kitchens as, 76; and private sleeping space, 69

Wright, Gwendolyn, 12–13

youth socialization, 123, 124

Zavisca, Jane, 6–7, 127

"Zona remonta" (*Rabonitsa* magazine), 31

zones, functional, 13, 14–15, 48–49, 126

CPSIA information can be obtained
at www.ICGtesting.com
Printed in the USA
LVHW040140240723
752905LV00031B/146/J